RENEWALS 458-4574

DATE DUE

Liberals,
the Church,
and Indian Peasants

Liberals, the Church, and Indian Peasants

Corporate Lands and the Challenge of Reform in Nineteenth-Century Spanish America

Edited by Robert H. Jackson

UNIVERSITY OF NEW MEXICO PRESS   /   ALBUQUERQUE

©1997 by the University of New Mexico Press
All rights reserved.
First edition

Library of Congress Cataloging in Publication Data

Liberals, the Church, and Indian peasants : corporate lands and the challenge of reform in nineteenth-century Spanish America / edited by Robert H. Jackson.—1st ed.
  p. cm.
Includes index.
ISBN 0-8263-1762-6 (cloth)
1. Land tenure—Mexico—History—19th century.
2. Land tenure—Andes Region—History—19th century.
3. Liberalism—Mexico—History—19th century.
4. Liberalism—Andes Region—History—19th century.
5. Indians of Mexico—Land tenure—History—19th century.
6. Indians of South America—Land tenure—Andes Region—History—19th century.
I. Jackson, Robert H. (Robert Howard)
HD325.L45 1997
333.3′0972′09034—dc20   96-25225
                                                      CIP

Contents

Illustrations	vi
Introduction	3

1. Dealing in Real Estate in Mid-Nineteenth-Century Jalisco
    The Guadalajara Region
    Robert J. Knowlton
	13

2. The Decade of Revolt
    Peasant Rebellion in Jalisco, Mexico, 1855–1864
    Dawn Fogle Deaton
	37

3. Liberal Theory and Peasant Practice
    Land and Power in Northern Veracruz, Mexico, 1826–1900
    Michael T. Ducey
	65

4. Liberal Modernization and Religious Corporate Property in Nineteenth-Century Guatemala *Hubert Miller*	95
5. Liberalism and Indian Communities in Peru, 1821–1920 *Nils Jacobsen*	123
6. Liberalism and the Land Question in Bolivia, 1825–1920 *Erick D. Langer and Robert H. Jackson*	171

7. Community and Hacienda in the Bolivian Highlands
    Changing Patterns of Land Tenure in Arque and Vacas
    Robert H. Jackson
	193

Conclusion	207
Index	217
Note on Contributors	227
About the Book and Editor	229

Illustrations

Figures

1.1	Plan of the Third District of Guadalajara	16
2.1	Population of Jalisco 1821–1869	42
2.2	Peasant Rebellions in Jalisco 1825–1885	43
2.3	Rebellions in Jalisco (per year)	43
2.4	Chronological Breakdown of Rebellions	44
2.5	Peasant Rebellions in Jalisco by Region	45
2.6	Peasant Rebellions by Region, 1855–1864	45
2.7	Causes of Peasant Rebellions, 1825–1885	49
2.8	Causes of Peasant Rebellions, 1855–1864	49
2.9	Participants in Peasant Rebellions	50

Tables

1.1	Table of Measures	33
1.2	Orozco Property Transactions	34
3.1	Amounts of Communal Lands	68
4.1	Conversion of Religious Facilities	115
6.1	State-Owned Lands in Cochabamba	185
7.1	Tributaries by Category in Cantón Capinota	195
7.2	Tributaries by Category in Cantón Quirquiavi	196
7.3	Structure of Land Tenure in Cantón Capinota	197
7.4	Structure of Land Tenure in Cantón Vacas	200
7.5	Structure of Land Tenure, Estancia Muyocchipa	202
7.6	Structure of Land Tenure, Estancia Yanatama	202
7.7	Selected Haciendas in Arque Province Divided for Inheritance	203
7.8	Transactions Involving Hacienda Sicaya	203
7.9	Number of Properties in Arque Province	204

Liberals,
the Church,
and Indian Peasants

Introduction

In the period between 1809 and 1825, most of Spain's colonies in the Americas won their independence following prolonged civil war. Leaders of the independence movements agreed on the goal of political separation from Spain, but not on the future of the nations they were creating. Spanish American leaders discussed different government plans, economic models, social structures, and even the role of the Catholic church in the new republics.

The debate over the future of the Spanish American republics frequently became divisive, especially when advocates of retaining much of the colonial-era social structure clashed with moderate and radical liberals who saw the future in patterns of development similar to Great Britain and the United States. By the last decades of the nineteenth century, elites in many Spanish American countries adopted reform and development programs influenced by liberal economic and social thought.

Brought together in this volume are a collection of original essays offering detailed case studies. Each represents the latest advances in the study of liberal policies that affected corporate landowners (such as the Catholic church), charitable institutions (such as orphanages and hospitals), and corporate indigenous communities. In their drive to modernize Spanish American societies and economies, liberals sought to liquidate what they considered to be unproductive capital held in mortmain; they sought to use the freed capital to spur economic development. Moreover, liberals attempted to integrate the indigenous population into national life and make its members socially productive.[1] Some liberals also believed that the liquidation of corporate indigenous community lands was essential to the modernization of agriculture; others advocated the creation of a class of yeoman farmers that, as in the thought of Thomas Jefferson in the United States, would form the backbone of republican society. Liberal theory and policy were at times contradictory and difficult to implement at the local or regional level.

In recent decades Spanish American nineteenth-century liberalism has received considerable scholarly attention. One area of inquiry has been liberal thought and politics, especially in reference to the Mexican experience.[2] Charles Hale examined the reformist ideas of the liberal ideologue José Mora in the three decades following Mexican independence. Others have examined the politics of Mexican liberalism. Richard Sinkin analyzed the voting records of liberal congresses after 1855 and viewed post-1855 liberalism as a process of nation-building. Laurens Perry looked at the functioning of politics during the Juárez and Díaz period and concluded that both leaders created political machines to maintain their power. More recently Donald Stevens presented a detailed and sophisticated study of Mexican political instability from the 1820s to the 1850s based on a prosopographic analysis of the background of politicians, including members of the cabinet. Stevens refines our understanding of the causes of instability and the class and regional backgrounds of conservatives and moderate and radical liberals. He concludes that wealth and status played an important role in later ideological orientation.

Economic liberalism, especially as related to trade and development policy, is a second area of study.[3] However, nineteenth-century liberal anticlerical and anticorporate indigenous community policies have also attracted attention, particularly in the Mexican case where liberal anticlericalism contributed to political polarization and instability.[4] In an important study published in English in 1971, Jan Bazant outlined the evolution of liberal anticlerical ideas, their implementation in the period of the so-called La Reforma, and the radicalization of the Juárez government during the course of civil war in the late 1850s. In studying anticlerical disamortization policies, Bazant focused on urban property in the central Mexican states. Among other findings Bazant pointed out that the Juárez government initially favored the sale of church-owned real property but, by the early 1860s, went one step farther and confiscated church wealth. Bazant also pointed out that liberal politicians themselves benefited from the sale of church property at discounted prices. Studies of the Andean region show more complex and nuanced consequences from the implementation of liberal economic policies, including anticorporate land policies.

The chapters in this book explore the development of liberal anticlerical and anticommunity policy and their practical application in two regions of Spanish America: Mesoamerica and the Andean region. These essays are microhistorical studies of discrete regions, as well as discussions of the formulation of national policy. They provide new insights to the formation and applications of liberal policy and especially to the resulting changes in patterns of land tenure and rural society. They provide additional case studies

INTRODUCTION 5

of the impact of liberal policies and offer new interpretations based on local variations or similarities in the implementation of liberal laws. Studies such as Bazant's analysis of liberal attacks on church wealth in Mexico generally focus on policy formulated by the national government. Studies in this collection show that national policies were frequently modified at the regional or local level.

The first group of chapters focus on Mexico and Guatemala. Robert Knowlton and Dawn Fogle Deaton examine two aspects of the impact of liberal policy in Jalisco. Knowlton documents the growth in the real estate market that resulted from the division of municipal and village ejidos in the Guadalajara region as a consequence of the Ley Lerdo of 1856. Scholars often allude to the growth of land markets following the implementation of reform, and Knowlton uses notarial records to study land sales in detail. Deaton documents peasant uprisings in the wake of the 1855 seizure of power by liberal politicians. She identifies a conjunction of factors, including growing commercialization of agriculture and resulting changes in land tenure, that contributed to rising levels of rural violence.

Michael Ducey studies liberal policy as applied to the corporate indigenous communities of the Huasteca region of northern Veracruz between 1820 and 1900. Ducey finds very complex patterns of change in community land tenure, ambiguity in the role played by the courts and local and state-level politicians and bureaucrats, and final liquidation of or significant reductions in community land tenure occurring in the Porfirian period only. One factor that limited efforts to divide community lands was the arming of rural residents during the War of the Reform (1858–1861) and the French Intervention (1862–1867). There were also conflicting interests within communities and between local elites, who may have wanted to acquire community lands, and government officials, who did not always implement reform legislation as intended or in some instances even increased community landholdings. Finally, the case of the Huasteca communities shows that the drive in the 1850s to liquidate corporate community lands was delayed in some parts of the country.

In some respects Ducey's chapter serves as a corrective to Florencia Mallon's recently published study of Mexico and Peru, which focuses in the Mexican case primarily on the Puebla Highlands in the 1850s and 1860s.[5] In a chapter entitled "The Conflictual Construction of Community," Mallon attempts to describe the nature of relations within communities without reference to the changes that resulted from the implementation of liberal anticorporate land policies. Community politics in central Mexico in the 1850s and 1860s and the direction of ethnic relations cannot be divorced from the context of liberal land policies, and any effort to explain ethnic relations without this context is meaningless. Ducey explores the intricacies of community politics and ethnic relations as related to the efforts to institute liberal anticommunity legislation using a detailed microhistorical approach that lends itself to a fuller understanding of the changes that actually did occur.

Almost by definition, the study of the impact of liberal policies on rural society must be quantitative. In both Mexico and Bolivia, for example, liberal policies attempted to modify landownership, and it was the threat to landownership that frequently incited community members to mobilize and violently resist government policies. An uprising by community members in the Bolivian altiplano in response to government-sponsored sales of community lands helped to topple the Bolivian dictator Mariano Melgarejo (1864–1871) from power. Long-term changes in land tenure can only be documented through painstaking research in notarial records and similar documents, employing quantitative methods.

Hubert Miller examines the question of Catholic property in Guatemala, focusing on the national debate and the views presented by liberals to justify the disamortization of church wealth. Guatemalan liberalism must be seen against the backdrop of the liberal–conservative struggle for control of the country, which lasted for some fifty years, and the influence of foreign ideas, particularly positivism with its credo of "order and progress," which influenced Latin American elites in the last decades of the nineteenth century. Liberals seized power in a violent fashion in 1871 and modified land laws to spur the development of coffee production. Triumphant Guatemalan liberalism promoted the development of an export-oriented economy that changed land tenure in the lower elevation districts but left the highland communities relatively intact to serve as a labor reservoir. In the coffee-growing regions, on the other hand, the new government promoted the division of state lands for coffee fincas and ignored community land claims.[6]

The second region examined in this volume is the one comprised of the Andean republics Peru and Bolivia, which, with extensive corporate indigenous community and church landholdings, evidenced similar challenges for liberal reformers. Two of the chapters in this section offer broad overviews of the evolution of liberal policy; the third offers a microhistorical case study.

Chapters by Nils Jacobsen and Erick Langer and Robert Jackson explore Peruvian corporate indigenous community policy and Bolivian community and government policy regarding the church. Jacobsen finds that liberal community policy in Peru was both complex and contradictory, reflecting the different goals of liberal politicians and shifts in perspectives and political alliances that included elite groups from both the coastal region and the Andes Highlands. Jacobsen constructs a chronology broken down into three periods. The first period, 1821–1854, is dominated by different Bolivarian policies that attempted to restructure Peruvian society, particularly rural society, but with limited results. The second period, 1854–1879, the author identifies as the high-water mark of Peruvian liberalism and especially liberal anticommunity policy and as including the influence of the 1848–1849 failed liberal revolutions in Europe. This period coincided with the guano boom, which provided Peruvian governments with new sources of revenue and the perception of prosperity, but ended with the disastrous War of the Pacific (1879–1883). Jacobsen believes that liberalism with a small l ended following the war. The final period, 1879–1931, witnessed the formation of a formal "Liberal" political party with an upper-case L, a development that was distinct from the older pattern of the influence of liberal ideas on political actors, some of whom also held conservative views on other issues. It also saw the emergence of new intellectual trends such as *indigenismo*. Jacobsen's essay also serves as a corrective to Mallon's recently published book by providing both a chronological and conceptual framework for understanding Peruvian corporate indigenous community policies, as well as to her first book published a decade ago.[7]

Langer and Jackson chart the course of Bolivian liberalism and make a distinction between the Bolivarian policies enforced by foreign leaders who liberated the country in 1825 and later policies formulated by native Bolivian political leaders. The chapter examines church policy and argues that reform measures instituted by followers of Simón Bolívar primarily affected the male regular orders, and that the female orders retained lands into the present century. Moreover, the anticlerical policies of the mid-1820s were also linked to efforts to fund the Bolivian debt and to exchange land for bonuses to be paid to foreign soldiers who helped liberate the country. The authors also outline the evolution of Bolivian community legislation during the nineteenth century, culminating with the 1874 law of *ex-vinculación* (disentailment) and the impact of community policy on land tenure in different parts of the country. In the Cochabamba region the law of ex-vinculación, coupled with fundamental changes in the structure of the regional economy, contributed to the growth of a class of smallholders locally called *piqueros*. The emergence of piqueros later led indirectly to the rise of peasant leagues called *sindicatos*, in the 1930s, and the 1953 Bolivian agrarian reform measure that transformed patterns of land tenure.

The final chapter by Robert Jackson presents a case study of the impact of community policy on land tenure in two highland districts, Arque province and Vacas, in Cochabamba department, Bolivia. Jackson links changes in community tenure to modifications of hacienda tenure and economic shifts that contributed to the fragmentation of agricultural land. In some regions of Bolivia, the final abolition of communities and communal forms of land tenure led to the creation of new estates and the expansion of existing haciendas at the expense of former community lands. The pattern in Cochabamba was distinct, as shown by the Arque case. Many of the former community lands remained in the hands of smallholders, and many haciendas experienced partition. The *piquero* class emerged especially in the valley districts bordering the Arque and Vacas highlands. In some parts of Arque haciendas continued to dominate, but there were also numbers of *piqueros*. In one district, Quirquiavi, community lands remained in a *pro-indiviso* (joint tenancy) communal tenure.

A number of similarities and differences emerging from the examination of liberal policies in Mesoamerica and the Andean region are examined in more detail in the conclusions. In all instances liberal anticlerical and anticommunity programs were initiated by political leaders who were not members of a formal political party in the modern understanding. Rather, coalitions of politicians found a common adherence to certain ideas and policies out of a desire to promote what they believed to be acceptable patterns of development as well as out of self-interest. In Mexico and Guatemala, groups with different views used force to seize and retain power, whereas in Bolivia and Peru, political instability was related to regionalism more than to ideological differences.[8]

Specific policies, while similar in some instances, were different in others. Bolivian and Guatemalan liberals legislated laws of *ex-vinculación* in the 1870s that stipulated that corporate indigenous community lands be divided into private property and that were similar to Bolivarian laws in Peru and Bolivia dating to the 1820s. Mexican liberals, on the other hand, passed legislation that more openly sought to strip communities of their land, while at the same time they supported the notion of the privatization of community lands. Mexican and Bolivian laws regarding church lands were likewise somewhat different. In Mexico, ownership was to have been shifted to private individuals, with a preference for the actual renters of the lands. Lands would be auctioned if the renter did not buy them. Unless auctioned, the purchase price was to have been amortized based on the rent paid at the time of the transaction, and the rent previously paid was to have been converted into a mortgage payment. As initially implemented, the church did not lose the capital value of affected lands, only ownership. The Bolivian legislation of the 1820s, on the other hand, confiscated church-owned lands, and sold the properties for the stated purpose of financing public education. The Bolivian government also converted some church-owned buildings to public use. However, the Bolivian law did not confiscate the lands of all convents and monasteries and, in most instances, left the female orders untouched. The law targeted the convents and monasteries with only a small number of residents, and it almost exclusively affected the male orders. In both Mexico and Bolivia, church land transactions were tied to liquidation of outstanding and generally depreciated debt certificates.

Finally, there was considerable difference between the letter and implementation of the law. In all cases laws were legislated at the national or state level, but the enforcement of the laws was delayed, in some cases for years, reversed, or subject to modification by local politicians or notables. With regard to anticommunity legislation, community members sometimes were able to delay or alter the impact of laws. Conflicting interests of local elites often modified the course of implementation of laws.

One final observation can be made regarding anticommunity legislation. The drive to privatize communal indigenous lands in the nineteenth century was not limited to Spanish America, as shown by two examples. In 1887, the United States passed the Dawes Severalty Act, which called for the privatization of reservation lands.[9] Similarly, the Glen Grey Act of 1894 attempted to convert tribal lands in South Africa to private tenures.[10] As liberalism became the established basis for economic theory in the Western world, communal tenures became anachronisms that blocked the goal of economic modernization.

A Note on Sources

The study of the impact of liberal policies on land tenure requires, by definition, an element of quantification, in addition to the analysis of legislation and the application of pertinent laws. The basic source for land transactions is the notarial protocol, which is a registered and duly legalized contract. Notarial records in some jurisdictions have been preserved that date back to the sixteenth century. The contracts contain a wealth of information on each transaction and the identities of the individuals involved. Wills also were registered with notaries and often contain itemized inventories and, in some instances, detailed maps of rural properties. My own research on the Cochabamba region of Bolivia turned up some inventories that listed the specific labor obligations of service tenants living and working on haciendas.[11] There were also nineteenth-century inventories of cacicazgos that were former community lands converted into private estates by *kurakas*, the hereditary ayullu head inthe Andean region.

In Bolivia, the government created a separate office, the *registro de derechos reales*, to register sales and rentals of real property and mortgages. There is an office in each department with records dating back to the 1880s. Following the passage of the law of *ex-vinculación* in 1874, the Bolivian government also established a separate register for transactions involving former community lands.

Other government records provide important information on land tenure patterns and changes in tenures that resulted from liberal legislation. Reports written by local or regional officials contain useful data. Tribute rolls are also an important source. Finally, cadastral surveys, usually instituted following the implementation of liberal reforms, provide detailed information on land tenure and on changes in tenure over time. The Bolivian government initiated cadastral surveys in the 1880s in tandem with the creation of a new land tax, although local surveys appear to have been taken as early as the 1840s, if not earlier. Government officials conducted surveys periodically, and the quality of information improved over time. The survey was most accurate for smaller properties. In his essay in this volume, Robert Knowlton uses a similar source from Jalisco, including maps showing property boundaries and the names of landowners.

The initiation of cadastral surveys also led to the introduction of a decimal-based system of land measurement. The Spanish land-measurement system of *fanegas* and *almudes* was based on the concept of the amount of land that could be sown by a measure of grain, and considerable variation existed between jurisdictions in the exact measurement of *fanegas* and *almudes*. The old Spanish system was replaced by a standardized measurement called the hectar. The hectar itself could be divided into smaller units called areas and centiareas, so that measurements reported in cadastral surveys would be recorded as hectares.areas.centiareas.

Court records and newspapers contain additional information on land tenure changes. Many land disputes ended in the courts, and nineteenth- and twentieth-century court records are generally underutilized by historians. Late nineteenth- and twentieth-century newspapers reported on aspects of changes in land tenure, instances of rural unrest, and also advertised land auctions. My own recently published study of land tenure change in the Cochabamba region includes a detailed analysis of advertisements of judicial land sales, and my study makes extensive use of newspaper articles that documented aspects of the implementation of anticommunity policies.[12] Again, newspapers are a source for Spanish American rural history underutilized by historians.

As argued above, the study of the impact of liberal anticorporate land policies depends on detailed microhistorical analysis using quantifiable information. The same generalization applies to discussions of changes in internal relations within communities and between the communities and local nonindigenous elites. Gender and race certainly are important elements, but the nature of these relations during liberalism's period of greatest influence was defined by the dynamic of changing access to and ownership of land.

Notes

1. On liberal ideas regarding corporate wealth and the role of the indigenous population in society, see Charles Hale, *Mexican Liberalism in the Age of Mora, 1821–1853* (New Haven, 1968).

2. See, for example, Hale, *Mexican Liberalism*; Richard Sinkin, *The Mexican Reform, 1855–1876: A Study in Liberal Nation Building* (Austin, 1979); Laurens Perry, *Juárez and Díaz: Machine Politics in Mexico* (DeKalb, 1978); Donald Stevens, *Origins of Instability in Early Republican Mexico* (Durham, 1991).

3. See, for example, Joseph Love and Nils Jacobsen, eds., *Guiding the Invisible Hand: Economic Liberalism and the State in Latin American History* (New York, 1988); Robert Potash, *Mexican Government and Industrial Development in the Early Republic: The Banco de Avio* (Amherst, 1983); David McCreery, *Desarrollo económico y politica nacional. El ministerio de Fomento de Guatemala, 1871–1885* (Guatemala City, 1981); Paul Gootenberg, *Between Silver and Guano: Commercial Policy and the State in Postindependence Peru* (Princeton, 1989); Paul Gootenberg, *Imagining Development: Economic Ideas in Peru's "Fictitious Prosperity" of Guano, 1840–1880* (Berkeley and Los Angeles, 1993); Tristan Platt, *Estado tributario y librecambio en Potosí (Siglo XIX). Mercado indígena, proyecto proteccionista y lucha de ideologias monetarias* (La Paz, 1986); Antonio Mitre, *El monedero de los Andes. Región económica y moneda boliviana en el siglo XIX* (La Paz, 1986).

4. See, for example, Jan Bazant, *Alienation of Church Wealth in Mexico: Social and Economic Aspects of the Liberal Revolution, 1856–1875*, ed. and trans. Michael Costeloe (Cambridge, 1971); Robert Knowlton, *Church Property and the Mexican Reform (1856–1910)* (DeKalb, 1976); Charles Berry, *The Reform in Oaxaca, 1856–76: A Microhistory of the Liberal Revolution* (Lincoln, 1981); Andres Lira, *Comunidades indígenas frente a la ciudad de México. Tenochtitlán y Tlatelolco, sus pueblos y barrios, 1812–1919* (México, D.F., 1983); Tristan Platt, *Estado boliviano y ayllu andino. Tierra y tributo en el Norte de Potosí* (Lima, 1982); Erick Langer, *Economic Change and Rural Resistance in Southern Bolivia, 1880–1930* (Stanford, 1989); Nils Jacobsen, *Mirages of Transition: The Peruvian Altiplano, 1780–1930* (Berkeley and

Los Angeles, 1993); Robert H. Jackson, *Regional Markets and Agrarian Transformation in Bolivia: Cochabamba, 1539–1960* (Albuquerque, 1994).

5. Florencia Mallon, *Peasant and Nation: The Making of Postcolonial Mexico and Peru* (Berkeley and Los Angeles, 1995).

6. David McCreery, "State Power, Indigenous Communities, and Land in Nineteenth-Century Guatemala, 1820–1920," in *Guatemalan Indians and the State: 1540 to 1988*, ed. Carol Smith (Austin, 1990).

7. Florencia Mallon, *The Defense of Community in Peru's Central Highlands: Peasant Struggle and Capitalist Transition, 1860–1940* (Princeton, 1983).

8. See particularly the sources listed in nn. 2 and 3.

9. For the impact of the Dawes Severalty Act on one tribe, see William McLoughlin, *After the Trail of Tears: The Cherokees' Struggle for Sovereignty, 1839–1880* (Chapel Hill and London, 1993), pp. 368–74.

10. Collin Bundy, *The Rise and Fall of the South African Peasantry* (Berkeley and Los Angeles, 1979), p. 135.

11. Robert H. Jackson, "Evolución y persistencia del colonaje en las haciendas de Cochabamba," *Siglo XIX* 3:6 (1988), 145–62.

12. Jackson, *Regional Markets and Agrarian Transformation*. The analysis of advertisements is found on pp. 144–49.

I
Dealing in Real Estate in Mid-Nineteenth-Century Jalisco
The Guadalajara Region
Robert J. Knowlton

On June 25, 1856, the liberal-reform government in Mexico City issued the Law of Disamortization, commonly called the Lerdo Law after Miguel Lerdo de Tejada, the minister of the treasury, the office responsible for the measure.[1] The law required that all rural and urban property owned or administered by civil or ecclesiastical corporations be sold to those renting the property; the annual rent paid was to be considered as six percent of the value of a property for sale purposes. Properties not rented were to be sold to the highest bidder at public auction. The law exempted from its provisions buildings devoted "immediately and directly to the service or object of the corporation." With respect to civil corporations (cities, towns, and villages) the exemption included jails, markets, and "the buildings, ejidos, and lands destined exclusively to the public service of the community (*poblaciones*) to which they belonged."[2]

The Lerdo Law was a significant piece of national reform legislation, which was enshrined in the 1857 Federal Constitution. With respect to civil corporate property, however, efforts to partition and individualize village lands had already been undertaken in various states, including Jalisco, since the time of independence. Furthermore, on December 12, 1855, the governor of Jalisco, Santos Degollado, ordered the sale of the municipal lands of Guadalajara.

The attacks on civil corporate property have raised various questions for scholars. For example, as is generally believed, did the partition of village lands contribute to the concentration of rural property in the hands of a relatively few private owners, especially during the long Porfirian Age, 1876–1911? Did villages resist the implementation of the laws because of the assault they represented on their traditional way of life? This essay is the third in a projected larger study of the effects of mid-nineteenth-century Mexican anti-civil corporate property legislation, a study that hopes to answer some of these questions.

Thus far, the research on Michoacán and Jalisco reveals that: (1) there was an apparently brisk business in Guadalajara municipal property (*ejidos*); (2) there was resistance to the individualization of village lands, though not to the purchase of urban *ejidos*, an inference drawn from the repetition of laws on village-land partition; (3) there was, perhaps, considerable "trafficking" in village lands, including some concentration of property; and (4) there also were many property transactions that were conventional, that is, not related to anticorporate legislation.

The first of the essays by this writer dealt with the individualization of property in Jalisco; it focused on the municipal lands of Guadalajara and the partition of the lands of Santa María, a village in the same *cantón* (*cantón* no. 1) as Guadalajara.[3] The second essay centered on the process of partition of the lands of various villages in the state of Michoacán.[4] This chapter, my third essay, returns to Jalisco to examine the operation and effects of legislation as revealed, particularly, in notarial records.[5]

Notaries historically played an important role in the lives of Mexicans, both the humble and the elite. Notaries, of course, plied their professions for a varying number of years and enjoyed varying degrees of popularity. For example, among those consulted for this essay, notary (*escribano público*) Martín Román's records fill forty-nine volumes (thirty-one of protocols and eighteen of supporting documents) from 1828 to 1866, while José María Rodríguez Blanco had only one volume, containing both protocols and documents, for the entire 1836–1856 period.[6] Notaries' work encompassed a broad range of matters, and the number of specific dealings varied greatly among the different types of business, for example, from one *codicilo* to fifty-eight *compraventas*.[7] Furthermore, the number of transactions involving property varied greatly.[8]

As noted, the Lerdo Law had excluded from its effects buildings, *ejidos*, and lands destined exclusively to the public service of the entity to which the property belonged. But well before that, the Jalisco governor's December 1855 decree had ordered the sale of the city's *ejidos*.[9] Those leasing the lands were to purchase them; the annual fee represented six percent of the value.[10] The proceeds were to be used to construct a theater, now the Teatro Degollado, worthy of the inhabitants of that "*populosa e ilustrada*" city. Six months later, following the issuance of the Lerdo Law, the *ayuntamiento* identified the first syndic as the official who was to issue the deed of sale (*escritura de adjudicación*) in the name of the *ayuntamiento* and subject to the Lerdo Law and other relevant measures.[11] Purchasers had the transaction formalized before a notary in detailed terms; one protocol stated, for example, that the syndic Lic. Don Amado Camarena was concluding a contract with Dario García who, "en virtud de la adjudicación que se hará en este instrumento, quedará dueño de un solar que es propiedad del Ayuntamiento" [in virtue of the adjudication that will be made in this instrument, he will remain owner of one solar that is the property of the Ayuntamiento].[12]

At times the purchase agreement stated that the money was to go into the construction fund for the theater; in other cases that was not stipulated. The disposition of the funds did not seem to depend upon whether the sale was concluded pursuant to the Degollado Decree or to the Lerdo Law. Whether the purchaser was taking a mortgage or paying the entire cost in cash "up front" may have been a consideration: if the entire amount was being paid at once the money often went into the theater fund, though this was not always the case; if a mortgage was taken, then the interest was paid to the *ayuntamiento*.[13] Just when proceeds from *ejido* land sales ceased to go into the theater fund is not apparent from these records, but reference to that use is limited to the earliest years. Notarial records also included later marginal notations on the original sale protocol, or agreement, stating that the mortgage had been paid off as agreed.[14] When *ejido* lands were not sold to tenants within the three-month time limit provided in the law or if they were not rented, they might be "denounced" by anyone and sold at public auction, for at least two-thirds of their assessed value. This was the case in November 1857 with vacant blocks (*manzanas*) 11 and 12 of the third district (*cuartel*).[15] (See Fig. 1.1)

What exactly defined an *ejido*? How many were there in Guadalajara for the *ayuntamiento* to dispose of? How large were they? What was their value? These questions cannot be answered with any precision—diversity and variation are often the most appropriate words. *Ejidos* were one type of common, or public, property. In the colonial period, Spanish settlements in Mexico, "in addition to the urban area divided into *solares* [building sites] and *suertes* [their corresponding farm plots], had the following properties of a communal nature: a) The *ejido* . . . which in the Spanish villages served so that the village might grow at its expense, as a field for recreation and sport for the inhabitants, as a threshing floor and as a pathway to drive the livestock to the *dehesa* [fenced pasture]. . . . b) The *Propios* [fields] were property which belonged to the *Ayuntamientos* and were used . . . [to defray] expenses of the Municipality and the provision of public services. . . . c) The *dehesa* [was] a fenced plot of ground that [was] to be used for grazing of livestock in Spanish villages."[16] In contrast, lands of the Indian villages established by the Spaniards consisted of the *fundo legal* (urban zone), which was "the place reserved for the houses of the village"; the *ejido*, which was "the field of land on the outskirts of the place," which was "not planted or worked"

Fig. 1.1
Plan of the Third District of Guadalajara

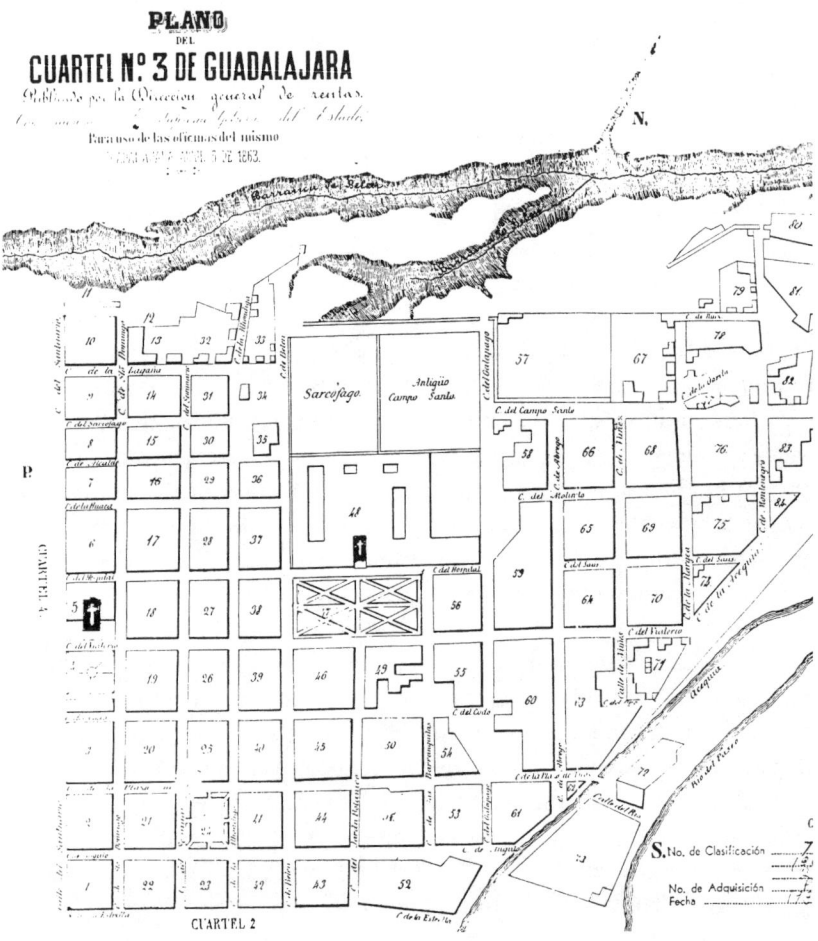

(Source: Lucía Arévalo Vargas, *Cartografía de Guadalajara* [Guadalajara, 1992])

and belonged "to all the inhabitants"; and the *propios,* which were "those lands belonging to the *ayuntamientos* the income from which was used to cover the public expenses of the community. They were granted to individuals under lease or for annual payment (*censo enfitéutico*) with the rent or the income being used to take care of public services of the community. *Tierras* [*de común repartimiento*] . . . were those which were divided into lots for the Indian families so that they might grow crops on them and support themselves with the products." Furthermore, "the *pastos* [pastures], *montes* [woodlands], and water supplies, because of their direct relation to raising livestock . . . belonged to all of the inhabitants."[17] In Guadalajara the term *ejido* applied to any property (*bien raíz*) that belonged to the municipality. The Degollado Decree, ordering the sale of *ejidos,* had exempted certain of the city's property: public plazas; avenues and walks; beds of rivers that ran through the city; and the land on which there were town halls and buildings dedicated to public charity.[18]

The number of *ejidos* belonging to the *ayuntamiento* of Guadalajara in 1855–1856 is not known precisely, but an 1823 report stated that there were 523 properties yielding 1,452 pesos in rent.[19] And a report on *ejidos* sold by the *ayuntamiento* between 1855 and probably September of 1859 listed some 517 *ejidos,* scattered over the nine districts of the city.[20] This number is deceptive, however, because of multiple listings of *ejidos* with the same numerical designation; that is, *ejidos* were sometimes divided and sold to different individuals. The *ejidos,* on which information is available, ranged in size from eighteen square varas to 7,747 square varas; few were under 100 or over 1,000 square varas, however.[21] The shapes of the *ejidos* and their value varied, and the value was not necessarily dependent upon size.[22] While values varied greatly, many were in the two- to three-peso annual rental range, meaning that their sale price was from about thirty-three to fifty pesos.[23]

These municipal *ejido* lands eventually passed to other owners by inheritance or resale.[24] Thus, a lot (*solar*) belonging to the municipality of Guadalajara was purchased in October 1856 by Rafael de la Peña. In September 1857 de la Peña sold the house and garden to Concepción Murillo for 250 pesos, the "fair and just value" of the property.[25] In March 1859, Murillo purchased another property from Ysidro Gudiño. Gudiño sold the house to Murillo—"realmente y para siempre" [effectually and forever]—was the typical terminology used, for 400 pesos, the just and legitimate value of the property.[26] In fact, Gudiño bought at least eight *ejidos,* four each in districts three and four.

Pursuant to the Degollado Decree, Nicanor Angel purchased an *ejido* in May 1856, on which he constructed a "comercio de licores" (liquor store). When he died intestate, his son and only heir, José María Angel, was obligated for his father's debts, one of which was one thousand pesos owed to Lic. Trinidad Bonilla. José María, in September 1861, put up the property as security for the repayment of the one-thousand-peso debt plus six percent interest.[27]

Purchasers of municipal *ejido* lands had to pay the customary five percent transfer of ownership tax (*alcabala*), as well as to prove that, as renters, they had regularly paid the municipal property tax (*contribución directa*); if not, they presumably would have to pay the delinquent taxes as well.[28] The legal sales agreement, prepared by the notary, invariably contained a statement identifying who was responsible for the costs related to the transaction. Usually the purchaser paid both the *alcabala* tax and the expenses of the *escritura*, but there were a number of other possibilities. Sometimes the seller paid both the *alcabala* and *escritura* costs; sometimes the costs of the *escritura* were the responsibility of the seller, while the purchaser was responsible for payment of the *alcabala*; sometimes buyer and seller split the *escritura* expenses, and the buyer paid the *alcabala*; sometimes the buyer paid for the *escritura* and the seller the *alcabala*.[29]

The expenses associated with concluding an agreement varied depending upon the value of the property and the complexity of the deal, but changing one's status from tenant to owner—the costs of proprietorship—could be an expensive proposition. Some costs are easily ascertained, others are not. The *alcabala* was 5 percent and the annual direct property tax was *tres al millar* (3 percent per one thousand pesos of value), but on land of little value, perhaps worth less than one hundred pesos, there was apparently no direct tax.[30] Also, a federal resolution of October 9, 1856, exempted from the *alcabala* and all other fees property worth less than two hundred pesos.[31] However, the resolution does not appear to have been observed in the sales under the Degollado and Lerdo measures studied here.[32] Additionally, there was at times another federal tax (*contribución federal*); there were the expenses borne by the seller for the "evicción, seguridad y saneamiento" (eviction, security, and guarantee) of the sale; and there was the cost of the *escritura* itself.[33] It is not known how frequently witnesses to the agreement were paid. Then there was the cost of the stamped paper used for the *escritura*; in *ejido* sales the paper cost one-half *real* per sheet (there were eight *reales* to one peso), while wills and other property transactions were on paper costing four *reales* (one-half peso) a sheet. A schedule of the notary's fees themselves has not been found; however, in one fairly elaborate and complicated case, which cost the individual a total of 54.25 pesos, the notary's portion was 16.25.[34] In another instance, notary Juan Riestra wrote a receipt declaring that he had received from his colleague, notary Jesús Durán, 3.75 pesos "por derechos de una escritura de venta" [for rights to a sales contract] in which José and Juan

García sold a lot and two small houses to José María Abreu. It is not known what Durán, the primary notary involved, received for his work.[35] In any event, the expenses of becoming a proprietor and maintaining ownership were considerable. As explained in this writer's study of church property, in the long run those costs inhibited achievement of the reformers' goal of creating a large new class of private individual owners.[36]

It is not surprising that many property transactions found in the notarial record that involve the inheritance of property and the purchase or sale of real estate do not relate either to the Degollado Decree or to the Lerdo Law. There was, after all, noncorporate real estate circulating in the market both before and after that legislation.[37]

Sales agreements often stated that the price was "el justo y legítimo valor ... el que en la actualidad no vale más [just and legitimate value ... currently]." Apparently the "just and legitimate" present value of a property could change quickly and dramatically. On September 7, 1857, Sra. María Anna Macías sold to Sr. Felipe Covarrubias a lot that bordered his property.[38] Macías sold the lot to Covarrubias for twenty-six pesos, its "justo y legítimo valor." On October 6, 1857, Covarrubias sold the same lot to Silvestre Ornelas for 100 pesos, "el justo y legítimo valor ... en la actualidad." And in August 1869 Merced Gonzáles, the widow of Ornelas, sold the lot to Casimiro Altamirano for seventy-five pesos, which was, of course, the "just and legitimate value of the lot which presently is worth no more."[39] Of course, the value of noncorporate property also fluctuated, and the market did not always favor the seller. In May 1857, Patricio Romero, a notary, sold a three-room house, which he had purchased in 1848, to Jacinta Feliciana Gutiérrez for 150 pesos. In January 1863 Gutiérrez sold the house to Ynés García for 120 pesos.[40]

In considering apparent changes in property values, it must be remembered that the *ayuntamiento* owned only the land; structures on a lot were the property of and built at the expense of the renter. Prior to the anticorporate property laws, renters of city *ejido* lands bought and sold the structures only.[41] After the laws were issued, when the *ayuntamiento* sold an *ejido*, the price was for the land only. When the owner later sold the property the price might be much higher if it included a house or other structure. For example, on November 4, 1856, Gregoria Ysaguirre purchased, as required by the Lerdo Law, a lot that she had rented from the *ayuntamiento*. The one-peso annual rent, capitalized, gave the *ejido* a value of 16.67 pesos. Two and one-half years later, in May 1859, Ysaguirre sold the lot with the house on it to Estanislao Macías for one hundred pesos.[42]

In late September 1861, José Veitia, the responsible municipal official, reported that sizable debts remained unpaid for *ejido* lands purchased under the 1856 Lerdo Law. Presumably, all those sold pursuant to the 1855 Degollado Decree had been paid for and the proceeds had gone into the theater construction fund. Veitia reported that the total amount outstanding was 2,173.08 pesos. He also declared that 310 *ejidos*, at least one in each of the city's nine districts, remained to be sold.[43] Unsold *ejido* lands and delinquent interest payments for *ejido* lands previously sold remained an issue for the *ayuntamiento* at least through the 1860s and into the 1870s.[44] Nevertheless, many purchasers of *ejido* lands either paid for them at once in cash or paid off their obligations promptly.[45]

The role of women is a striking feature in both rural and urban real estate transactions; however, if a married woman was involved, the agreement invariably stated that she acted with the prior consent of her husband. Consistently, too, women used their maiden names in those transactions.[46] In one list of forty purchasers of *ejidos*, for which this writer noted the names, ten were women.[47] Although not always the case, women frequently obtained property by inheritance—from a parent, a spouse, even a deceased son.

A sizable number of transactions simply documented earlier informal agreements that were perhaps undertaken in an attempt to avoid all the costs associated with a legal document. For example, on December 4, 1862, José Rubio "legalized" the purchase of a house that he had bought informally from Manuel Alvarado in 1860. About two weeks later Rubio used the house as security for a two-hundred-peso short-term loan from Justo Aguirre. Rubio probably formalized his earlier purchase at that particular time precisely so that he could use the house to secure the loan.[48]

Juan Orozco is a name prominent in the notarial records. He provides a good example of multiple property transactions, which are also relevant to the issue of trading in village lands. Guadalajara resident Juan Orozco came on the scene in July 1857, when he bought a part of La Mojonera ranch.[49] Orozco acquired the ranch, which consisted of at least thirty *fanegas* (about 107 hectares) of land in three transactions, one each in 1853, 1857, and 1858.[50] He used it as security for other land acquisitions in 1862 and 1866. As early as 1849, however, Orozco had been buying, selling, and exchanging Nestipac real estate. In 1861 Juan wrote his last will and testament.[51] A resident of Guadalajara, but originally from Arandas, Juan declared that he was the son of Tomás and Gregoria Orozco, both deceased. Eight children of Juan Orozco and his wife, Teresa Santa Cruz, survived infancy. At the time of their marriage, neither Juan nor his wife had any property (*bienes*), but he inherited 532 pesos upon the deaths of his parents. The property Juan acquired thereafter included: a ranch called La Mojonera, located in the jurisdiction of the village of Ocotán, with its livestock, tools (equipment), and other farming appurtenances;[52] four separate plots of land in the village of Nestipac; two houses in the town of Zapopan; and a house he built in Guadalajara, with its furnishings. Orozco declared that he had no debts, but rather was a creditor. He willed one-half of his estate to his wife and he noted that he had given some cash, to be deducted from their inheritance in order to be fair to all, to a son and a daughter; otherwise, Orozco made no specific distribution of his property in this will. The 1861 will proved to be premature and Juan continued his real estate transactions in the municipality of Zapopan.[53] As late as 1869 he paid one thousand pesos for a house in Guadalajara and in 1877 he paid off a debt.[54]

Many questions are left unanswered by the property transactions detailed here, which are based upon limited archival sources. The questions relate to the activities of individuals like Juan Orozco and to dealings involving lands belonging to communities. For example, what was the significance of the extensive dealings in Nestipac lands? Did village land come to be concentrated in a few hands following the state and national measures that individualized communal holdings?[55]

Nevertheless, a partial picture emerges from these fragments of information on the property transactions of one person in particular. Juan Orozco seems to have been a considerable entrepreneur. According to his premature 1861 will, he began married life with no appreciable material goods. He inherited a few hundred pesos and proceeded to accumulate considerable wealth in real estate within a decade or so. In the transactions presented here, over the years Orozco spent some 10,350 pesos to purchase property that included the hacienda of La Lentija and the ranch of La Mojonera; the latter consisted of about 107 hectares and Orozco used it several times as collateral for loans. In addition, Orozco acquired several houses and about 140 hectares of other land. All of the property mentioned in this paper was in Guadalajara and the district of Zapopan, in the villages of Nestipac and Ocotán, located in the municipalities of Tesistán and Zapopan. The fragments of land that Orozco acquired might or might not have been consolidated, or contiguous, but often descriptions note that a particular piece bordered on other land belonging to him. And Orozco was not just buying land, but selling and exchanging plots as well.

Indeed, in those years generally there seems to have been considerable buying and selling of real estate, both urban and rural. Legislation from the time of independence on provided opportunities for the ambitious and the astute to prosper: state laws partitioned and individualized Indian village lands (the Nestipac village lands referred to above probably had been acquired initially by individual villagers through distribution under state laws like those of 1825, 1828, and 1849); the 1855 Degollado Decree mandated the sale of Guadalajara's *ejidos;* the 1856 Lerdo Law required the sale of civil and ecclesiastical corporations' real estate. In addition, real estate other than that encompassed in those laws changed hands. At least some of the "entrepreneurs" did not tie up all of their capital in real estate, but retained some to lend to others. However, success, the growth of capital and wealth, probably did not always crown their dealings. One would think it particularly risky to deal in real estate in a period of political instability and market saturation, since there were large amounts of property available as a consequence of the Degollado and Lerdo measures.

The enduring uncertainty surrounding property transactions during politically uncertain times is pointed up by José María Pérez Maldonado's sale for two hundred pesos of a lot in Guadalajara's third district to Sra. Margarita Santa Ana on October 11, 1866. Maldonado had purchased the lot from the *ayuntamiento* on November 22, 1856, under provisions of the Lerdo Law. Nearly a decade later the transaction was submitted to review under the Imperial Law of Revision of February 26, 1865, and the sale was validated on May 26, 1866.[56] The Law of Revision required that all property transactions carried out under the liberal laws be submitted to imperial review. If it was found that the transactions had been concluded in accordance with provisions of those laws, the imperial authorities ratified them; if they were not carried out in conformity with the laws, they could be made to conform, for a fee, and were then ratified. Meanwhile, the peripatetic Republican government of Benito Juárez prohibited all dealings with the empire and promised to punish any who collaborated.

This was just the last act in a decade, 1857–1867, during which Mexico endured political upheaval and economic dislocation. First, the country was engulfed in three years of civil war, the War of the Reform, between adherents of the liberal reformers and their conservative opponents. Then, shortly after the liberal victory in December 1860, foreign intervention occurred: a French expeditionary force occupied much of the country (1861–1864), followed by the imposition of the Austrian Archduke Maximilian's empire (1864–1867). Nevertheless, despite the warfare and seemingly chaotic conditions in much of Mexico, life seems to have gone on "normally" as far as property transactions were concerned. However, particularly in the case of ecclesiastical property, the notarial records reflect political changes. There was great activity in corporate real estate (civil and ecclesiastical) after the issuance of the Lerdo Law in mid-1856, following the conservative annulment of that law in early 1858, and then again on the heels of the liberal victory in the civil war at the end of 1860 with implementation of the 1859 nationalization decree.[57]

With regard to lands belonging to communities inhabited by "los que antes se llamaban indios" [those who before (independence) were called Indians] the notarial archives add to the information contained in this writer's 1978 essay on Jalisco and the partition of village lands that was mandated at various times in the nineteenth century, notably in 1825, 1828, and 1849.[58] That essay showed, with respect to Guadalajara, that there were

> striking similarities in the history of the disamortization of civil and ecclesiastical corporate property with respect to the lack of knowledge about what property the corporations owned, lack of documentation on antecedents, continuing problems over liquidation of debts, lenient payment terms, the use of special agents to search out corporate property, imperial revision of transactions, and disputes and litigation over ownership of property. Yet another similarity was the confusion over what municipal property was exempt from disamortization, despite seeming clarity of the law.

With regard to village lands, specifically Santa María, the documents revealed "internal village disputes between the elected Commission [charged with effecting partition of lands] and dissident villagers, the conflict between a neighboring *hacendado* and the village over land ownership, the uncertainty of boundary lines, and the fertile field for litigation and lawyers' services, which perhaps contributed to the durability of the controversies and certainly contributed to the financial problems of the community." The impact of political changes and turbulence on village lands is difficult to determine. At least in the case of Santa María, there is little reference to political changes influencing village property. What does emerge is "bureaucratic red tape, intra-village animosities, hacienda-village frictions, constant petitioning and argumentation between local and higher authorities. Certainly one of the constants over the decades was the invariable response of state authorities to village petitions and complaints—'take the matter to the courts.'" Nevertheless, the evidence *does* suggest that political events of the 1850s and 1860s "not only delayed or obstructed implementation of laws, but that some laws, notably the 1856 Lerdo law, did affect and complicate the process of village land division and contribute to controversies at the local level." The 1978 essay also cited the need for further investigation into the racial implications of village controversies, the effect of disputes on the distribution and control of land, the significance of personality conflicts, and the real meaning of individualization of communal property. Thus, the 1849 Jalisco state decree permitted joint possession of the land distributed among individual villages. That "joint possession, as well as undivided property and unalienated property administered by the *ayuntamiento*, continued long after the promulgation of the Lerdo law and the 1857 Constitution."

A particular value of the notarial documents is the information they provide regarding changes in property ownership after partition and disamortization were decreed. The dealings of Juan Orozco and others reveal some of that process. One consequence of partition, which the Orozco case suggests, was the opportunity it provided for individuals to accumulate village lands, as in Nestipac. The 1825 state law, however, prohibited the acquisition of village lands by large landholders. It is not yet clear whether that prohibition was flouted; nor is it often known what prompted villagers to sell their plots or how they spent the pesos that they received from the sales.

For example, José María López, a native (*indígena*) of the village of Analco, through partition received a piece of land in April 1814. The plot was held in "quieta y pacífica" (undisturbed and peaceful) uninterrupted ownership for more than forty years. In April 1859, by which time Analco had been absorbed into Guadalajara as District 8, the widow Jacinta Guevara, who had inherited the land from López, her father, sold it for fifty pesos.[59] Other pieces of land in Analco, apparently obtained through purchases from the beneficiaries of the partition of village land in the 1820s and inherited by the children of the purchasers, were being sold in 1860, perhaps to nonresidents of Analco. Prices ranged from sixteen pesos and thirty pesos for two small plots to one hundred pesos for a more sizable piece.[60] Reasons for the sales, after the lands had been in the same families for so many years, are not specified. The sales, however, took place during the War of the Reform, and during the imperial period in the 1860s there continued to be sales of lands that had been acquired through village land partition and held for many years.[61]

These examples confirm the generalization that the notarial documents usually provide no explanation for the transactions involving former civil corporate property beyond citation of specific laws and inheritance. There is usually no hint that sales were prompted by financial difficulties, by poor economic conditions, or by political upheaval. However, there did seem to be continuity in the anti-communal property policies of successive state governments from independence through the mid-century reform era. Although there were variations in the laws, repetition may be accounted for, in part, by inhabitants' opposition to any law that attacked their communal ownership; an opposition long asserted by scholars. Scholars have also maintained that privatization of village lands facilitated encroachment on those lands by outsiders, or even by "enterprising" villagers, resulting in greater concentration of rural landownership. Although there was much trafficking in corporate real estate, and some individuals accumulated sizable holdings, much more research and analysis of data will be required to substantiate the standard beliefs.

Notes

1. Funds provided by the Center for Latin America at the University of Wisconsin, Milwaukee, and the University of Wisconsin, Stevens Point, helped support the research for this article. Special thanks are due the staff of the historical documents section of the Archivo de Instrumentos Públicos for their assistance, especially Lic. Mayra González Jaime, the head of that office. The plans from the *Cartografía de Guadalajara* are used courtesy of the Archivo Histórico de Jalisco. I am also indebted to my wife, Barbara, for invaluable research and editorial assistance.

2. Corporations were defined as "all the religious communities of both sexes, confraternities and archconfraternities, congregations, brotherhoods, parishes, municipal governments (*ayuntamientos*), colleges (*colegios*), and in general every establishment or foundation of perpetual or indefinite duration. Luis G. Labastida, *Colección de leyes, decretos, reglamentos, circulares, órdenes y acuerdos relativos a la desamortización de los bienes de corporaciones civiles y religiosas y a la nacionalización de los que administraron las últimas* (México, 1893), pp. 3–4.

3. "La individualización de la propiedad corporativa civil en el siglo xix—notas sobre Jalisco," *Historia Mexicana* 28:1 (1978), 24–61.

4. "La división de las tierras de los pueblos durante el siglo xix: el caso de Michoacán," *Historia Mexicana* 40:1 (1990), 3–25.

5. The state decrees relative to village, or community, lands most cited in the documents used in this article are:

Decree 2, February 12, 1825, which stated that "the ones formerly called `indios' are declared to be owners of the lands, houses and lots which they currently hold individually whether in the urban zones of the villages or outside of them" (art. 1). "The `indios' are forbidden to alienate their holdings ... to those land owners who have one or more `sitios de ganado mayor'; the latter will not be allowed to acquire those lands directly or indirectly at any time or through any instrument" (art. 3). (One *sitio de ganado mayor* equals 1,755.61 hectares and one hectare is approximately 2.47 acres.) *Colección de acuerdos, órdenes y decretos sobre tierras, casas y solares, de los indígenas, bienes de sus comunidades y fundos legales de los pueblos del estado de Jalisco* (Guadalajara, 1849–1880), vol. 1, "Decretos del Honorable Congreso", pp. 131–32.

Decree 151, September 29, 1828, which provided that "the real estate purchased by those formerly called `indios' and known under the name of communal holdings are their [the indios'] property" (art. 1). "The government will arrange for the cession to the respective communities of the properties which have been under the jurisdiction of the municipalities so that they [the communities] can then proceed to their distribution" (art. 2). Ibid., pp. 133–34.

Decree 121, April 17, 1849, which reiterated that "the urban and rural real estate bought by the natives . . . , which up to now has been recognized as communal, is their property as of September 29, 1828" (art. 1). "In the partition the goal will be the greatest equality possible in quality and size of the parcels" (art. 7). "The natives who want to hold jointly the properties that are theirs through the division may do so after they have been distributed, under the legal agreements that they reach among themselves as individuals" (art. 24). Ibid., pp. 152–56.

6. The records of some notaries mentioned in the transactions of other notaries, for example, Vicente Munguía, Patricio Romero, and José María Mireles, are not available in the archives where they ought to be housed; perhaps they were misplaced, or perhaps those notaries failed to forward their records to the archives. Archivo de Instrumentos Públicos, Guadalajara, Jalisco (hereafter cited as AIP).

7. AIP, Garibay, Protocolos, vol. 7 (1864), vol. 8 (1865), vol. 9 (1866). His index for 1865 includes: Adjudicaciones (2 items), Arrendamientos (5), Ampliaciones (1), Cesiones (8), Compromisos (3), Convenios (3), Contrato de mutuo (1), Compañías (2), Codicilos (1), Donaciones (1), Fianzas (13), Finiquitos (1), Hipotecas (32), Obligaciones (7), Poderes (60), Protestos (6), Protocolizaciones (23), Particiones (3), Prorogas (2), Reconocimientos (2), Ratificaciones (4), Retroventa (1), Recibos (1), Subarriendos (1), Testamentos (27), Transacciones (1), and Ventas (53). AIP, Garibay, Protocolos, vol. 8. Unfortunately, not all notaries so thoughtfully provided indexes.

8. In the years 1856–1858 Jesús Durán handled seventeen property sales, at least twelve of which were of ecclesiastical property; the others were of noncorporate real estate; in 1859, twelve sales, one of former municipal property; in 1860, seventeen, one of which was former municipal property; in 1861, forty-one, none municipal, virtually all ecclesiastical; in 1862, eleven transactions, most former ecclesiastical, only one former; meanwhile, Mariano Hermoso's books for 1856 and 1857 are filled with sales of Guadalajara *ejidos*.

9. "Se dispone la venta de egidos . . . por decreto del 12 de diciembre del corriente año, expedido por don Santos Degollado" (1855), Archivo Municipal de Guadalajara (hereafter cited as AMG), caja 1, legajo 72.

10. The legal term for these arrangements was *emphyteusis*, that is, while the corporation actually owned the land, it gave long-term "use ownership" (*dominio útil*) to individuals who paid an annual "rent" (*canon*).

11. "Sobre varias disposiciones relativas al cumplimiento de la ley de 25 de junio de 1856," AMG, caja 1 (1856), September 30, 1856, p. 2.

12. AIP, Luis G. Arreola, Protocolos, vol. 11 (1856), October 29, 1856, pp. 394–96. This notary is referred to in the records as both Luis G. Arreola and Luis Gonzaga Arreola; henceforth, the citation used will be Arreola.

13. AIP, Juan Riestra, Protocolos, vol. 11 (1856): Doña Teresa García, November 6, 1856, p. 565; Doña Jacoba Rivas de Figueroa, November 6, 1856, p.

568; Doña Josefa Figueroa y Rivas, November 6, 1856, p. 570; Don Gabriel Cárdenas, November 21, 1856, pp. 591–92; Sra. Doña Refugio Gutiérrez, December 9, 1856, p. 619. See, also, AIP, Hermoso, Documentos, vol. 4 (1856–1859), Doña Ysidora Ramos, December 29, 1857, p. 261. But see AIP, Hermoso, Protocolos, vol. 24 (1856), Doña Gregoria Ysaguirre, November 4, 1856, pp. 334–35, for a case of a mortgage taken with the interest going to the theater fund.

14. For example, AIP, Hermoso, Protocolos, vol. 25 (1857), January 8, 1857, p. 7.

15. AIP, Francisco Riestra, Protocolos, vol. 1 (1857–1863), January 24, 1858, pp. 11–12. See, also, the case of Cándido Domínguez, who denounced and purchased an *ejido* for 41.66 pesos. AIP, Mariano Hermoso, Protocolos, vol. 25 (1857), September 15, 1857, p. 212.

16. Raúl Lemus García, *Derecho agrario mexicano (sinopsis histórico)* (México, 1975), pp. 115–16.

17. Ibid., pp. 117–19.

18. "Se dispone la venta de egidos . . . " Degollado, art. 1. As will be recalled, the Lerdo Law exempted buildings and other property belonging to *ayuntamientos*, like *ejidos*, and lands destined exclusively to the public service of the population. The specific exemption of *ejidos* was omitted from article 27 of the 1857 Constitution which dealt with property; it exempted only "los edificios destinados inmediata y directamente al servicio u objeto de la institución [the structures immediately and directly destined to the service or object of the institution]." Donald Frazer maintains that, despite the apparent omission in article 27, *ejidos* continued to be exempt. As proof, he cites a June 15, 1857, communication from the minister of hacienda to the governor of Zacatecas, stating that "the ejidos of the municipalities destined to the `beneficio común' are included in the exceptions granted under article 8 of the Lerdo Law." Frazer also cites the concession granted for the establishment of three towns in Tehuantepec: they were to have "a fundo legal of one square league and ejidos that measured 838 meters on a side." Donald Frazer, "La política de desamortización en las comunidades indígenas, 1856–1872," *Historia Mexicana* 21:4 (April–June 1972).

Also, in an 1871 *amparo* case involving the sale of lands of the village of San Lorenzo Ixtacoyotla (Hidalgo state) the district judge, in his sentence, stated that the village had individualized the major part of those lands, "retaining the character of common or undivided the wood lots, ejidos and running waters, that is, the land expressly excepted from disamortization because it is of public use, art. 8 of the June 25 Law and the Supreme Resolution of August 20, 1856." "Juicio promovido ante el juzgado de Distrito del Estado de Hidalgo por el C. Juan José Quiroz . . . vecinos de San Lorenzo Ixtacoyotla . . . , " *Semanario judicial de la Federación*, 1st epoch, vol. 2 (1871), p. 711.

The common interpretation of the prohibition of corporate property ownership and the exemption clause was that expressed by Luis Labastida, stating that "once the urban area has been laid out and the part intended for cemeteries and other public uses set aside, the remainder will be divided and distributed among the fathers or heads of family" (p. 21). Thus, apparently, only those *ejidos*, or parts of *ejidos*, not used for public purposes were to be partitioned and reduced to individual ownership. However, federal circulars sent to state authorities dated October 28, 1889, and May 12, 1890, were more broadly framed; the former stated that federal authorities were to "promote before the respective local authorities the distribution of ejidos in accordance with the provisions of laws issued to this end as well as [the distribution] of other similar properties." The local authorities declared: "Because of such a decisive order, it is clear that neither the ejidos nor the lands known as 'terrenos de común repartimiento' can endure under the ownership arrangements that most of them currently enjoy and that it is a duty of the appropriate authorities to proceed to the conversion of the aforementioned ejidos and properties into private property, with their alienation free of any restraints." Labastida, *Colección de leyes*, pp. 47–48.

There were other clarifications of article 8, as well as of other articles of the law. For example, a resolution of August 20, 1856, declared that the *montes* of municipalities were to be included in the exemption from disamortization (art. 8) insofar as "the greater part of their use is directly by the citizens of each municipality, even though some of the exploitation of those wood lots, such as felling of large trees, are granted through rental." Labastida, *Colección de leyes*, p. 50.

19. "Estado relativo a los egidos pertenecientes al muy ilustre ayuntamiento de esta capital" (1823), AMG, Egidos no. 2, leg. 210.

20. "Noticia de los egidos del Ayuntamiento que han sido vendidos desde el año de 1855," AMG, caja 2.

21. One *vara* equaled about thirty-three inches, or 2.75 feet, or 0.835 meters.

22. For example, one *ejido* of 3,382 square *varas* (38 by 89) sold for 300 pesos; another of 4,420 square *varas* (52 by 85) sold for 150 pesos; another of 6,020 square *varas* (86 by 70) sold for 200 pesos. While many *ejidos*, like those just cited, had fairly regular shapes, there were also some curiosities (for example, 32.75 by 53.75 by 36.5 by 15.75 by 70 by 68.75). "Legajo de recibos y planos de poseedores de egidos" (1856), AMG, caja 2, leg. 2.

23. See, for example, AIP, Hermoso, Protocolos, vol. 25 (1857), p. 212, and AMG, Egido y Agua (1873).

24. For example, AIP, Garibay, Protocolos, vol. 8 (1865), August 21, 1865, pp. 370–71, and AIP, Garibay, Protocolos, vol. 10 (1867), July 6, 1867, pp. 342–43.

25. AIP, Garibay, Protocolos, vol. 1 (1857–1858), September 3, 1857, pp. 20–21.

26. Gudiño had bought the *ejido* from the *ayuntamiento* on June 17, 1856, and had built a house on it. AIP, Garibay, Protocolos, vol. 2 (1859), book 1, March 2, 1859, pp. 11–12.

27. A notation in the margin of the agreement (*escritura*) on August 2, 1864, canceled the mortgage (*hipoteca*) because the debt had been paid. AIP, Garibay, Protocolos, vol. 4 (1861), September 7, 1861, pp. 251–52.

28. AIP, Hermoso, Documentos, vol. 4 (1856–1859), June 3, 1857, pp. 107–8, August 18, 1857, pp. 136–37, March 9, 1859, pp. 526–27.

29. AIP, José María Muro, Protocolos/Documentos, vol. 7 (1858–1860), January 30, 1858, p. 6; January 31, 1859, pp. 6–7; February 4, 1859, p. 9; February 7, 1859, pp. 9–10; February 26, 1859, p. 11; November 18, 1859, p. 38.

30. AIP, Rodríguez Blanco, Protocolos/Documentos, one volume (1836–1856), December 22, 1852.

31. The resolution stated that "each property whose value does not exceed $200, in accordance with the law of June 15, is to be sold to the respective renter whether the latter receives it through partition, since it belongs to the *ayuntamientos*, or through some other means of disamortization; and the renters will not be charged the alcabala or any other tax." Resolución de 9 de octubre de 1856, Labastida, *Colección de leyes*, p. 13. The sign $ refers to Mexican pesos which, during this period, were on a par with the United States dollar.

32. For example, see AIP, Hermoso, Documentos, vol. 3 (1856).

33. Receipts dated July 22, 1861, and December 5, 1862, from Administración Principal de Rentas in AIP, Tomás Bravo, Protocolos, one volume (1851–1862), pp. 5 and 62.

34. AIP, Tomás Bravo, Protocolos, one volume (1851–1862), p. 34.

35. AIP, Durán, Protocolos/Documentos, vol. 12 (1859–1862), September 7, 1859, p. 5.

36. See Robert J. Knowlton, *Church Property and the Mexican Reform, 1856–1910* (DeKalb, 1976).

37. For example, see AIP, Garibay, Protocolos, vol. 4 (1861), February 9, 1861, p. 34, Lizana selling to Cárdenas, and AIP, Notary Juan Nepomuceno Esparza, Protocolos, vol. 2 (1858–1861), Lizana buying from Francisco Real, February 4, 1860, pp. 4 and 7; AIP, Garibay, Protocolos, vol. 5 (1862), January 3, 1862, pp. 3–4, Romualda López selling to Dolores and Jesús Prieto, and AIP, Notary Esparza, Protocolos, vol. 2 (1858–1861), López buying from Antonia Robles de Peres, April 16, 1861, n.p.; AIP, Garibay, Protocolos, vol. 6 (1863), June 22, 1863, p. 211, Muñiz selling to Cobián, and AIP, Notary José María Muro, Protocolos/Documentos, vol. 7 (1859), December 31, 1859, p. 46, Cobián buying from Dávila.

38. The lot had been purchased in March 1821 by her husband, Iván José Meza (d. 1845), from his brother, who had acquired it in the partition of lands among the villagers of Mexicalcingo. Mexicalcingo had been a separate village that was later absorbed by Guadalajara.

39. AIP, Arreola, Protocolos, vol. 12 (1857), September 7, 1857, pp. 236–39; October 6, 1857, pp. 252–54; AIP, Garibay, Protocolos, vol. 12 (1869), August 23, 1869, p. 294. The September 1857 sales agreement was signed by Jesús Meza for his mother and by a witness, Ygnacio Orozco, for Covarrubias because neither one could write. Witnesses also signed the October 1857 agreement for the principals. The parties to the 1869 agreement, Merced Gonzáles de Ornelas and Altamirano, signed for themselves.

40. AIP, Ramón Barboza, Protocolos, vol. 6 (1857–1859), May 28, 1857, p. 11, and AIP, Garibay, Protocolos, vol. 6 (1863), January 12, 1863, p. 13.

41. For example, on June 9, 1830, Agapito Velasco sold to Pedro Días de Sandí twelve "piezas techadas" located on land that he rented from the *ayuntamiento*. AIP, J. V. Tapia, Protocolos, one volume (1829–30 y 31), pp. 77–78.

42. AIP, Hermoso, Protocolos, vol. 24 (1856), pp. 334–35, and AIP, Juan Riestra, Protocolos, vol. 14 (1859), book 4, May 14, 1859, p. 14. For an example of the text see AIP, Hermoso, Protocolos, vol. 24 (1856), October 30, 1856, pp. 281–82, and AIP, Juan Riestra, Protocolos, vol. 12 (1857), July 17, 1857, p. 303.

43. For example, he reported one remaining in District 2, three in District 1, ninety-six in District 5, and fifty-four in District 3. "Noticia sobre egidos y documentos entregados a la mayordomía por el C. José Veitia . . . " (1862), AMG, caja 2, leg. 164.

44. "Venta de egidos—noticia de los que se han hecho en el presente año" (1871), AMG, Egido y Agua, 57.

45. See, for example, AIP, Arreola, Protocolos, vol. 11 (1856), October 29, 1856, pp. 394–96, 398–99, and 399–401; AIP, Hermoso, Protocolos, vol. 24 (1856), October 30, 1856, pp. 280–81 and 281–82, and December 9, 1856, p. 490; and AIP, Muro, Protocolos, vol. 7 (1858), February 11, 1858, pp. 14–15.

46. For example, "Sras. Doña Josefa y Doña Angela Leñero, de esta vecindad, mayores y la primera libre de matrimonio y la segunda casada con Don José María Fernández, quien le concede la licencia necesaria para este contrato . . . , " AIP, Muro, Protocolos/Documentos, vol. 7 (1858–1860), January 30, 1858, p. 6. *Libre de matrimonio*, free of marriage, apparently did not mean that the woman had never been married, simply that she was not married at the time of the transaction. In this case, the two women, as required by the Lerdo Law, had purchased from the *ayuntamiento* on November 27, 1856, a lot they had rented for two pesos a year. They therefore paid 33.33 pesos for the *ejido*. On January 30, 1858, they sold the lot with a small two-room house for 100 pesos to Teodocio García. AIP, Hermoso, Protocolos, vol. 24 (1856), November 27, 1856, pp. 405–6, and AIP, Muro, Protocolos/ Documentos, vol. 7 (1858–1860), January 30, 1858, p. 6.

47. The list included a total of 147 receipts for *alcabala* payments dated between October 30 and December 30, 1856. AIP, Hermoso, Documentos, vol. 3 (1856). For other examples of women buying or selling property, see

AIP, Muro, Protocolos, vol. 7 (1858–1860), January 27, 1858, p. 5, July 8, 1858, p. 22, December 31, 1859, p. 46; and AIP, Desiderio Mejía, Protocolos/Documentos, vol. 3 (1858–61), September 29, 1859, pp. 63–64.

48. Alvarado had purchased the house, standing on a municipal *ejido*, on June 1, 1849, from José María Ruiz; following promulgation of the Lerdo Law, Alvarado bought the land from the *ayuntamiento* on October 25, 1856. In August 1860, Rubio bought the house and part of the lot for one hundred pesos; that contract was formalized in 1862, just before the loan agreement. The loan was to be repaid in six months at three percent interest per month. AIP, Tomás Bravo, Protocolos, one volume (1851–1862), December 4, 1862, pp. 60–64, and December 17, 1862, pp. 64–65.

49. The land, located in the municipality of Tesistán, district of Zapopan, was purchased from José María Leal, and it bordered other property on the north, south, and west belonging to Juan Orozco. AIP, Arreola, Protocolos, vol. 12 (1857), July 28, 1857, pp. 209–11.

50. One *fanega de sembradura* equals 3.5661 hectares; one hectare is approximately 2.47 acres.

51. AIP, Garibay, Protocolos, vol. 4 (1861), pp. 159–62. Although Orozco declared that he was in excellent health at the time, he drafted his will because "one can never tell."

52. There may well have been *two* ranches called La Mojonera, one in Ocotán, the other in Nestipac. See Figure 2 for the locations of Nestipac, Ocotán, and Mojonera (Zapopan, nos. 35–36).

53. AIP, Garibay, Protocolos, vol. 4 (1861), pp. 171–72, vol. 5 (1862), pp. 28–31, 93–94, 240–44, 417–19, and vol. 9 (1866), pp. 49–50, 327–29, 345–47, and 393–94. As noted earlier in this essay with regard to Guadalajara *ejidos*, Juan Orozco's acquisitions of rural lands varied in size and value, as would be expected, but they also varied in the regularity of their dimensions, which might not be expected. AIP, Arreola, Protocolos, vol. 12 (1857), July 28, 1857, pp. 209–11. He paid fifteen hundred pesos for a pasture in Ocotán that measured some 1,766 *varas* by 390 *varas* by 659 *varas* by 3,036 *varas*. AIP, Arreola, Protocolos, vol. 12 (1857), October 7, 1857, pp. 254–56. In 1866 Orozco purchased lands in Nestipac, one piece for 225 pesos measuring 800 by 370 by 482 by 808 *varas*, and the other, for 80 pesos, measuring 512 by 412 by 286 by 298.5 *varas*. AIP, Garibay, Protocolos, vol. 9 (1866), January 24, 1866, pp. 49–50, and August 4, 1866, pp. 393–94.

54. AIP, Garibay, Protocolos, vol. 12 (1869), March 10, 1869, pp. 106–8. He gave the house to his daughter, Perfecta, as part of her inheritance; she was to pay six percent annual interest, however, until the death of either of her parents. Perfecta was the wife of Marcelino Zavala.

55. According to one source, the village of Nestipac had 216 inhabitants in 1838 and 250 in 1858; the town of Zapopan, 1,274 in 1838 and 1,421 in 1858; and the village of Ocotán, 458 in 1838 and 509 in 1858. These com-

munities were in the sixth department (*partido*) of the *cantón* of Guadalajara; the *partido* had 13,432 inhabitants in 1838 and 14,940 in 1858. The city of Guadalajara's population was 45,544 in 1838 and 75,000 in 1858. The Guadalajara *cantón* had a population of 146,355 in 1848 and 165,574 in 1858; the entire state population for the same years was 778,646 and 829,716. Longinos Banda, *Estadística de Jalisco, formada con vista de los mejores datos oficiales y noticias ministradas por sujetos idoneos, en los años de 1854 a 1863* (Guadalajara, 1873), pp. 44, 84–85.

56. AIP, Garibay, Protocolos, vol. 9 (1866), pp. 464–65.

57. Examples of post-civil war activity may be found in AIP, Durán, Protocolos/Documentos, vol. 12 (1859–1862).

58. See Knowlton, "La individualización."

59. The uncultivated plot was approximately 2,200 square *varas* in size. AIP, Garibay, Protocolos, vol. 2 (1859), book 1, April 5, 1859, pp. 40–41.

60. AIP, Garibay, Protocolos, vol. 3 (1860), part 1, September 13, 1860, and part 2, May 9, 1860, pp. 53–55.

61. For example, in October 1864 Nicolás and Antonio Ríos, inhabitants of the village of San Agustín residing at the time in Guadalajara, sold two pieces of land to Eligio Calderón. The Ríos brothers had inherited the lands from their mother, a native of the village of San Agustín; she had acquired them pursuant to the 1825 state decree, one plot in 1834, the other in 1848. One piece of land, two *fanegas* eight *almudes de sembradura* in size, called Tierra Salada, bordered Calderón's property on one side; the other smaller plot, three-fourths of a *fanega de sembradura*, bordered Tierra Salada on one side. The "just and legitimate" sale price of the two properties was four hundred pesos. AIP, Garibay, Protocolos, vol. 7 (1864), October 10, 1864, pp. 331–32. One *almud* was equal to from one-half to one *medida*; one *medida* equaled 0.2934 to 0.5867 acres.

Appendix: Table 1.1

Table of Measures[1]

Length
1 league = 1,290.00 meters
1 *vara* {2.75 feet} = 0.838 meters
1 *cordel* = variable[2]

Area
1.424 square *varas* = 1.00 square meters
1 hectare (10,000 square meters/2.47 acres) = 14,240.0657 square *varas*
fundo legal for a village = 101.12 hectares or 1,200 square *varas*
1 *caballeria* (0.024 square leagues[3]) = 42.795 hectares or 1,104 x 552 *varas* or 427,953 square meters
1 *fanega de sembradura de maiz* (7.2 acres) = 3.5662 hectares
1 *solar* for a house (50 x 50 varas) = 0.1755 hectares
1 *cuartilla de sembradura* (4.39 acres) = 1.75 hectares or 250 x 100 *varas*

    1. Unless otherwise noted these equivalences are based upon Alberto J. Torres, *Peso y medidas antiguas en Mexico*.
    2. There is some disagreement over the length of a *cordel*. Silvia Herminia Contreras Ojeda, in her 1991 thesis for the licenciatura at the University of Guadalajara, cites a measure given by Manuel Carrera Stampa of 8.38 meters (10 *varas*), but she also cites a figure given by Manuel Orozco y Berra of 41.90 meters (50 *varas*). Carrera Stampa states in "Evolution of Weights and Measures in New Spain" that in addition to the *cordel* of 10 *varas* (used principally in measuring the *criadero*), a *cordel* of 50 Mexican *varas* (0.8359 meters) was employed in laying out plots of land and a *cordel* of 69 *varas* applied to the measurement of *caballerias* of land." (*Hispanic American Historical Review* 29:1, p. 11.) The last was probably used in at least some cases referred to in this article because some measurements had *cordeles* plus *varas* which exceeded 50.
    3. Charles Gibson, *The Aztecs Under Spanish Rule: A History of the Indians of the Valley of Mexico, 1519–1810* (Stanford, 1964), p. 276.

Appendix: Table 1.2

Orozco Property Transactions

Date/Property	Measurement	Price in Pesos
A. Juan Orozco Acquisitions		
July 28, 1857/Part of Mojonera[1]	4c 23v x 19c 3v x 19c 3v[2] (a *cordel* here equalled 50 *varas*)	400
August 7, 1857/Exchange in Nestipac	11c x 12c 9v x 4c 29v x 6c 15v	100
October 7, 1857	25c 41v x 5c 45v x 9c 38v x 44c	1,500
April 7, 1858	one *fanega* and one *cuartilla de sembradura de maiz*	100
July 11, 1860/Two pieces of land in Nestipac	a) one *fanega de sembradura de maiz*; b) 41v x 41v x 600v x 600v	81 / 60
January 21, 1862/Three sections of pasture, part of Mora ranch	size not given	3,800
June 26, 1862/Hacienda La Lentija (5 pastures) in Partido of Zapotlanejo	size not given	3,000
January 24, 1866/Land in Nestipac	800v x 370v x 482v x 808v	225
August 4, 1866/Land in Nestipac	512v x 412v x 286v x 298 1/2v	80
March 10, 1869/House in Guadalajara	Entry, living room, two bedrooms, dining room, three other rooms, kitchen, patio, corral, upper level straw loft, well and laundry room	1,000
B. Martin Tello e Orozco Acquisitions		
March 17, 1856/Land in Nestipac	a) 5c 16v x 5c 16v x 6c 21v x 6c 27v; b) 3c 13v x 2c 55v x 7c x 6c 46v	75
September 26, 1856	152v x 250v x 234v x 250v	30
April 10, 1860/Three pieces in Nestipac sold by Juan Nepomuceno Orozco	a) 360v x 390v x 221v x 183v; b) Three pieces: 250 square *varas*; 230v x 230v x 265v x 300v; 250v x 250v x 348v x 383v; c) *rincon e la Mojonera*: one *fanega de sembradura e maiz*	269
April 10, 1860/Two pieces sold by Antonia Lozano	a) three *cuartillas de sembradura de maiz*; b) 180v x 328v x 180v x 303v, plus a *rincon* on the south angle of 240v x 273v x 134v x 153v	140
July 1, 1866/Two plots of Nestipac land	a) irregular features; b) seller had bought six pieces from Nestipac natives	600 / 300

Orozco Property Transactions (continued)

Date/Property	Measurement	Price in Pesos
A. *Juan Orozco Acquisitions*		
C. *Juan Nepomuceno Acquisitions*		
October 19, 1857/Three pieces of Nestipac land (sold in 1860, see above)	a) 250 sq *varas*	30
	b) 230v x 230v x 265v x 300v	30
	c) 250v x 250v x 384v x 383v	20
October 26, 1857/Two pieces of Nestipac land (sold in 1860 to Juan Orozco)	a) 1.5 *fanegas de sembradura de maiz*	40
	b) 179v x 179v x 161v x 161v	30
November 2, 1857/Nestipac land in rincon de la Mojonera (sold in 1860)	*one fanega de sembradura*	30

1. La Mojonera ranch consisted of at least 30 *fanegas* or about 107 hectares. Orozco acquired the ranch in three parts: in 1853 from several people named Morales; in 1857 from Jose Maria Leal; and in 1858 from Antonia Morales. Orozco used the ranch as security for lands in 1862 and 1866.

2. c = *cordel*; v = *vara*

2
The Decade of Revolt
Peasant Rebellion in Jalisco, Mexico, 1855–1864
Dawn Fogle Deaton

Violent social protest in the Jalisco countryside erupted without comparison in the years 1855–1864. Jalisco's "decade of revolt" witnessed massive peasant mobilizations more frequently and in greater numbers than during any other time in the state's history.[1] In the sixty-year period, 1825–1885, the documents record twenty-seven peasant (primarily indigenous) rebellions in the state.[2] Yet seventeen of the twenty-seven occurred within one decade, 1855–64. Within that decade, ten occurred in one year—1857. This essay addresses the question of why the years 1855–64, and especially 1857, witnessed so much tumult and became "the decade of revolt." Another major issue this study addresses, which follows logically from the fact that 1857 recorded the most unrest, is whether or not the promulgation of Ley Lerdo (1856) contributed to the wave of rebellion.[3]

Caught in the flux of nineteenth-century Mexico and its move from independence to nation-state, the western state of Jalisco experienced many waves of unrest, popular protest, and open rebellion. These conflicts arose out of political and social struggles among classes and between classes. The countryside witnessed an exponential increase in popular protest from that which the state had seen during the colonial period.[4]

A confluence of factors explains why peasant rebellion—violent, collective acts of protest—soared during the nineteenth century. The commercialization of the economy, especially in agriculture, and the movement toward "modernization," as well as their concomitant effects on land tenure, land use, labor patterns, and communities, demanded fundamental changes in peasants' lifestyles. Often these brought with them the seeds of discontent.[5]

Together with the economic changes came the political—both on a superficial level and at the very core of society. During the sixty-year period of 1825–1885, Jalisco witnessed many modifications to government imposed from Mexico City, especially the continuous seesaw from centralism to federalism and back again. This incredible instability directly influenced patterns of rebellion. This chapter will show how these forces came together to make the years 1855–1864 the most rebellion-ridden years of the entire period. It will also illustrate that peasant unrest during the nineteenth century, including those crucial years of La Reforma, constituted not merely reactive protest but also offensive action in which peasants, primarily indigenous communities, used every opportunity to exact their demands.

The decade of revolt witnessed many significant events at the national level, which very clearly had an impact on what occurred in the state. On the political scene, the liberals ousted long-time *caudillo* Antonio de Santa Anna. Centralists and federalists (also cast as conservatives and liberals) battled for power not only at the ballot box but in a bloody civil war from 1858 to 1861, in which Jalisco became a major theater. Military leaders from the west/central Mexican states played a decisive role in the Revolution of Ayutla. Among those who would later influence events in Jalisco were Melchor Ocampo, who governed the neighboring state of Michoacán, and Santos Degollado, a law professor from Morelia who succeeded Ocampo in the governor's chair, later taking refuge in Guadalajara.[6] Leading the Revolution of Ayutla, Juan Alvarez garnered support from Degollado's "formidable rebel army" in Jalisco.

In 1861, France, England, and Spain invaded Mexico, ostensibly to force debt payment. However, when the latter two powers withdrew shortly after landing on Mexican soil, the French—with eyes on empire—moved to incorporate Mexico. The struggle between liberals and conservatives then metamorphosed into the fight against the French. Many in Jalisco saw it as merely a continuation of the recently concluded and devastating War of the Reform.

Jalisco itself experienced no fewer than eighteen transfers of power in the ten-year period, as liberals and conservatives (and sometimes liberals against liberals) vied for control of the state political apparatus. Armed bands, ranging from "mere bandits" to pseudo-military forces, roamed the state. Often, the distinction blurred and these *gavillas* wreaked their own havoc, threatening towns and persons, sacking, destroying crops, and looting. Forced loans and conscription by both *gavilla* and government troops brought hardship and fear to those caught in the way.

Santa Anna's flight from Mexico on August 9, 1855, on the heels of several liberal victories, including some major ones in Jalisco, secured the state's leadership for the liberals. Ignacio Comonfort, who had been instrumental in Juan Alvarez's ascendancy to the interim presidency, remained in Jalisco and, together with Santos Degollado, set about restructuring the state government along less-centralist lines. Later that year, Comonfort himself assumed the presidency.

During the 1850s, Jalisco's political life was quite tumultuous. In addition to liberal–conservative controversies and pro- and anti-Santa Anna conflicts, the liberals themselves began to factionalize. By late 1855 the pace of reforms enacted by the liberal government slowed in the face of new, primarily political rebellions. In December, Santos Degollado traveled to Tepic in an effort to "impose order" following an "armed uprising" led by the commander of the "Libres de Jalisco" battalion, Ángel Benitez.[7] Triumphant, Degollado returned to Guadalajara, offering the "City of Roses" as a refuge for President Comonfort and the national government should any of the "brotes de inconformidad" [buds of disagreement], which had erupted throughout the country, pose any threat. In mid-July, he resigned from the governorship after "revolutionary movements" challenged his power, setting in motion yet another power struggle between two liberal factions, the *moderados* and *radicales*.[8]

The struggle for control between the two liberal factions even involved President Comonfort and the military, who tried to broker an agreement. The national government went so far as to send General Anastasio Parrodi with a brigade to take over the state, end the liberal rebellion, and set up a provisional government.[9] Parrodi faced problems of his own in Jalisco: a military revolt led by Blancarte, a peasant uprising on the banks of Lake Chapala, lack of political consensus, and other reaction to federal laws. Nevertheless, the governmental "musical chairs" continued as Parrodi put on his military coat, set off to quash political revolts, and named Gregorio Dávila *gobernador sustituto*.[10]

At the federal level, the national Constituent Congress had convened on February 18, 1856. Because of the turmoil in Jalisco, the state's delegation could not take its place until early August 1857. Therefore, the most significant legislation of the early Reforma, coming in mid-1856, would be promulgated without Jalisco's participation. The two most famous initiatives of this period, Ley Juárez and Ley Lerdo, played a direct role in the national power struggle and intra-elite competition, filtering down even to the local level. Both passed during the time of the *jaliscience* delegation's absence and Jalisco's "decade of revolt."[11]

Ley Juárez itself caused political problems in Jalisco.[12] Guadalajara's bishop, Pedro Espinosa y Dávalos, opposed its provisions and admonished his clergy to disregard it. The liberals in the state applauded its provisions for equality under the law. Ley Lerdo complicated matters because it further challenged the hegemony of the church and civil corporations (municipalities and indigenous communities) and provoked more strife and, at times, open conflict.[13] On top of the turmoil caused by these liberal laws came the new national Constitution, approved on February 5, 1857, again before Jalisco's delegation joined the Constituent Congress. Later that month it was proclaimed in Jalisco, and to Jesús Camarena, *gobernador sustituto* in Parrodi's absence, fell the task of swearing allegiance to it, guarding it, and ensuring that all military and civil employees did the same. The state celebrated the Constitution with a holiday on March 29, 1857.[14]

Yet numerous conflicts between ecclesiastic and public authorities loomed, as did those between supporters of the new Constitution and its detractors. The church hierarchy in Jalisco opposed implementation of the Constitution and its related regulations. Bishop Espinosa y Dávalos actively challenged imposition of the new laws and asserted divine right to freedom from temporal rule.[15] The air of festivity and celebration that surrounded the declaration of the new Constitution soon began to wane. The façade of unity faded. The country erupted into the War of the Reform only a few months later. By 1858 Jalisco had become one of the principal scenes of the civil war.[16]

In April 1857, political and military discord broke out in Lagos, San Juan, Mascota, and Guadalajara. At the same time, the number of robberies and crimes escalated "as banditry rose with roving bands assaulting travelers, haciendas, and towns."[17] Throughout 1856 and 1857, reports of encounters between government forces and various *gavillas* came in from points all over Jalisco. The danger of *gavilla* attacks prompted *tapatío* liberals to join *comerciantes* in proposing a security force to protect towns and cities from the "attacks of *bandidos* who swarm[ed] the state."[18] Financial difficulties, however, caused state authorities to appeal to the *comerciantes*, industrialists, and the like to establish a fund for creating and sustaining such a force.

Banditry, civil war, financial crises, natural disaster, combined with political and administrative disarray at all levels of government, created conditions conducive to rebellion, within which the peasantry acted. Accounts of the period depict a state on the verge of anarchy. Calls for the use of force to regain public peace often met with government apologies and denials of assistance because of lack of resources. This, in turn, seems to have led to further chaos or arming of nongovernmental entities such as *hacendados*, and most probably the peasantry, as certain accounts of rebellion imply.

Government inability to guarantee safety in person and property contributed to massive migration from the countryside to the cities as well as from the state's urban areas to those outside Jalisco—further tattering the social and economic fabric of *jaliscience* society through loss of productivity, capital, producers, and consumers, and the creation of a mass of disconnected humanity, many of whom joined *gavillas* and possibly rebellions. The blurring of the lines between "mere bandits," *gavillas,* and pseudo-military and military forces proved a serious challenge to the maintenance and restoration of the *seguridad pública* and cannot be underestimated.[19]

Arming the populace, not merely in the face of *gavillas,* but also as a thought-out political tactic of mobilization, especially in the Wars of the Reform and against the French Intervention, provisioned the lower classes with weapons and skills for rebellion. The incorporation of *gavillas* (many of them peasant bands or made up largely of that segment of the populace) into the broader military structure blurred distinctions further and legitimized peasant insurrection. Peasants could act within a structure already founded upon violence.

Political and military problems alone did not account for all of the chaos in Jalisco during these turbulent years. The 1850s opened under a cloud of hunger and disease, with a devastating drought and cholera epidemic—clearly inauspicious beginnings. The deprivation that resulted from this deadly combination continued until at least the mid-1850s, as demonstrated by reports of rising corn prices, hunger, and seed shortages in 1854.[20] The nationwide agrarian crisis of 1856 further compounded Jalisco's problems, and reports of peasant rebellions in the latter 1850s, especially in 1857, demonstrate that hunger remained a severe problem—at a time when Jalisco witnessed a significant rise in population—perhaps generating conflicts over land and scarce resources. (See Figure 2.1) Typhoid struck Jalisco in 1860–1861, dealing yet another blow to the state's beleaguered populace.

Adding to nature's fury and that of general chaos were severe economic problems and the carnage, despoilment, and despair accompanying successive conflagrations of civil war and foreign invasion. Because Jalisco became one of the principal scenes of the civil war, it is not surprising that a record number of peasant rebellions occurred in the year the war erupted, 1857. Taken together, the three years of civil war account for the highest number of revolts of the decade. The fact that the number dropped significantly in 1858 and 1859 may indicate that peasant protest became channeled into the larger conflict (or perhaps that officials were so caught up in the war that they simply did not have time for "mere" peasant rebellions when faced with larger issues.)

The *jaliscience* economy itself suffered a *"pésima situación"* exacerbated by the need to expend precious funds for defense, military supplies, or forced loans to one faction or another.[21] Liberals now faced increasing social, political, and economic chaos. By way of example, in November 1857 the state Congress granted Governor Anastasio Parrodi extraordinary powers to organize the national guard "and pursue the thieves and those who disrupted the public order."[22] Two days later, he exacted an "extraordinary tax aimed at generating thirty thousand pesos a month as a war subsidy." In February

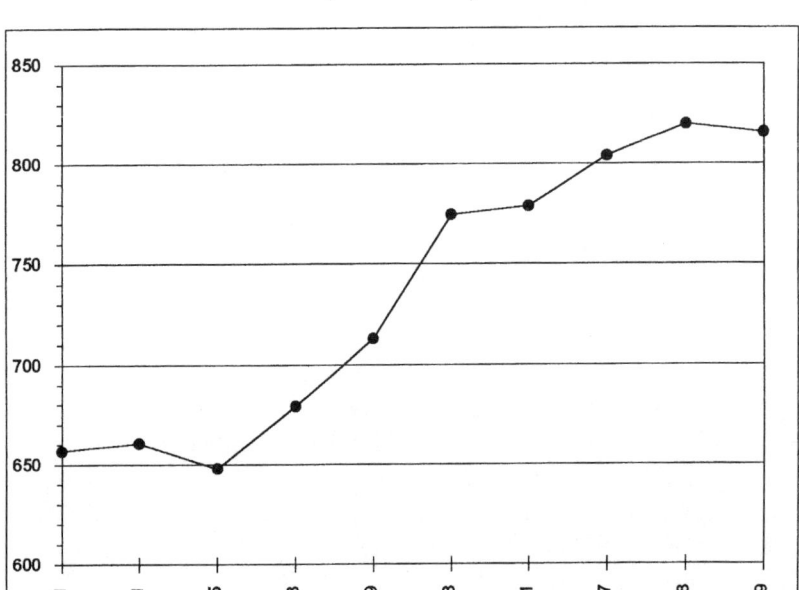

Fig. 2.1 Population of Jalisco, 1821–1869 (in thousands)

(Source: *Historia de Jalisco*, p. 100)

1858 shortly after Benito Juárez assumed the presidency, he relocated his capital in exile to Guadalajara. On March 1 he imposed the first national loan for the war and sent word to all the country's governors. To Jalisco, never really on sound financial footing, fell the burden of 80,000 pesos—35,000 of which was to come from the *cantón* of Guadalajara.[23]

As stated initially, Jalisco witnessed twenty-seven rebellions during the years 1825–1885, with seventeen occurring in the decade 1855–1864. Within this period, the majority occurred prior to 1861, with a grouping during the years from 1857 to 1860, and some extending from one year to another. Those continuing beyond 1861 had begun in 1857. Two rebellions, in fact, extended from 1857 until 1874 and 1881 respectively. (See Figs. 2.2–4)

(Sources for Figs. 2.2 through 2.9: author's statistics gathered from records found primarily in the AHJ Ramos: Gobernación, Asunto Indios, Seguridad Pública, Tranquilidad Pública, and Tierras.)

My warmest thanks to my husband, Mark, for his constant support, careful editing, and tireless effort on the graphs.

Fig. 2.2 Peasant Rebellions in Jalisco, 1825–1885

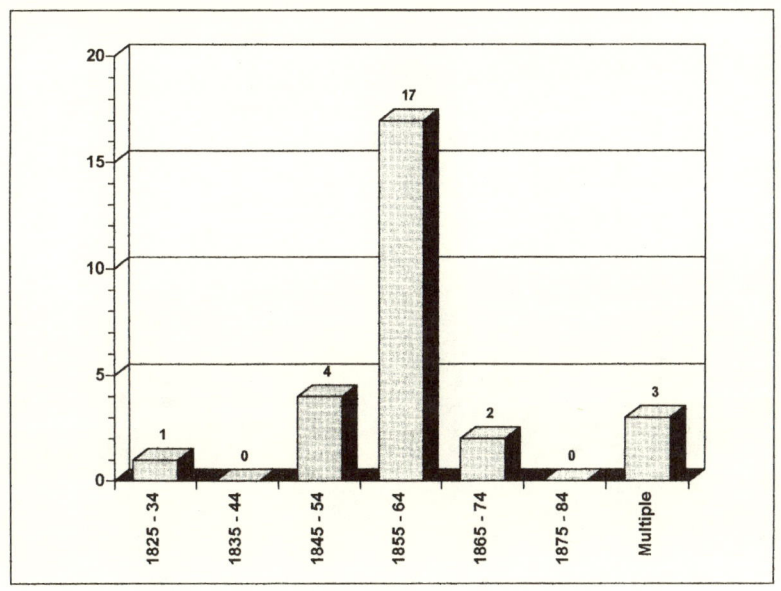

Fig. 2.3 Peasant Rebellions in Jalisco, 1855–1864

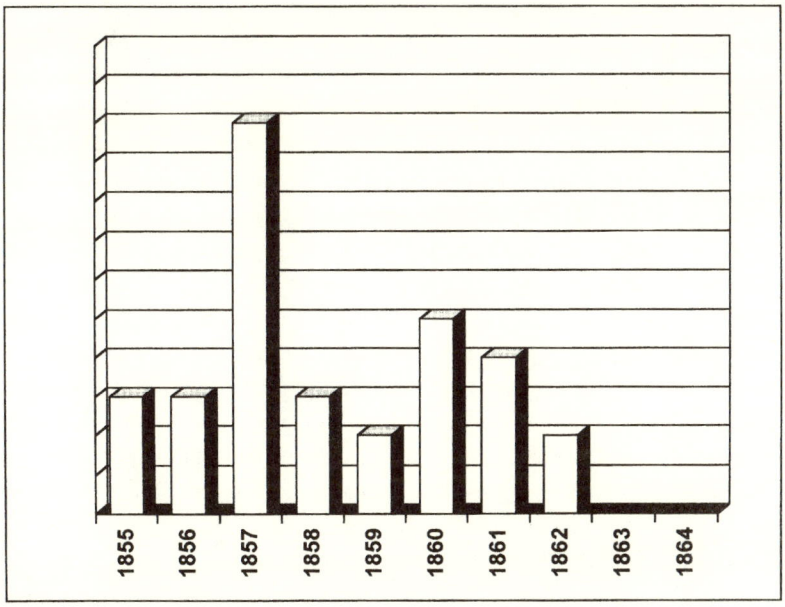

Fig. 2.4 Chronological Breakdown of Rebellions

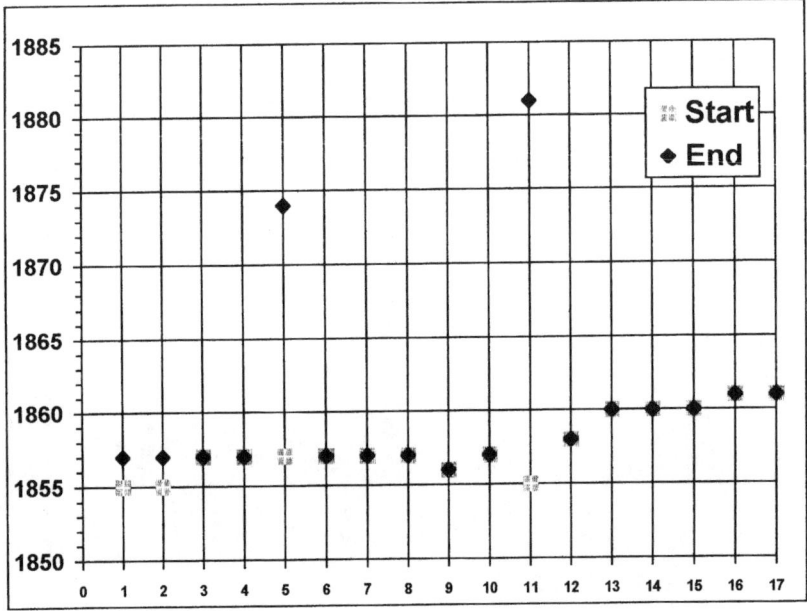

As shown in Fig. 2.5, geographically almost the entire state felt the heat of revolt, with the exception of Los Altos (eastern Jalisco).[24] During the decade of revolt, as seen in Fig. 2.6, the burden of rebellion was shared almost equally across the state, with the area around Lake Chapala and the central region seeing slightly more unrest and some rebellions crossing regional borders.

The chronology of the rebellions in the decade of revolt is striking. The year 1857 clearly saw the greatest number of rebellions, recording ten. At first glance, it would seem easy to correlate that record number with promulgation of Ley Lerdo, which had come the previous June, or with the implementation of the new Constitution in early 1857. Traditionally, there has been an assumption in the literature that Ley Lerdo provoked massive protest because it sought to alienate communal properties. However, an examination of the rebellions considered here does not demonstrate such a relationship, and in the case of Jalisco, this thesis is not borne out. Rather, this study supports Meyer's assertion of only a partial link in one or two cases.

The idea of dissolving communal lands and making them individual commodities did not originate with Ley Lerdo or La Reforma. Rather, Ley Lerdo culminated at a national level what states across Mexico, twelve of them by the late 1820s (among them, Jalisco), sought to accomplish.[25] Jalisco itself

Fig. 2.5 Peasant Rebellions in Jalisco by Region

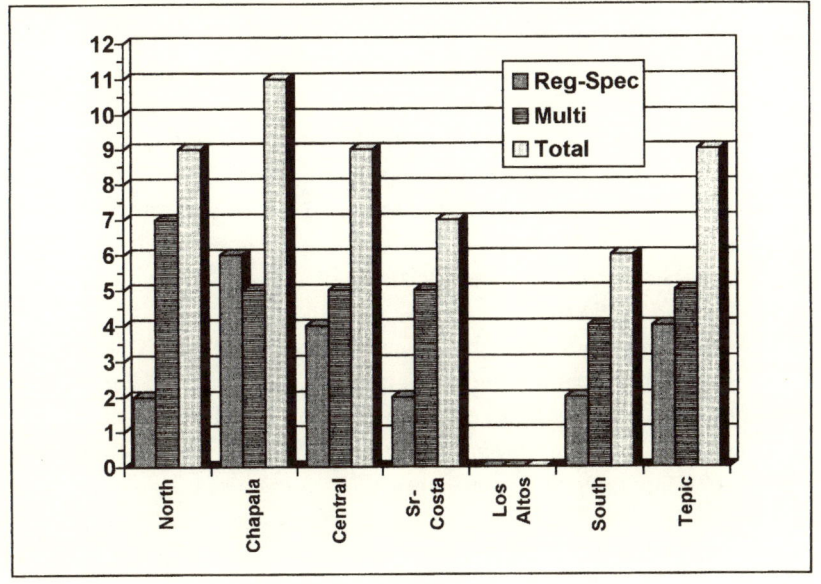

Fig. 2.6 Peasant Rebellions by Region, 1855–1864.
Includes cross-regional rebellions.

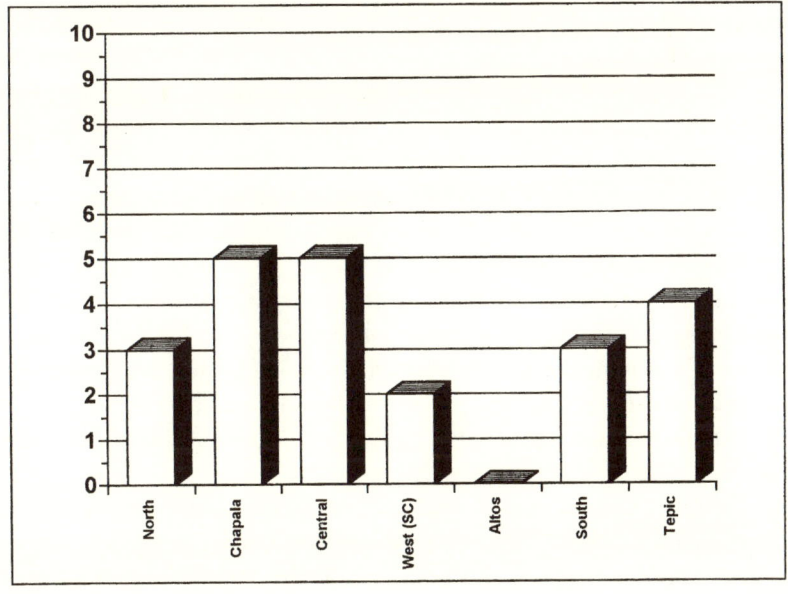

had laws in effect from the 1820s, which called for Ley Lerdo–type changes in communal property.[26] As Meyer correctly points out, "*Ley Lerdo* (1856) came at the end of the process. It is enough to consult the six volumes of the *Colección de Acuerdos* . . . to understand that the corporate properties of the *repúblicas pueblerinas* had suffered definitive condemnation well before the *Reforma* proceeded to its famous disamortization."[27] He traces the disentailment of communal property back to the colonial era, at least to 1806, and focuses on decrees issued in 1822 by the Cortés Extraordinarias. Among the most significant pre–Ley Lerdo initiatives, which retained their importance into the decade of revolt, counted Decreto No. 2 (1825), Decreto 151 (1828), and Decreto 121 (1849).[28]

Meyer further argues that the "disamortization in Jalisco began long before *Lerdo*, yet that does not mean that it had been completed before 1856."[29] For that reason, he states that Ley Lerdo could not have been the direct cause of the uprisings of the *pueblos indígenas*.[30] This study affirms these assertions. First, only a few cases of the seventeen refer to the above legislation. None mentions it as a reason for revolt. Also, an evaluation of peasant protests and pleas of the period shows that in many cases, rather than objecting to it, they demanded "*reparto*" according to Ley Lerdo and the existing state laws.[31] Third, as was the case in Chalco, the divided, at times almost impotent, state government could not effectively implement policy, as many officials lamented.[32]

That is not to say that there were no post–Ley Lerdo protests resulting from the legislation or that property disputes did not contribute in a very real way to peasant unrest. Rather, the rebellion occurring post–Ley Lerdo, especially in 1857, did not represent a massive reaction against the law itself.[33] A brief review of the stated causes of the rebellions under consideration and a subsequent examination of a few key rebellions in greater detail will provide a clearer picture of peasant dissent in the decade of rebellion, 1855–1864.[34]

In 1855, two thousand indigenous peasants took up arms in the *cantón* of La Barca and under the leadership of Lugardo Onofre, assaulting the hacienda of Gachos, appropriating the deeds and requisitioning the harvest. A year later, in September 1856, the organizers reunited in Onofre's house, proclaiming reclamation of the land that previously had been theirs and inviting other peasants to join the armed struggle. The dispute arose over property that the peasants had sold "some time ago" to the "landowners," but for which they had not yet received payment. Military forces apprehended Onofre, executing him immediately.

Following Onofre's capture, leadership passed to Octavio Cevellos. With troops unable to contain them, the *insurrectos* took the pueblos of Tamaní (Jamay), Tala, and Otatán, and attacked surrounding haciendas.[35] The struggle continued until the military successfully defeated the uprising in La Barca in March 1857 and the troops retook Tamaní. Upon surrendering themselves, their arms, and horses, the *revoltosos* (rebels) received pardons but were held liable for claims of the *terratenientes* (hacienda owners). Prisoners of war were deported to the Californias and the *levantimiento* (uprising) came to an end. Despite insistence that the peasants accede to the haciendas' demands, the military section chief urged the minister of war to avoid excessive exactions because hunger was intensifying in the region and he feared the peasants would rebel again.[36]

Throughout 1857, other peasants in the southern Chapala region and into the south of Jalisco (Jamay, Tomatlán, Tuxcacuesco, and Tizapán el Alto) launched various armed attacks against haciendas over land. They rose up in arms, seizing some properties that were disputed, and solicited properties that had once been communal lands and now fell within the boundaries of haciendas. Finally, these peasants protested yet another hacienda's usurpation of a *fundo legal*, a complaint first issued in 1802.[37] These *brotes* met with amnesty in one case and armed force in the others. Another observation recorded in the same documents comes from a local judicial official who stated, "All the pueblos of the littoral are up in arms except the one under my command." He urges, "Give them back land. Keep them peaceful!"[38]

As these two brief examples point out, peasant revolt in the post-Ley Lerdo era cannot simply be reduced to reaction against it. Rather, they reveal some of the complexities. Clearly, as best seen in the second example, much more was operating here. These instances alone show peasants taking offensive action (not merely reacting) against what they perceived as an injustice. Claims that they made for return of property did not commence with disentailment through Ley Lerdo. Rather, the usurpation had occurred more than fifty years previously, or in "*tiempo atrás.*" Also, contested lands which at the time fell within hacienda borders, could very easily have become property of the *hacendados* because of peasant-population declines that resulted in so-called *pueblos extinguidos* (extinguished villages).[39] This occurred beginning in at least the eighteenth century and continued into the early nineteenth, when indigenous populations began to recover.[40] Perhaps population growth and lack of resources provoked conflict where it had not existed previously and where no truly illegal action had been taken by the hacendado. The instance of the *fundo legal* dispute existing from colonial times demonstrates that Ley Lerdo did not cause all the peasants' problems.

Both of these accounts give some insight into the social and economic situation that the peasantry faced. Each warns of further disorder if needs such as hunger and land are not addressed. Clearly, the state and military apparatus saw the peasantry as empowered and capable, not to mention armed. Force versus force in peasant rebellion signified a momentous change from the predominantly nonviolent ritualized protests of the colonial era. Circumstances unique to this period in Jalisco's history undoubtedly added fuel to the fire.[41]

A brief survey of the stated reasons for rebellion in the seventeen instances reveals that the issue of causation is extremely complex and that the documentation is merely a starting point. Much remains outside the accounts, and many plausible explanations for this exist. First, the bulk of the documents reflects the view of the government officials who authored them. Authorities may have misunderstood what was happening. Together with this, their task was one of reporting what occurred to their superiors, not one of explaining why. Also, a consensus on some points may have caused their deliberate omission from the documentation. Misunderstandings and errors exist whenever one segment or culture tries to define another's action. Because they were official documents, they may have understated or overstated the situation depending on the officials' motivation (for example, to make himself look good or to receive assistance.) Additionally, the peasants may not have adequately articulated their reasons for action. Finally, historical hindsight may allow us to see factors that the participants and observers themselves could not ascertain.

As is seen in Figs. 2.7 and 2.8, over half of the accounts that specified a motive acknowledged some dispute over or demand for land: eight out of seventeen (total) but eight out of thirteen (specified); some included multiple causes. Yet none specifically protested alienation under Ley Lerdo. Of those remaining, seven referred to political or religious motivations, and two appear to be racial or ethnic in origin and with political overtones. Four accounts did not actually specify reasons for rebellion but demonstrated actions related to robbery of arms and war materiel and other goods, possibly a joining of social and political protest because of their targets.

Another point which needs to be stressed is that peasant rebellion during this decade involved massive numbers of *insurrectos* and could not easily be ignored. The sheer number of *revoltosos* demonstrates that problems existed within society that provoked violent outbreaks of discontent by huge numbers of the lower class, and their great numbers made them a powerful force with which to reckon.

Of the seventeen revolts considered, ten accounts do not specify numbers of *revoltosos*. They do, however, provide a sense for the many or the few: a band, a plague, entire *pueblos*, a *gavilla*, *insurrectos*, and others. These qualifications, together with the duration, actions taken, and means of quelling, give some insight into the size of the uprising. Despite the fact that ten of

Fig. 2.7 Causes of Peasant Rebellions, 1825–1885

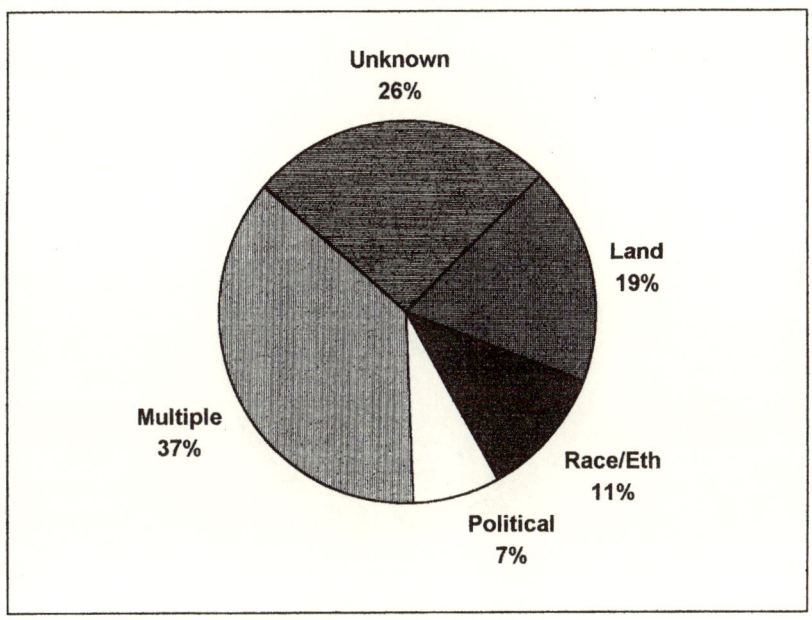

Fig. 2.8 Causes of Peasant Rebellions, 1855–1864

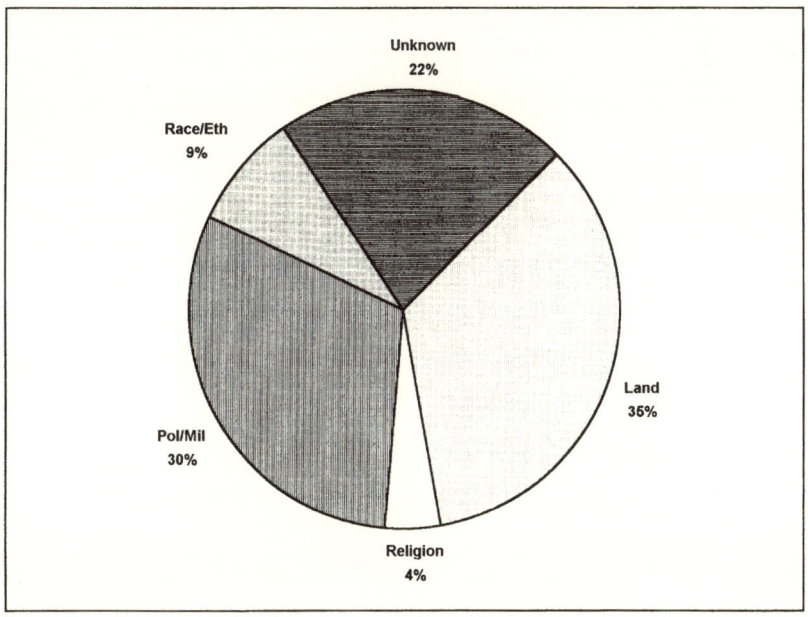

Fig. 2.9 Participants in Peasant Rebellions
.000 = 2; >800 = 1; 400–500 = 3; <70 = 2; unspecified = 10

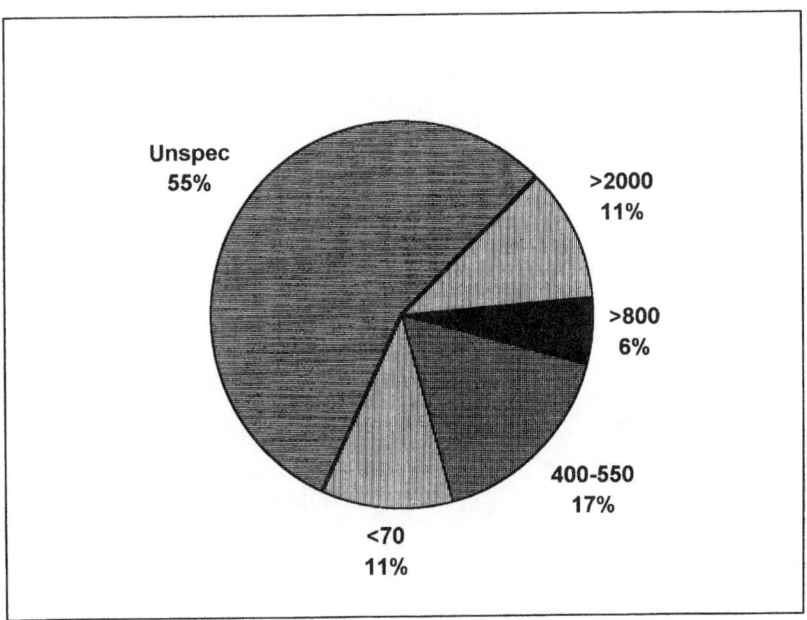

the seventeen provide no precise number of participants, the remaining seven show a tremendous range.[42]

Two of the accounts report participant numbers in excess of two thousand (and in one of these the number reaches nearly three thousand). At the other extreme, two revolts counted about thirty to thirty-five. And the remaining three or four (some overlapped) had between 400 and 800 *revoltosos* (and in one case, 100).[43] (See Fig. 2.9.)

With this brief overview of the decade of rebellion, its causes, and its participants, we may now consider some revolts in slightly more detail as a way of pulling together the acts of rebellion themselves and the broader social and political milieu in which they occurred. Such evaluation and synthesis will present a truer picture of why the years 1855–1864 saw such widespread popular unrest and the effects that such dissent had on state and national policy.

Los Revoltosos

Manuel Lozada led the most widespread and longest rebellion in the nineteenth century, precisely within Jalisco's decade of revolt.[44] His rebellion

THE DECADE OF REVOLT   51

(1857–1881) not only touched the seventh *cantón*, Tepic, but also Colotlán and the northern region, the *sierra-costa* (west), and the *Centro* (the area around Guadalajara). It alarmed officials in the states of Zacatecas, Durango, Aguascalientes, Querétaro, and Sinaloa as well. At one point, eleven thousand peasants, mostly Indians, took up arms under Lozada and various sub-captains.[45] The mountainous geography of large portions of Tepic helped preserve the social and cultural traditions of the Indian communities that came into conflict with the expanding non-Indian population, primarily *criollos* and Europeans engaged in commerce and contraband.

The region of Tepic is presently the state of Nayarit. Indigenous people, primarily Coras and Huicholes, constituted the majority of the population, and it appears that more Indian communities existed in Tepic than in any other part of the state of Jalisco.[46] Communal villages shared the land with haciendas. A large affluent European community resided in the area.

Tepic's economy differed markedly from that in other areas of the state. An international business community earned its living from commerce, shipping, banking, gold and silver exportation (contraband), textiles, mining, and land (haciendas.) Revenues from the port of San Blas played an important part in the economy of the region. Tepic's political situation was often chaotic and ties to Guadalajara often tenuous. In 1867, the federal government separated the region from the state of Jalisco and made it a military district "directly dependent upon the Supreme Government of the Republic," an action deeply resented to this day by the *jaliscienses*.[47]

The Lozada rebellion provides a strong example of the "complexity of causation" and the ties between politics, instability, and rebellion. The scope of this movement was unparalleled in nineteenth-century Jalisco. Lozada frequently changed his stance on the government, at times supporting it and at others, opposing it. He also joined forces with those advocating the independence of Tepic from Jalisco, especially the European commercial interests.[48]

Although Lozada and his followers were frequently classified as bandits, the movement insisted that it aimed "not at robbery but at changing the system." Recovery of peasant lands, one of the *lozadistas*' major objectives, became not only a way to gather popular support, but also a basis upon which to make alliances with political factions. Lozada made alliances with both liberals and conservatives that lasted only as long as they were faithful to the stated objective of obtaining lands.[49]

In June 1862 Lozada declared that he no longer recognized other authority and set up his own government. Three years later in 1865 and again in 1866 Maximilian won Lozada to his cause by decreeing land to the peasants. Because Maximilian had given land, Lozada withdrew from the fight, stating that he no longer had a motive for confrontation. However, *gavillas* continued, and in the 1870s armed rebellion reignited.

In addition to regional political struggles that Lozada frequently used to his advantage, the national political scene was wrought with confusion and struggles between liberals and conservatives that only hampered the national government's ability to control the *revoltosos*. A state congressional initiative dated September 10, 1861, bemoaned the difficulties that the nation faced and put forth a plan to prevent indigenous uprisings:

> On top of the disgraceful situation in which the Nation finds itself because of the "war of extermination," that for three years it had to sustain with the "reactionaries" to the point of leaving them humiliated and conquered on [that] glorious day,[50] it has been necessary . . . to continue the war, without yet bringing the various *gavillas* which operate in different points of the Republic to order, that so many times have been pardoned and whose clemency has done nothing more than to always be betrayed and revive rebellion and disorder everywhere.
>
> In the middle of so many difficulties, with which the entire public fights to destroy once and for all the sworn enemies of their liberty . . . , even for the triumphs of the State's forces over the "bandits of Alica" [Lozada and followers], as well as that of the General Government's forces over the detestable monster of Tacubaya, there appears in the state a greater calamity, that requires the united forces of *Jalisciences*, in order to exorcise [them] and not leave the reactionaries the hope of achieving that for which they have worked so hard, without stopping the blood and the extermination of the state, that would be the unavoidable consequence.[51]

The congressional letter went on to lament that Indians in different parts of the state continued to threaten life and property on the pretext of recovering lands that had been theirs previously without regard for the rights of those who possessed the lands at that moment. In order to repel the growing threat of a general Indian uprising, the Congress declared that the state would have to "abandon the Campaign of Tepic, leaving those towns exposed to all the depredations of the bandit Lozada or wait for forces from the neighboring states, which would not allow enough time to impede the complete destruction of the towns, which soon the *indígenas* could invade like a plague."[52] It demanded that the state take "violent measures" and that "reconcentration of power [was] the only way to save the situation."[53] The political upheaval and the effects of civil war were clearly linked to peasant rebellion in Tepic and across the state.[54]

Another point that cannot be overlooked with regard to the rebellion in Tepic is the effect of an essentially peasant rebellion on national policy. As mentioned previously, Lozada's revolt spanned the years 1857–1881, a tumultuous epoch. The confluence of the federalist/centralist struggle and the Lozada rebellion caused the Juárez government, on August 7, 1867, to decree Tepic a "Military District, directly dependent upon the Supreme Government of the Republic."[55] From 1868 to 1878, Jalisco sought the reincorporation of the seventh *cantón*. In 1885, the Law of the Organization of the Territory of Tepic finalized the separation of the region. By promising land Maximilian had also acceded to the *lozadistas'* demands: The movement could hardly be ignored.

While the strength, duration, and severity of the Lozada revolt set it apart from most other peasant rebellions in the state during this era, smaller, short-lived rebellions present a similar picture of the causes and nature of revolt and the connection between political stability and peasant protest. In April and May of 1860, "*indios insurrectos*" assaulted the village of Chapala. At the same time, not far away, a separate group from Mezcala took up arms. The government withdrew from the region because it did not have enough troops to fight. In a communication, it also noted the probability that the rebels joined other *pueblos* because the rebellion in Nayarit and Tepic was spreading.[56]

In early July of that year, the *indígenas* of Mezcala requested that the government send arms and a force to fight "the enemies of order (Rojas and Rochín)" who opposed the government. Despite some conflicts between "*vecinos*" and "*indígenas*," they joined in calling for an armed force because Rojas and Rochín had assaulted several towns, including an attack by one thousand men on the *pueblo* of Mezcala. They feared the same would happen in Ajijic. Although the account is unclear, it seems that the government responded to this plea.[57]

The situation changed in late July, and a communication dated July 21, 1860, reinforces the relationship between the larger political scene and peasant rebellion. It appears that the government had changed hands because it granted a pardon to "all *indígenas* of the town of Mezcala who return to order and peaceful life and turn in their arms."

The vacillation of the authorities over several months, with an about-face in less than a month, demonstrates the instability on the political scene. It is possible that in early July the government had armed the peasants, not only to protect its citizens but in an effort to reach an accommodation with the *indígenas*, who had themselves rebelled the previous April. It is also conceivable that having rebelled earlier and knowing the government's inability to put them down, the peasants took advantage of the situation to get arms.

In early 1857, officials in the town of Tonalá expressed fear of a band of *indios insurrectos* (nonmilitary infantry and cavalry) numbering about seventy who had assaulted several haciendas and neighboring towns, taking prisoners, stealing horses, saddles, bits, and arms and were three leagues away. Santa Anita had also been attacked by a group of 150, "with the character of thieves," who sacked homes, taking clothing and whatever else they could. They also seized arms from the local jail and released prisoners, and robbed the municipal treasury of all funds.[58] Similar reports poured in.

Antonio Godines led a *gavilla* of twelve mounted and armed *indios insurrectos* in an attack on the bridge of Tolotlán, an important thoroughfare. Diego López, along with Antonio N. and Fernando N., captained a force of three hundred mounted *"indios insurrectos y indígenas sublevados"* armed with guns and lances, who attacked and robbed in what officials called a *"conspiración de indios."*[59]

A major area of peasant rebellion occurred in the "frontier zone" between the states of Jalisco and Zacatecas. This area, characterized by steep cliffs, offered the perfect escape for rebels from one part or another because of the ambiguity of the border and the political and military authority to control it. Officials from both states blamed the other's inability to maintain peace when faced with outbreaks of banditry and open rebellion. The *cantón* Colotlán and the cities of Bolaños and Huejuquilla saw many of these confrontations.

One such revolt, headed by Carlos Rivas, grew larger and stronger by the day because of the promise of restitution of lands that had been sold to the "so-called *vecinos.*"[60] By the time of the report, the *revoltosos* had taken the seed stores of the towns of Totatiche, Bolaños, Chimaltitán, San Martín, Mamatla, Mezquitic, and Huejuquilla and the indigenous inhabitants of these *pueblos* had joined the cause. One of the major sparks for this revolt involved a land conflict between the Indians and haciendas. Lamenting the "complete ruin of all the towns in the sierra of Alica because of the prolonged war" and recognizing the power that the *"facsioso* [sic] Rivas" derived from promising land, the reporting official acknowledged that the Indian's needs required attention:

> He who writes [José Valadés] believes that the claims of the Indians of San Luis and of other towns are for the most part just, because the Indians on more than one occasion have been scandalously pillaged by the haciendas. But some such claims are also exaggerated and in some cases [are] entirely unfounded ... because the lands that they reclaim have really belonged to the Haciendas from the beginning or because they had passed to them after being

sold or because they really don't belong to one or another but rather are national property.

[We should] concede [land] to the *pueblos de indios*, [because] they do not have enough for planting and cattle, a part of the vacant lands that without a doubt will be found to be with the supposed limits of the haciendas when the survey is taken—[but] this concession should be made with a clause considering these new lands as *fundo legal* of the *pueblo* without legal authorization to transfer their domain.[61]

This rebellion, which actually may have been several at the same time, also combined political and religious motivations and most probably had links to Lozada's revolt. By way of example, Rivas is referred to in the report as "*el facsioso*," which usually refers to a political opponent. Second, in Tala, another site of unrest in this account, the question of land gets tied up with the issue of religion, a modus operandi attributed to Lozada on various occasions. Third, the large numbers of participants, in one place 800 and in another over 2,000, certainly presented a force with which to reckon. As a matter of fact, *jaliscience* authorities requested assistance from the governments of Zacatecas and Durango. Fourth, in addition to armed repression, several factors came together that helped calm an extremely vicious rebellion: a trade embargo with the *lozadistas*, rumor of Lozada's death, a decree of extinction of the *pueblos*, and "naming of a commission to examine claims brought by San Luis Pochititan, San Pedro Tequepespan, and others that have pending disputes with the *hacendados*."[62]

Several other accounts draw attention to the lack of defense in the towns that the *indígenas* attacked and the request for state assistance. Miguel Barrucha, Cocula's political authority, warned,

> For three months there have been frequent alarms and many rumors that the *yndígenas* of this place allied with other *pueblos* are preparing for an attack. I'm sorry to have to bother [you for] your attention but if disgracefully this disastrous case occurs, we are firmly resolved to defend ourselves, by armed hand, when we are attacked in the same way. Nevertheless, we do not have any other arms except those which each one of the *vecinos* has for his own defense like pistols, shotguns, etc.[63]

Officials in Hostotipaquillo received word to request help from the surrounding towns to put off the *indios sublevados*.[64] The *jefe político* of the first *cantón* reported to the secretary of *gobierno* of Jalisco that there was a "revolution among the *indígenas* of the *pueblos* of Mazamitla, Zacoalco, and Tamazula" and he would "take whatever means necessary to repress the *revoltosos* and restore public tranquillity."[65] But perhaps the communication from Teul most poignantly expresses the frustration with the chaos and lack of government control. When faced with a *gavilla* of 400 to 500, its officials wrote, "We are poor, with scarce arms, but we will resist. It's about time you established a respectable force in this area to keep people from attacking our peaceful [town]."[66]

Conclusion

Peasant uprising during Jalisco's decade of revolt far outpaced that of any other time in the years from 1825 to 1885. Banditry, civil war, financial crises, and natural disaster, together with political and administrative disarray at all levels of government, created an atmosphere conducive to rebellion. In the final analysis, rural unrest during this decade cannot be linked to one solitary cause, not even to the promulgation of Ley Lerdo and the policy of disamortization of communal peasant lands.

There is ample evidence to show that the overall chaos, war, and devastation of that ten-year period made it ripe for insurrection. Hunger, financial devastation, insecurity in home and in person, political mayhem, depredation, and casualties of war affected the entire state. Population growth and scarcity of resources combined with real grievances, sometimes long-standing ones, to provoke discontent. Mobilizations at the hands of competing factions facilitated access to arms and fighting skills. The resulting power vacuum created by such political and social strife provided many opportunities for action by *"los de abajo."*[67]

Van Young points out that during the waning years of the colonial period, *pueblos* and haciendas both began using marginal lands because of the increased population's demands for new resources. It appears that much the same occurred in the decade of revolt. Rebellion accounts describe peasant attempts to regain land that had once been theirs and without regard to the present owner. There are numerous references to the resurgence of *"pueblos extinguidos."* Even government authorities seem to acknowledge the paucity of resources and the need for access to food and land. Population statistics continue to post a rise over the course of the 1850s, showing a significant jump in 1857 and 1858 and a slight decline in the late 1860s.[68]

Emigration, another coping strategy of mid-century *jalisciences*, from the countryside to the cities as well as from the state's urban areas to those outside Jalisco, had several major effects on its social and economic structures. First, such an outflux must have had some effect on the productive unit of the countryside. Second, this mass of disconnected humanity fed the confusion of an already unsettled urban environment. Many participated in *gavillas* (both political and "bandit" gangs), and possibly in rebellions. Officials frequently recorded the depopulation of towns because of violence and the migration of those who had survived. The massive exodus to surrounding states, such as the migration of the weavers and artisans to Guanajuato, deprived Jalisco of both producers and consumers.

The *gavillas* themselves wrought havoc on society by attacking civilians, sacking homes, and destroying property, crops, and foodstuffs. Towns and governments used scarce resources for defense. Forced loans and conscription by both *gavillas* and government troops caused much alarm and hardship. Taxes levied on major sources of income, such as mescal, compounded an already difficult economic environment.

Calls for the use of force to regain public peace often met with government apologies and denials of assistance because of lack of resources. This, in turn, seems to have led to further chaos or arming of nongovernmental entities such as *hacendados*, and probably the peasantry, as the accounts from Chapala imply.

In governmental ranks, distinctions disappeared as political and military leadership often went hand in hand. Anastasio Parrodi, the frequently in-absentia governor of Jalisco, relinquished his political command at a moment's notice to take charge of military forces sent to save the nation. Even when the government was not seesawing between liberals and conservatives, which occurred with sufficient frequency, the stability of the political structure could not be taken for granted. Clearly such an environment of violence and disruption would have fostered a climate of rebellion.

Because Jalisco became one of the principal sites of the civil war, it is not surprising that a record number of revolts occurred during the year the war erupted. When taken together, the three years of civil war registered the highest number of revolts of the decade. The discontent demonstrated through massive rebellion dwarfs the years prior to and following the War of the Reform. Even the period of the French Intervention comes nowhere close to the same scope of revolt. Significantly, even the decade after the liberal state regains primacy during the Restored Republic (1867) and is able to set about implementing the new Constitution and the reform laws, including Ley Lerdo, does not witness a significant rise in peasant uprising, further supporting the contention that Ley Lerdo alone did not provoke the widespread rebellion witnessed in the year after its promulgation.

With the upheaval of war and the worsening of Jalisco's already *pésima* economic state, the War of the Reform and against the French robbed the state of needed resources in order to support the national cause, a frequent complaint of state officials. Without sufficient military and financial resources they could not hope to improve the situation or guarantee security. It is fairly certain, then, that the liberal administration in Jalisco did not have the state apparatus to fully implement the reform laws. Despite the promulgation of Ley Lerdo, it appears that some of what Tutino described for Chalco occurred in Jalisco, and that the legislation itself did not produce major peasant rebellion. Those revolts considered here certainly do not show a correlation.

Peasants advocated for *reparto* rather than protesting it, and in many cases the government replied that no further division could take place because the *reparto* had been completed. Other cases show that peasants complained because the surveys and other administrative work had been done, but they had not yet received their titles. Commercialization and the notion of land as a commodity developing at this time in Mexican history does seem to have affected the peasantry. Access to land does fuel the fire of rebellion. Yet alienation of property under Ley Lerdo does not appear to have contributed to the explosion of peasant rebellion between 1855 and 1864.

Rather, the combination of war, pestilence, disease, land disputes, racial and ethnic struggles, political instability, and lack of economic and military resources set the stage for peasant action during Jalisco's decade of revolt. The revolts considered above clearly show that dissatisfaction ran deep, and that the circumstances of this decade provided the peasantry with a chance to take the offensive. Throughout the period 1825–1885, the scope and intensity of peasant rebellion cannot compare with the years 1855–1864. Yet no other epoch witnessed such a lethal combination of factors.

Notes

1. The work presented here represents part of a larger study that examines the theoretical bases of peasant rebellion in the western Mexican state of Jalisco during the years 1825–1885. By analyzing factors such as land patterns, tenure and use, increasing commercialization (especially in agriculture), *mestizaje*, economic changes, and political instability across seven distinct cultural and geographical regions over time, that investigation has drawn some conclusions about the nature of "rebellious causation" in Jalisco during Mexico's transition from independence to nation-state. The present study further analyzes a significant finding of the broader investigation. For a discussion of the regional breakdown of Jalisco and more on the theoretical application of the broader study, see the author's "La protesta social rural durante el siglo XIX en Jalisco" in *Élite, clases sociales, y rebelión en*

Guadalajara y Jalisco, siglos XVIII y XIX, ed. Carmen Castañeda (Guadalajara, 1988). See John Tutino, *From Insurrection to Revolution in Mexico: Social Bases of Agrarian Violence, 1750–1940* (Princeton, 1986) for an excellent synopsis of theories regarding rebellion and causation. Also, see Friedrich Katz, ed., *Riot, Rebellion, and Revolution: Rural Social Conflict in Mexico* (Princeton, 1988).

2. Findings for this study come primarily from information found in the Archivo Histórico de Jalisco and corroborated in other sources such as the Biblioteca Pública del Estado de Jalisco (BPEJ). Colección de Misceláneas (primarily manuscripts) and various governors' *Memorias* or *Informes de Gobierno*. The documents I consulted in the Archivo Histórico de Jalisco (AHJ) consist mainly of government reports and correspondence from local state officials to their superiors on matters such as public security, public peace, Indian affairs, land questions, and so forth. See forthcoming dissertation for more detail.

3. Leticia Reina has asserted that such a correlation exists. See especially Leticia Reina, *Las rebeliones campesinas en México, 1819–1906* (México, D.F., 1980), and Reina, *Las luchas populares en México* (México, D.F., 1985). Jean Meyer disagrees somewhat; see Jean Meyer, *Problemas campesinos y revueltas agrarias* (México, D.F., 1973), and Meyer, *Esperando a Lozada* (Zamora, 1984). Also, see subsequent discussion herein. Additionally, there seems to be a general, if often subtle or understated, sense in texts on Mexican history that this occurred.

4. The best sources for an overall history of the state of Jalisco remain Luis Pérez Verdía, *Historia Particular del Estado de Jalisco* (Guadalajara, 1951), and José María Muriá et al. *Historia de Jalisco*, 4 tomos (Guadalajara, 1980).

5. The results of the broader investigation suggest that communal landholders with a low degree of social and cultural *mestizaje* in regions of high commercialization rebelled during times of political instability.

6. Degollado's subsequent glory in Jalisco would be immortalized in the fine arts theater that still bears his name.

7. For more extensive discussion of the reforms in Jalisco, and political contests and revolts, see Muriá et al., *Historia de Jalisco*, tomo 3.

8. Many of these men had a long history in *tapatía* politics and would continue to wield influence throughout the nineteenth century.

9. See Muriá et al., *Historia de Jalisco*, 3:157ff.

10. Ibid. The political intrigues of this era often read like a suspense novel. Accounts of officers revolting, pressing civilians into service, and exacting protection money or taxes from the populace give one a sense for the uneasiness that must have been felt in Jalisco during these chaotic years. Faced repeatedly with the threat of invasion from its own *militares*, the *tapatía* capital used scarce resources to fortify the city.

11. These laws and their repercussions in Jalisco will be dealt with subsequently in more detail. See also Robert Knowlton's essay in this volume.

12. Ley Juárez abolished military and ecclesiastical *fueros*. The provisions therein would provoke military and clergy alike, who would at times rally the peasants within their domains to enter the struggle (especially during the Three Years War) on their behalf.

13. See Knowlton's essay in this volume. Also see Muriá et al., *Historia de Jalisco*. Later in the text this essay will discuss how this legislation directly influenced patterns of rebellion.

14. Conversations with María Teresa Fernández Aceves, former director of the AHJ and author on the subject of the 1857 state Constitution. The *jaliscience* Constituent Congress debated the new state Constitution throughout 1857, not passing it until December. Some speculate that if Jalisco had participated in the federal Congress, the national Constitution may not have been so radical. State congressional debates show that some representatives had a true states' rights attitude—let them do what they are going to do in Mexico (City) but it will not happen in Jalisco. In actuality, the *jaliscience* Constitution was less radical than the national. This undoubtedly contributed to lax enforcement of the federal mandate.

15. For further discussion of reaction against the Constitution, especially the actions of the church, see Muriá et al., *Historia de Jalisco*, 3:173–80.

16. Ibid.

17. Ibid., pp. 178–79.

18. Ibid.

19. Artisans, weavers, and other skilled laborers fled to "other cities in the Republic offering a more tranquil climate." This source estimates that an exodus of twenty thousand persons went to the state of Guanajuato alone. Muriá et al., *Historia de Jalisco*, 3:240–41.

20. Ibid., 3:128. Early in the "year of hunger," cholera outbreak hit the *cantones* of Lagos and La Barca. By April the population of Guadalajara had felt it. The year brought a disastrous drought that ruined the harvest. Fear of hungry masses prompted action by *hacendados*. "The proprietors themselves, fearing that the indigent hordes, despairing because of hunger, would revolt and occupy their properties, taking their goods, took the initiative to constitute commissions charged with finding solutions to the agricultural crisis." This included establishing the Banco de Beneficia to buy seeds with the purpose of selling them at low prices. This law also assigned a tax of 18.75 percent to seeds taken outside the state. By February 1851 the situation had not improved dramatically, and new legislation "definitively prohibited" the removal of seeds from the state. "As a consequence of the seed scarcity, groups of peasants emigrated from the countryside to the city in search of the means of survival while others moved to the *barrancas* to feed themselves with natural products.... Despite the fact that the rainy season of 1852 and 1853 was beneficial for cultivation, the rise in the price of corn was constant. On July 25, 1854, the government threatened to punish profiteers, speculators,

and dishonest *comerciantes* who raised the prices of articles of first necessity without authorization."

21. Ibid., pp. 128–80. For discussion on independence-era banditry and revolt, see William B. Taylor, "Banditry and Insurrection: Rural Unrest in Central Jalisco, 1790–1816," in Katz, *Riot, Rebellion, and Revolution*, pp. 205–46. Also in the same volume, see Eric Van Young, "Moving toward Revolt: Agrarian Origins of the Hidalgo Rebellion in the Guadalajara Region," pp. 176–204.

22. Muriá et al., *Historia de Jalisco*, 3:178–80.

23. Ibid., 3:186. This is also an excellent source for discussion of how the civil war played out in Jalisco, especially in Guadalajara. It details political, military, economic, and social cause and effect. Once again, it reinforces the degree of insecurity at all levels and the tremendous effects on society. Battles broke out all over the state, and the capital itself was besieged. Intense battles ensued. Attacks and counterattacks, two governments (one liberal and one conservative) claimed title to the government. Scarce resources targeted mainly at the troops became even scarcer. The church–civil struggle intensified, especially in the face of increased exactions and rents on ecclesiastical properties. And the liberals exacted yet another loan of 150,000 pesos from the city (late 1858). Following the liberals, Miramón's conservatives gained power and levied yet another forced loan of 100,000 on the *comerciantes tapatíos* and another of equal amount on the *cabildo eclesiástico*.

24. Los Altos remains the exception throughout the entire period of the broader study.

25. See especially John Tutino, "Agrarian Social Change and Peasant Rebellion in Nineteenth-Century Mexico: The Example of Chalco," in Katz, *Riot, Rebellion, and Revolution*, pp. 95–140 for an excellent, detailed discussion of what occurred in Chalco. Also, see Knowlton in this volume, and Robert Knowlton, "La individualización de la propiedad corporativa civil en el siglo XIX, notas sobre Jalisco," *Historia Mexicana* 27:1 (1978), 24–61.

26. See especially, Knowlton, "La individualización," Muriá et al., *Historia de Jalisco*, and Meyer, *Esperando a Lozada*.

27. Meyer, *Esperando a Lozada*, pp. 111–12.

28. Further detail on these decrees can be found in Knowlton's work, that of Meyer, and the BPEJ's *Colección de acuerdos, órdenes y decretos sobre tierras, casas y solares de los indígenas, bienes de comunidad y fundos legales de los pueblos*, 6 tomos (1849–1882). These volumes contain legal documents, relating to indigenous land and other matters, dating from the colonial period. My research shows that in cases where peasants solicited *reparto* of corporate or state properties they did so under the authority of state legislation, and only based their claims on Ley Lerdo occasionally and after they had cited state law. By the same token, state officials seem to have relied more heavily on Jalisco's pre-Ley Lerdo statutes.

29. He further asserts that disamortization did not end until after 1915. See Meyer, *Esperando a Lozada,* p. 135. While my research does not extend to that date, I have found that as late as the 1880s communities were complaining that *reparto* had not yet been carried out despite the fact that all the preliminary work such as surveys had been concluded. Another problem that arises in the documentation is that government officials argue that *reparto* could not occur because communities and individuals lacked titles to disputed lands. See especially *Colección de acuerdos.*

30. Meyer, *Esperando a Lozada,* pp. 135–36

31. *Colección de acuerdos.*

32. AHJ: Ramo de Gobernacion, Asunto Indios, 1857–1862 (hereafter cited as G-9-857, or as applicable) also Ramo de Gobernacion, Tranquilidad Pública, 1855–1862 (hereafter cited as G-15-855, or as applicable). Also, see Tutino in Katz, *Riot, Rebellion, and Revolution.* In fact, Tutino notes that by October 1856, a mere four months after the promulgation of Ley Lerdo, "peasants were generally ignoring the reform law," causing the treasury ministry to selectively abrogate parts of the legislation. "The new ruling eliminated the need for active implementation of the Lerdo law as it applied to small peasant holdings of community lands. The liberals could simply announce the completion of the reform, and peasant communities could carry on locally as usual, effectively ignoring the new property law" (pp. 120–21). It appears that this occurred in Jalisco as well. Peasants who requested *reparto* received word that all property had been divided up and therefore none remained for partition. In response, peasants went to court to show this was frequently not the case. See especially *Colección de acuerdos.*

33. Most of my sources for this assertion come from records found in the AHH and from the six-volume *Colección de acuerdos.*

34. This does not even consider the number of disputes that were addressed through the courts or other legal means.

35. Meyer notes, in *Esperando a Lozada,* that Jamay is the actual word and that Tamaní (Reina's transcription) is wrong. While such accuracy is important, I will use Tamaní because my description of the events relies on Reina's account. Nevertheless, one must note that other towns around Jamay rose up at the same time, as the AHJ documents point out.

36. See especially Reina, *Las rebelliones campesinas,* pp. 143–53.

37. AHJ: G-9-856

38. Ibid.

39. Many of the documents allege that lands in question belonged to towns that no longer existed and therefore rightly belonged to the haciendas within whose bounds they now were found. Eric Van Young discusses the population decline of the *jaliscience* peasantry during the colonial period in *Hacienda and Market in Eighteenth Century Mexico: The Rural Economy of the Guadalajara Region, 1675–1820* (Berkeley and Los Angeles, 1981). It seems

a fair assumption that many of the lands disputed in the decade of revolt passed into *hacendado* hands during times such as those detailed by Van Young.

40. Ibid.

41. William B. Taylor, *Drinking, Homicide, and Rebellion in Colonial Mexican Villages* (Stanford, 1979).

42. The author again notes that the accounts may not be entirely accurate for a variety of reasons: lack of statistical reliability for crowd estimates in the mid-nineteenth century, official exaggeration or diminution, and so forth.

43. See n. 69, below, on sources for charts.

44. The following discussion of the Lozada revolt, which haunted Jalisco off and on for years and had tremendous consequences for the state's history, highlights significant points about revolt during the years 1855–1864. Yet because it has been treated in great detail by others, this essay focuses on it only briefly. See especially Mario Alfonso Aldana Rendón, *Rebelión agraria de Manuel Lozada* (México, D.F., 1983). Also, see Aldana Rendón, *Manuel Lozada y las comunidades indígenas* (México, D.F., 1983); Aldana Rendón, "El liberalismo y la propiedad indígena en Jalisco (1855–1858)," in *Desarrollo rural en Jalisco: contradicciones y perspectivas*, ed. Alcántara Ferrer, Sergio and Enrique Sánchez Ruíz (Guadalajara, 1985); and Meyer, *Esperando a Lozada* (Guadalajara, 1984).

45. Among the peasants were six thousand Huicholes and three thousand Coras—indigenous groups who had long fought integration into Hispanic society.

46. See especially Longinos Banda, *Estadística de Jalisco, 1854–1863*, 2d ed. (Guadalajara, 1982); and Mariano Bárcena, *Ensayo Estadístico del Estado de Jalisco*, 2d ed. (Guadalajara, 1983). Both of these are reissues of contemporary statistical accounts, containing data on everything from population, geography, and physiography, to agriculture and economy. See also Meyer, *Esperando a Lozada*, and the works of Aldana Rendón for more specifically on Tepic.

47. Meyer, *Esperando a Lozada*, p. 223. See also Muriá et al., *Historia de Jalisco*.

48. Meyer details the "economic hegemony of the Barrón Forbes Company and the inevitable relations between the *cacique* Manuel Lozada and the local elite." Jean Meyer, "La Casa Barrón Forbes y Compañía: Formación y desarrollo de una empresa en México en el siglo XIX," in his *Esperando a Lozada*, pp. 197–98. Some of the accounts read like intrigues of present-day commercial espionage or best-seller thrillers.

49. AHJ: G-15-857 JAL/3148. See also works by Muriá et al., Reina (especially *Las rebeliones campesinas*), and Meyer (especially *Esperando a Lozada*).

50. This refers to the Three Years (Civil)War between liberals and conservatives (federalists and centralists).

51. AHJ: G-15-861

52. Ibid.

53. Ibid.

54. The government and military officials also frequently generalized the Lozada threat and attributed numerous revolts or attacks to his contagion even if no proof of a link existed.

55. Meyer, "La cuestión de Tepic: El sentido de la separación de facto del 7º cantón en 1867," in his *Esperando a Lozada*, p. 223.

56. Reina, *Las luchas populares*, pp. 113–14. Also, see AHJ: G-15-860 CHA/2277.

57. AHJ: G-15-860 CHA/3154.

58. AHJ: G-15-857 GUA/254.

59. AHJ: G-15-857 GUA/252.

60. As one account notes, and common usage affirms, *vecinos* refers to those who were not Indian.

61. AHJ: G-15-857 JAL/3148. *Fundos legales* were inalienable communal properties to be used for sustenance of the *pueblo*.

62. AHJ: G-15-857 JAL/3148. In the case of San Pedro de las Lagunillas (SPL), the slaughter was particularly brutal. "The assault of the bandits of Alica on SPL has produced the result of having sacrificed in cold blood and with the most savage ferocity about 260 persons of that town, dead by the knife. Almost all the population that remained alive has emigrated *en masse*." Further atrocities noted by the official caused the people of Tala to organize their own defense. "Upon occupying said towns, they rob and assassinate the major part of the populace and set fire. Upon leaving, they carry off women, boys, girls, cattle, pigs, horses, and mules.

63. AHJ: G-15-861 COA/2273.

64. AHJ: G-9-861.

65. AHJ: G-9-861 JAL/1259.

66. AHJ: G-15-857 ZAC/251.

67. Jean Meyer argues that a power vacuum in the period 1854–1855 facilitated peasant uprisings. See his *Esperando a Lozada*, p. 125. I believe that this continued at least into the 1860s and that the power vacuum combined with other factors to produce the explosion of the late 1850s to mid-1860s.

68. Because of the absence of data between 1858 and 1869, it is difficult to tell exactly when the decline occurred. My guess would be over the entire period, with a major dip during the war years, 1858–1861, and perhaps to a slightly lower degree during the fight against the French.

3
Liberal Theory and Peasant Practice
Land and Power in Northern Veracruz, Mexico, 1826–1900
Michael T. Ducey

Introduction

The following pages describe the policies and attitudes of liberals toward the communal property of the indigenous villages of Northern Veracruz, Mexico. In addition to outlining the liberals' aims in their land policies, this chapter addresses the issue of how the municipalities actually implemented changes in land tenure. The case study undertaken here indicates that a wide gap often separated the objectives of the liberal legislation and the manner in which local officials and villagers enforced the laws. Local villagers often delayed the implementation of the laws or greatly modified them before allowing the government to privatize their land. The case study begins by considering the state of village landholding in the early nineteenth century. When one observes the changes in land tenure under the Mexican republic it appears that there was little encroachment on peasant lands before the 1870s. In fact, local governments often acted to preserve or expand communal landholdings. In stark contrast to actual practice, liberal legislation developed by the state Congress often decreed that municipalities should convert their communal property into private land as quickly as possible. In spite of liberal intentions, change in landownership came slowly. It is only in the late nineteenth century that the liberal property regime became a system for the widespread expropriation of peasant producers.

The land-tenure legislation also raises some questions concerning the relationship between the liberals and indigenous communities. Historians have generally assumed that liberals ignored peasant interests and point to the land issue as an example of such attitudes.[1] The land question raises a fundamental problem in Mexican history. How did the liberals win enough support in the countryside to ensure victory against the conservatives and their foreign allies if liberal policies had such a negative impact on the peasantry? This question finds a resolution when one considers the way in which liberal politicians applied the new land laws to the benefit of members of the communities in the Huasteca. Only recently Florencia Mallon, Guy Thomson, and others have proposed the existence of a "popular liberalism" that bridges the gap between peasants and liberal ideologues.[2] In the peripheral areas of Mexico, where liberals counted on strong support, peasant communities did not lose access to land until well into the Porfiriato. This occurred partly because community members won the power to control the implementation of the new laws in their localities. Liberal policy also addressed critical issues of rural life popular with village residents. Local politics often consisted of conflicts within the town and between *cabeceras* (the seats of municipal government) and *sujeto* communities (settlements dependent on the government in the *cabeceras*) and between municipal/district functionaries and local Indian officials. Liberals adroitly exploited the divisions of "ins" and "outs" and tensions within local communities to create a constituency for their party. The history of the land laws is one illustration of how local liberals achieved this support.

This chapter describes the agrarian history of the municipalities of the Huasteca *veracruzana* and evaluates the manner in which local governments applied judicial innovations between 1820 and 1900. The first section estimates the amount of land controlled by several communities in the early nineteenth century and describes the methods villagers used to expand their landholdings. I have also included a discussion of how the municipal governments administered communal lands during the republican period, paying particular attention to the different uses of communal property. The core of the essay analyzes the liberal project and describes how local communities frustrated and transformed liberal laws in practice. The paper ends with a description of the fate of village lands under the Porfirian government. Landownership ultimately rested on the political independence of peasant communities, and control of local governments often seemed as important to villagers as their ancient land titles. Ultimately what sealed the fate of indigenous control of land was the villagers' declining political weight under the modernizing regime of Porfirio Díaz.

Communal Land in the Nineteenth Century

One of our first tasks is to determine how much communal land the villages in Northern Veracruz controlled during the nineteenth century. Such a task is more difficult than it seems. No systematic surveys of communal land existed before the late nineteenth century, when local governments measured the land in order to enforce the liberal land laws. The surveys themselves were often contentious events. Community members resented having to pay for them and they often challenged the results.[3] Villagers had good reason to do so since the surveyors were not always competent. In one case, villagers claimed that the surveyor never visited the lands he claimed to have measured. Twentieth-century agrarian reform officials compiled a report that discovered Carlos Toledano's 1892 survey of Texcatepec to be seriously deficient. The survey had major flaws: when compared to "more trustworthy maps," Toledano's map overlooked at least five thousand hectares.[4] "Consequently," the report concluded, "the legal transaction [of land division] was nothing more than a formula or rather a farce."[5] Furthermore, surveys often reported their results in the rather imprecise terms of *sitios de ganado mayor*, the large traditional unit of measurement equal to 1,750 hectares.

Although unreliable, the numbers presented can at least give an indication of the amount of land held by the indigenous communities into the 1880s. The table consists of lands subject to the liberal legislation and includes both land bought by the community and granted in vicegeral titles.[6] When at last the Porfirian government began to divide the native lands, the inventories of the quantity of land controlled by the communities was impressive.

The titles and expropriation complaints in state archives reveal the vitality which the communities demonstrated in the years following the achievement of independence. The amount of land at the disposal of peasant populations in northern Veracruz actually expanded in the period between 1821 and 1870. This expansion occurred by three processes: the communities bought lands, they won them in legal challenges, or they simply took them in invasions.

Temapache was one of the peasant communities that bought an estate soon after independence. In 1826 the ex-marquesa of Uluapan (María Josefa Rodríguez de Uluapan) sold the hacienda of Buenavista to the indigenous villagers of Temapache, who had previously exploited the same lands as tenants. According to the title of sale, the owner sold the estate, consisting of 15,380 hectares, for 3,120 silver pesos in two payments. The Indians raised the money by means of a collection of 20 pesos from each of 187 members of the community.[11]

Nor was Temapache the only community to buy lands in the republican period; the largely *mestizo* "commons" of Tuxpan also increased its lands at the expense of private property. In 1846 the municipal government of Tuxpan bought two estates from the descendants of President Guadalupe Victoria. The heirs of the haciendas, Asunción and Santiago de la Peña, sold them for

Table 3.1: Amounts of Communal Lands ca. 1880

Municipality (*sujetos* in italics)	Amount of land (in hectares)
Coahuitlán	3,510[7]
Coatzintla	21,875
Coxquihui	8,351
Chicontepec	29,989
Sasaltitla	1,117
Chila	430
Chumatlán	1,050
Huayacocotla	45,234
El Espinal	6,492
Ixcatepec	18,695
Otlamalacatl	6,180
Santa Cruz	2,140
Papantla	81,650 approx.
Temapache	15,360
Texcatepec	7,000 approx.
Amaxac	2,177
Tihuatlán	16,289[8]
Tuxpan	84,070
Zontecometlán	1,905[9]
Zozocolco *Tres Cruces*	7,000[10]

Sources: ACAM, expedientes 8, 14, 42, 45, 48, 51, 61, 67, 68, 73, 76, 80, 81, 88, 242, 297, 300, 306, 341, 382, and 1188; Archivo del Registro Público de la Propiedad (hereafter cited as ARPP), sección Papantla, deeds of December 23, 1875, and February 29, 1880, numbers 57, 58, and 59; 1882, f. 30, 37, 49, 51. ARPP, sección Tuxpan, deed of September 2, 1878.

14,580 pesos. Apparently the municipality raised the money for the purchase by means of a popular subscription among the *tuxpeños*.[12] As a result of this transaction, almost all of the land within the municipality's boundaries now belonged to the corporation.[13] Santa María Ixcatepec also assured its access to land by the purchase of an 18,695-hectares estate for the price of 7,500 pesos in 1867. Later the community organized these lands as a *condueñazgo*, which sustained the agricultural life of Ixcatepec's many Indian settlements during all of the nineteenth century.[14]

Peasants also used another more direct means to gain access to land. Peasants in El Espinal, a pueblo near Papantla, invaded the lands of the hacienda de la Jamaya during the first years of the republic. When the owners of Jamaya attempted to exercise their property rights in 1849, the municipality of El Espinal began a legal action to protect the villagers' possession of the contested lands. The legal conflict continued until 1892, when the community agreed to pay six thousand pesos to buy their rights to the land. The document that described the transaction noted that the price was only half of the true value of the property.[15] This example illustrates how peasants combined different techniques to accumulate lands. First the peasants invaded the lands, and later, after a long legal suit, they offered to buy them. Something similar happened in Tuxpan, where the purchase title mentions that Indians from the hamlet of Ojite had already invaded part of the lands sold.[16] Evidently, the peasantry of the nineteenth century could threaten landlords and the latter sometimes preferred to sell instead of running the risk of losing everything.

Violence could also influence the action of the republican courts. In Amatlán the townspeople had long-standing claims against the hacienda of San Benito and won a favorable hearing in court after a bloody outburst of violence. The members of the community worked the land as tenants of the estate, and contemporaries believed that the tensions between these people and the owners contributed to the causes of the so-called caste war that laid waste to the entire Huasteca in the years 1847–1849. In the 1850s, the court decided in favor of the community renters and ordered the hacienda to cede a good portion of land to the Indians of Amatlán.[17] What remained of the hacienda of San Benito underwent another subdivision in the late nineteenth century. In the 1930s, when the Agrarian Reform Commission studied the municipality to determine if there was a property large enough to form an *ejido* under the new agrarian laws, the municipal president informed the secretariat's representative that the estate had disappeared in 1895. "The lands of the hacienda San Benito de Amatlán ... were divided up among its former tenants ... in general the lots were divided into plots of thirty seven hectares and the smallest lot received six and a half hectares."[18] The Amatlán decision indicates that courts often considered popular interests when determining land disputes, a tendency that also appears in the courts' interpretation of liberal land legislation.

Uses of Communal Land

There is a considerable lacuna of information concerning the manner in which the communal property operated in the nineteenth century. Who determined access to community lands? Who administered the lands? During the colonial period, the indigenous town councils known as *repúblicas de indios* supervised community goods.[19] After independence, the new constitution suppressed the *repúblicas* in favor of municipal governments, but unlike colonial governments non-Indians often dominated town councils. The manner in which republican local governments administered the goods inherited from their colonial predecessors is largely unknown. Laws passed by state governments often delegated the old functions of the *repúblicas* to the new municipal governments, but the process was slow and uneven.[20] Municipalities claimed powers, such as labor drafts and control of communal land, that had belonged to *repúblicas*. But while the law often put community resources at the disposition of the municipalities, in practice traditional forms of control of communal lands endured. Indigenous peasants retained traditional forms of organizing production and fiercely rejected attempts by municipalities to intervene in the lands at the center of peasant life.

As Brigida Von Metz has shown, community life revolved around the division between *cabeceras* and the dependent *sujeto* communities.[21] Differences between *sujetos* and *cabeceras* become particularly apparent in questions of land. The spotty nature of municipal archives and the state's tenuous control over Indian community affairs has produced very limited documentation of land use in Indian communities. However, several examples in the Huasteca *hidalguense* provide some clues as to how communities regulated land access. As Powell noted, Indian pueblos had different categories of lands destined for distinct uses.[22] The *fundo legal* consisted of the original "six hundred *varas*" [six hundred-yard] square that served as the town site. Closely related to the *fundo*, *ejidos* served as common pastures and forest lands also located near the town. Many communities in the Huasteca did not have a separate *ejido* delineated on their community lands. The two most important categories of land for the towns in the Huasteca consisted of the *propios* and the *tierras de repartimiento*. Communities owned the *propios* and rented the land out as a source of municipal revenue. The *tierras de repartimiento* were the most important lands for the Indian peasants. Peasant agricultural production actually occurred on these lands. The communities divided up these lands among the members of the villages and farmed them in family plots. A certain sense of ownership developed among the indigenous peasantry since sons inherited the family plots from their fathers.

The manner in which villages and municipalities administered the different categories of land reveal power relations in the countryside. The new municipalities of the republican period generally inherited the *propios*. The municipalities rented out the lands to raise funds for their treasuries. Following colonial precedents, local governments made the land available to the wealthier residents and to individuals with influence in town councils.[23]

The rents were often nominal: the municipalities rented most of the estates for amounts between ten and twenty pesos a year. In other regions similar cases, where landlords rented lands from municipalities for relatively small amounts, also occur. Thus a large portion of "communal" lands had already escaped the control of the peasant members of the communities long before the liberal innovations of the mid-nineteenth century.

Not surprisingly, the *propios* comprised the lands that local elites alienated most often in the region during the liberal period. In Huautla, for example, five individuals claimed six properties under the Ley Lerdo in 1856.[24] The alienation of the *propios* economically strengthened local landowners since it provided them with a more secure form of tenure. Schryer also notes that the new land opportunities allowed wealthy Indians to fortify their positions as *rancheros*. The loss of these lands did not affect peasant production but, rather, the coffers of the municipalities.[25] While the income from the rents greatly interested some individuals, indigenous peasants did not directly benefit from the land rents. As Lira points out, towns often used the rental income to pay the fees of the clergy.[26]

The *tierras de repartimiento*, however, largely remained beyond the administration of the local municipalities. The peasant communities within the municipalities largely regulated the access to *repartimiento* lands themselves. Few documents concerning the administration of these lands have survived, but during the republican period the several attempts to intervene in the administration of the lands produced information concerning who actually controlled the *repartimiento* lands. An unusually detailed account comes from a municipality with a large amount of land on the western edge of the Huasteca, Mextitlán. In the 1830s, the government imposed a national land tax in order to pay for the expedition against Texas and ordered municipalities to collect the tax from the occupants of communal lands in their jurisdictions. Mextitlán officials therefore attempted to carry out a survey of the town's communal land to assess the tax. While the earliest laws of the state of Mexico ordered that the lands formerly held by the colonial *"pueblo" "pasan a ser propios de los fondos municipales,"* [became communal lands of municipalities] in practice the municipalities exercised only limited control.[27] The municipality stated that it could not carry out the survey due to the great number of farmers on the land and because the Indians denied they possessed the land in order to avoid the tax.[28] "[T]he Indians believe that in practicing the land survey (*avalua*) the town council will commit some evil and supposing that it [the survey] is the result of the council's orders, they have even threatened to bring suit to the supreme government against the municipal corporation."[29]

The way in which the community parceled out the lands indicated great wealth differences between the *comuneros*. The municipal government reported "great irregularities" in the way the Indians had divided the land. "There are individuals that have as much as twenty *fanegas de sembradura* (about sixty hectares) while others barely have six or eight furrows (*surcos*) of twenty to thirty yards, and some not even that." The wealthy Indians had monopolized lands and they "never confess to the total of their possessions."[30] Again, access to official positions in village administration and traditional status as elders gave peasants the means to build up their *ranchos* on communal lands.[31] Evidently, community members bought, sold, rented, and even mortgaged usufruct rights, which made the accumulation of wealth within the community possible. The municipality noted discontent within the Indian community over the current division of lands. The municipal officers complained that Indians jammed the local court with legal disputes between members of the community over possession of land.

Villagers had a strong sense of usufruct rights to the *tierras de repartimiento*. The villagers owned these lands communally in large undivided lots, but they often had a fierce sense of personal control over specific plots. The ambiguities of Republican municipal control over resources also caused discord between *cabecera* governments and Indian peasants. One may observe an example of these disputes in the lawsuit brought by a hamlet called Temazola. The residents of the hamlet complained that the town council had wrongfully rented out part of the lands they claimed as their *tierras de repartimiento*. Such a rental "was contrary to the laws that protect the rights of property that regulate communal lands."[32] The petitioners continued, "if the municipal government thinks that because the lands are *de repartimiento* they can dispose of them as they will . . . it has erred."[33] The case gives some information about how the residents thought the villages should manage their lands. They note that the *tierras de repartimiento* "are as equally hereditary" as private property and that the municipality should not intervene in the disposition of land acquired by inheritance. Part of the debate evidently stemmed from the powers of the district *jefe político* to distribute "unoccupied" lands. The town council did not question the hereditary nature of *repartimiento* lands; rather, they replied that the petitioners were not the traditional occupants of Temazola, but had only recently started exploiting the land and that one or two troublemakers had "seduced them to sign [the petition] by trickery."[34]

Remarkably, members of *sujeto* communities continued to use the colonial titles of *gobernador*, *viejos*, and *principales*.[35] Oftentimes they coincided with new posts in local government, such as justice of the peace and *subregidor* (a municipal representative resident in a *sujeto* community). Throughout the nineteenth century Indian officials continued to have influence as representatives of villages or hamlets in dealings with higher levels of government and in controlling certain resources, as in the case of the communal lands in Mextitlán. Colonial terminology and offices also continued to function in the indigenous community of Temapache. Indian communities retained some elements of their colonial organization, although they lacked any constitutional basis for their existence.

The Liberal Project

When Mexican elites searched for the causes of the nation's "backwardness," they quickly found fault with peasant agriculture. Conservative observers tended to blame the very nature of the Indian population. The department governor (centralist) blamed the Indians for the decadent state of Veracruz's agriculture in 1844:

> The material exercise of agriculture is left to the native class in most of the Department who are occupied as laborers in the estates both big and small, cultivating those which they possess themselves in community; but never in greater extension than that which satisfies their limited necessities, and to put on the market the surplus for their religious expenses of the same community and other functions they have as customs in which they invest all which they have gained, causing abuses of drunkenness and others no less pernicious.[36]

Since, in the conservative view, the incorrigible laziness of the Indian villagers was the central issue, they recommended tighter controls over peasant communities, less autonomy, and a return to colonial orderliness.

Liberals took a different approach, concentrating their criticisms on the system of land tenure. For example, the liberal governor, Juan de la Luz Enríquez, identified the communal tenancy system as the source of disorder and economic stagnation. "Mexico's difficult situation since independence to the present day," said Enríquez, "is due only to the circumstance that we have not divided our property."[37] He continued with a description, in the style of classical liberalism, of the wonders that would come with the division of lands into individual private plots. Almost every governor after 1856 expressed similar sentiments.[38] For the liberals who aspired to promote "progress" in the Mexican countryside, communal land and undivided properties created brakes on individual innovation and, therefore, a barrier to the promised land of progress. In the words of Manuel Soto, a member of the

Constitutional Congress of 1857, "To give the Indians property is to tie them to the land which is theirs exclusively. Private interest will work with them to better it, and once improved it will rise in price and the desire to profit... will act as a stimulus to make them hard working, active and economic."[39] Thus, in the liberal view, the Indians were lazy only because they did not own private property.

This intellectual environment produced an extensive amount of legislation designed to convert communal lands into private property. The opinion of the state's political elite ran against municipal ownership of land and the usufruct rights enjoyed by the mostly indigenous peasantry. The local legislature passed a simple yet far-reaching law that formed the legal basis of the state's land policy until the end of the Porfiriato. This law of December 22, 1826, ordered that "all community lands of the natives, forested or not, shall be reduced to private property, divided up with equality to every person... belonging to the community."[40] The law encompassed all of the community land that originated in colonial land grants or purchases by the community, with the only exception a small parcel set aside to serve as an *ejido*. State legislatures passed similar laws in Jalisco, the state of Mexico, Michoacán, and other states, calling for local governments to distribute their lands to the indigenous inhabitants.[41] The law left many problems unanswered that later frustrated attempts to implement privatization. It did not specify who paid the expense of surveying and administering the division of the land. The law had no provisions determining who had rights as community members to the land. Another problem stemmed from the fact that villages often engaged in land disputes over the borders of the community properties and no division could take place until the towns and their neighbors settled the lawsuits.[42]

Besides the state laws, liberals at the federal level formulated legislation against community ownership in the famous Ley Lerdo of June 25, 1856. This law declared that tenants and usufruct-rights holders on communal lands (or church properties) could claim the lands by means of an "adjudication" before a notary, thus converting communal tenancy into private property. The Ley Lerdo further stipulated that any lands not adjudicated could be claimed by any other individual once a period of three months had passed after the promulgation of the law.

The number of laws concerning land division increased as the century wore on. The government of Ignacio de la Llave promulgated a law in 1856 that aimed at resolving the boundary disputes that had stymied the land divisions in many municipalities.[43] The law established a system of arbitration to rapidly resolve land disputes and avoid the costly and prolonged court process, thus freeing up the land subject to the law of 1826. Many more laws followed, some even including Draconian enforcement measures. For example, the law of March 17, 1869, specified that the state would declare all of the communal lands vacant (*baldíos*) and property of the government if the villages did not divide them into private plots within six months.[44] Evidently, the leaders in the state Congress felt that the indigenous peasantry needed incentives to comply to the law.

In spite of eloquent exhortations of liberal ideologues, state governments only found frustration in their efforts to divide up communal properties. In 1844, Antonio María Salonio reported that the government had only carried out one land division in the entire state, eighteen years after the law of 1826.[45] Apolinar Castillo, governor in 1882, gave an equally bleak report—only four or six towns had carried out the land division laws or privatization.[46] Evidently, these few land divisions took place in the early 1860s, in the area around the state capital, at the initiative of members of the communities themselves.[47] The towns that applied the laws first were generally *mestizo* communities, close to the center of political and commercial activity in the state. The number of laws passed ordering the immediate division of land indicates that the state had little power to enforce the division in regions far from the capital. The profusion of laws did not aid the land division. According to Enríquez, "the accumulation of decrees expedited to extend enforcement periods, modifying previous laws, and eliminating articles of other laws is such that one is barely able to dictate a resolution without the danger of forgetting some legal precept."[48]

Frustration of the Liberal Project

Once such extreme laws were on the books one would expect communal ownership to evaporate, but the results of the liberal legislation were more mixed than the inflexible articles of the laws suggest. Even with threats of expropriation, the villagers stalled the application of the laws before 1880. Two cases where the federal Ley Lerdo appeared in the land records of northern Veracruz illustrate the ability of Indians to conserve their traditional system of tenancy and to manipulate the laws in their favor.[49] The law permitted occupants of communally owned land to purchase the property, but it also stipulated that outsiders could "denounce" any land not claimed by the occupants after a few months. However, attempts by outsiders or villagers to claim *tierras de repartimiento* under the law were very rare.[50] Villagers used the Ley Lerdo to revalidate old titles. In 1856, the inhabitants of San Gerónimo, a *sujeto* of Chicontepec, went before a judge and claimed "a piece of land valued at 300 pesos." The Indians declared that although they had the legitimate ownership, they had lost their title deeds and they needed new documents to protect their possession.[51] From their declarations before the notary it is apparent that the Indians used the law only to get a title to protect their ownership. "The present step is a sacrifice," declared the Sasaltitleños to the notary, "but it is inevitable, to provide for their well-being and although they recall having had titles to said lands, these have disappeared without any trace."[52] Incidentally, an adjudication without titles, as in this case, violated provisions of the law.

In another case from Chicontepec, Ignacio Marcos Zavala and José Raphael Luvían attempted to grab the lands of Cececapa and Santa Cruz (two tracts of communal land belonging to the town) by using the Ley Lerdo. The effort failed. The Indians hired a lawyer and appealed to a local *juez de primera instancia*, who quickly rendered a decision favorable to the Indians. The judge, Manuel Ramos, doubted that the law of June 25, 1856, encompassed the lands used by Indian producers as *tierras de repartimiento*. He also observed that Zavala and Luvían had received their deed from a justice of the peace and not a notary or *juez de primera instancia*, thereby making the title void. Thus on December 26, 1856, the judge declared the adjudication invalid.[53] In San Gerónimo the villagers used the law to get new valid titles to communal land, and in the Cececapa the village successfully proposed that the *tierras de repartimiento* were not subject to the law. The cases suggest that local officials bent to the will of the Indian population when they interpreted the federal law.

State land law, especially the law of 1826, ultimately had more impact on communal landholding than the Ley Lerdo, and had more advantages for villagers. The law recognized Indian *comuneros* as the owners of the land and, unlike the Ley Lerdo, required no payment. Before the 1880s, local officials made the law even more agreeable by applying it according to the criteria of the Indians themselves. In 1875 Papantla divided its lands, but it did so by creating twenty-five "large lots" (*grandes lotes*), three *fundos legales,* and an *ejido*. The liberals granted each of the municipality's villages a large parcel. The Indians organized the large lots as "agrarian associations" or *condueñazgos*, with the land held *pro-indivisa*, or in other words, without division into individual plots.[54] The result did not conform to the ideals of individual property that the urban liberals desired.[55] A three-member "committee of *indígenas*" took the authority to carry out the division of Papantla's lands. Included in the committee were two Indians who had led a rebellion against the Austrian garrison in April of 1866, Simon Tiburcio and Pablo Hernández. The committee justified its decision to adopt the system of large lots with the argument that they could not easily survey the irregular and hilly land, but more importantly, the *condueñazgos* easily accommodated the system of agricultural rotation practiced in the region. The new system of lots eliminated any interference of the *cabecera* municipal government in the administration of land. Such a result could well have had a favorable impact for the majority of the Indians who lived and worked in the *sujetos*. Now the *sujetos* controlled their own economic resources as independent agrarian societies.

Liberals designed the land laws to eliminate conflicts that emerged from within communal properties by converting tracts of unsurveyed land into many small, well-defined plots. However, when indigenous peasants opposed such privatization solutions local administrators accommodated them. Temapache is an example of how Indians modified liberal intentions in practice. Land conflicts emerged within the town because when the indigenous community bought the hacienda de Buenavista, the non-Indian residents did not participate in the purchase. As a result of their decision not to join the Indians in the purchase, the *mestizos* remained on the lands as tenants, dependent on resources now in the hands of Indians. This situation produced frequent clashes of interest between the two populations. In 1841 the Indians attempted to resolve the conflict between the two "republics,"[56] selling usufruct rights to half of the territory to the *"común de la gente de razón"* for two thousand pesos. But, according to one local official, this sale only aggravated the competition between the two communities, "to the level of disrupting the public tranquillity of this district."[57]

One of the principal points of dispute originated from the *mestizos* grazing cattle on the lands, even when a clause of the 1841 sale prohibited the use of the land as pasture. When the *mestizos* violated this clause, the Indians resorted to the judicial system on two occasions, in 1845 and in 1856. In both cases they won favorable results, as the courts ordered that *mestizos* retire the offending cattle from Buenavista.

However, the courts did not resolve the dispute definitively until 1868. Under the auspices of the Liberal Restored Republic, each community chose an arbiter with the authority to reach an agreement. But when the two representatives failed to settle, the governor designated Lázaro Muñoz, *jefe político* of Papantla and a liberal with impeccable credentials, as a binding arbiter.[58] Muñoz decided wholeheartedly in favor of the indigenous community, declaring the sale of 1841 invalid and ordering the Indians to return the two thousand pesos the non-Indians had paid twenty-seven years earlier. At the same time the *mestizos* lost any rights they had to the land of Buenavista. The decision completely ignored the arguments of the arbiter for the *mestizo* community, Joaquín del Valle. He wanted to convert the usufruct rights that the *mestizos* had bought in 1841 into property rights. He also recommended that the courts divide the estate into lots for each community. Del Valle's proposal, in effect, called for the application of liberal property laws. After all, forty years of laws ordered that villages transform usufruct rights into simple private-property tenure wherever possible. Del Valle protested against the Muñoz decision, stating that it was merely an "echo" of the Indians' position and "an attack against property rights." The ideas Muñoz used to justify his decision are even more interesting. Muñoz used several principles rooted in colonial precepts concerning village land rights rather than liberalism. Muñoz stated that since there were more indigenous community members than *de razón* villagers, the Indians had more need for the land. Muñoz also reasoned that the *mestizos* had operated "in bad faith" when they introduced cattle onto the lands of Buenavista. The *jefe político* of Tuxpan, Manuel Gorrochotegui, also endorsed the opinion, in spite of the fact that he was a *mestizo* landowner in Temapache.[59]

Thus some local officials of the Restored Republic made an effort to keep the land undivided and in the hands of the indigenous community. Ironically, the liberal governor of Veracruz in 1856 had originally promoted the system of arbitration used in Temapache with the objective of facilitating the conversion of communal lands into private property. The case at hand offers an excellent example of why scholars should not write the history of land tenancy by consulting law books. Local officials often ignored the land laws of the early nineteenth century or applied them in such a way as to take the interests of villagers into account.

Reasons for Delay

Governments proved unable to divide peasant land before the 1880s, and in most cases outsiders did not interfere until the last decade of the nineteenth century. In the following pages one must address two questions: why the delay and what happened to community lands once the authorities began to enforce the laws? I suspect that the very local functionaries who had the duty to enforce the laws made them ineffective. They simply let time pass without attempting to apply the laws. In respect to the decisions handed down in Temapache and Chicontepec the judges and *jefes políticos* went even further and actively decided in favor of the communities. Such a supposition is logical if one considers that local officials did not have the necessary police to force the application of the laws if the Indians refused to accept them. Thus when the governors tried to explain why they had failed to divide the communal land, they resorted to the time-worn refrain of "the ignorance of the indigenous class and the bad faith of some individuals who live exploiting this ignorance" as the cause of their failures.[60] The governors attributed the delays to ignorance, when in reality the Indians' perception of their own interests caused the slow pace of change.

How did villagers defend and even expand their communal lands in the first two-thirds of the nineteenth century? First, contrary to what is generally affirmed, the war of independence brought important social and economic changes that allowed the growth of the *pueblos*. These changes did not take the form of a pro-peasant or *indigenista* government; rather, it occurred at the level of the economic base of the landlord elite. The wars left the landlords in a state of decay; Bellingeri and Gil Sánchez estimate that the production of the great estates declined by at least half of the level they had attained at the end of the century.[61] Although there is no solid study of the haciendas of the Huasteca in the nineteenth century, reports from the region indicate that these estates had stagnated. In the properties of the Huasteca coast, where cattle was the typical product, observers complained that "they [the land owners] have not been able to introduce any advancement in agriculture, and the cattle and horse stock daily tend to degenerate. Everything, in a word, has been abandoned to nature."[62]

Given the decline that Mexico suffered, private landlords had little incentive to invade communal lands. This economic situation changed the balance of power in favor of the communities. The cases described above were a natural result of the decadence of the great estates: impoverished *hacendados* sold their lands in order to get funds to finance other activities, or they simply did not have the resources to resist the advances of the communities on their lands.[63] Thus the rural elite, far from being strengthened by independence, found themselves in dire straits.

The lower classes in rural Mexico, both hacienda tenants and members of Indian communities, undermined the economy of the estate owners. The fear of peasant revolutions affected agricultural production and social relations in the countryside. In the Huasteca these fears became reality on various occasions, but especially from 1847 to 1849, when peasant rebels destroyed many properties. In the municipality of Amatlán, for example, local insurgents destroyed the estates of San Benito and San Jerónimo. Eduardo Fages, a contemporary, commented that at the hacienda of San Benito the insurrectionists "did not leave one stone laying on another."[64] Rebellion increased the risks for great estate owners, while the rebels were relatively risk free. During the "caste war," when the Mexican government finally concentrated enough troops to put down the disorders, the peasant armies disintegrated.

The rebels surrendered, requesting and receiving generous amnesties whenever they confronted superior army forces. The governor of Puebla even allowed the so-called *cabecillas*, captured by government forces, to go free when he decreed a general amnesty.[65] This policy of conciliation resulted from the governor's knowledge of the state's weakness. The government did not have the ability to maintain the forces necessary to establish garrisons throughout the countryside. Peasants discovered that they could carry out their actions against the landlords with little risk to their own interests.

Instability and the economy may have provided general causes for the slow pace of privatization, but to understand land tenancy one must consider the relations between villagers and liberal officials. Local functionaries rendered ineffective the laws expropriating the villages that delayed in dividing up the land. The officials simply let time pass without attempting to apply the laws. While in part the local government realized that it did not have the police power to dictate tenure changes, a popular element within the liberal camp also created a political space for indigenous small producers. Thus, local liberals before the Porfiriato did not apply the laws ordering the expropriation of land. Instead, they carried out the laws ordering the division of communal lands into small properties. Generally, towns transformed the communal land tenure into nominally private *condueñazgos*, with little disruption of possession or agricultural practices.

The ten years of war following 1856 created an armed peasantry, which provided the basis for the liberal victory in 1867. But it also meant that peasants in places like the sierra de Puebla, the Huasteca, and Guerrero had greater influence to determine how their communities functioned. In Temapache, the Indians mobilized in the Guardia Nacional used their military force to influence the decision of the courts in 1868. Del Valle, the lawyer representing the *gente de razón*, complained that the mostly Indian Guardia Nacional confiscated the cattle of his clients.[66] The Indians imposed their will precisely because of the military and political power they had won during the civil war. In the words of Del Valle:

> The deplorable state in which the very lands of the so-called *de razón* exist is due to the preponderance that the indigenous class has taken. For causes that are not necessary to describe and principally because the Indians are accustomed to being in the vanguard of all the political revolutions, as a result the majority of the *de razón* have had to emigrate and live in the ranchos.[67]

The influence that Papantla's Indians exercised in carrying out the first division of lands into large lots resulted from the military role they played in the rebellion against the Austrian garrison occupying their town. In fact, a previously unknown Indian, Simón Tiburcio, and a sublieutenant in the national guard, Rosalindo Fajardo, organized the revolt without the support of the more respectable liberals in the town.[68] No doubt the prestige they had won in the rebellion gave them the influence to control the land-tenure change. Elites and representatives of the state had to negotiate their authority with village communities during the decades of the 1860s, and land-tenure changes could not simply be legislated without taking account of local realities.

Prudence appears to have been the liberal characteristic most common in questions referring to communal tenancy in the towns. Up to a certain point, an alliance between liberal politicians and the peasantry existed. In some regions of Mexico liberals could count on rural followers largely because they reinterpreted their own laws to the benefit of the villagers. Peasant discontent often had its roots in the ambiguous power relations within municipalities. Besides taxes, head towns demanded labor services from *sujeto* communities, which Indians considered especially burdensome. The municipalities of independent Mexico extensively used this prerogative (formerly belonging to Indian *repúblicas*) to make their municipal budgets go further. Municipalities did not equally divide up tax burdens within the towns, and tax differences often served as a point around which local politicians could organize supporters. Thus, when liberals stated that they wanted to liberate the Indians from "the cruel yoke of the community," it was not necessarily a discourse alien to the experiences of Indians.[69] Often in the name of the community, local elites exacted labor and taxes from the peasantry.

In the 1820s, the republican government superimposed the dichotomies of Indian/*mestizo* and municipality/*república de indios* on the *sujeto/cabecera* split. Liberals and political officials on the local level had to function within these divisions.[70] In applying the land laws the liberal government removed the administration of communal resources from the town councils based in the head towns and turned them over to *condueñazgos* based in the *sujeto* communities. The new system eliminated any interference of the head-town municipal government in the administration of land. Such a result could well have had a favorable impact for the majority of the Indians who lived and worked in the *sujetos*. The *condueñazgos* had notarized agreements regulating the use of land and communal resources such as forests. The regulations established governing bodies elected annually to enforce community decisions and administer sales of forest products.[71] These councils had to approve any sales of land or shares in the *condueñazgo*, for shares could not be sold to outsiders without first being offered to community members. These rules permitted peasants to continue exploiting the land, and in essence, villagers won new private titles to communal tenure patterns.

Greater autonomy of the *condueñazgos* made them quite popular with the Indian members of the communities. The way in which land laws functioned indicates that liberals allowed the Indian members of *sujeto* communities to continue to possess the land they tilled. Furthermore, it gave them greater autonomy, resolving the conflict between *sujeto* and *cabecera* for control of community resources in favor of the former. In fact, the case of Papantla shows that Indians not only controlled the first land division, but they also used the occasion to establish three new pueblos by setting up town sites.

The Porfirian Onslaught

Liberal governments allowed for local autonomy in the form of *condueñazgos* until the 1890s. To bring this discussion to a close, one must touch on the fate of these forms of ownership as the Mexican economy grew and a more powerful central state emerged under the leadership of Porfirio Díaz. During the period from 1890 to 1910 non-Indian elites began to turn the tide against peasant communities and their lands. Several characteristics of the assault on peasant access to land are evident in the towns of the Huasteca. First, the indigenous peasantry did not simply accept its fate when faced with the maneuvers of the landlords; villagers fought back with lawsuits in the courts and sometimes with rifles in the fields. Occasionally, villagers succeeded in defying would-be land grabbers. The Porfirian *despojo* was not universal. Second, villagers tended to lose their lands through political machinations, especially by the intervention of *jefes políticos* rather than the simple forces of the market—that is to say, market forces had a human face. More often, local officials of modest origins turned themselves into great landlords at the expense of peasant lands. The expropriation villagers suffered in these years resulted from the growing autocracy of the Porfirian dictatorship. The method of accumulation of land also reveals that the economic elite of the Porfiriato relied on state power to create its wealth.

To illustrate how the loss of peasant land occurred, several examples follow that describe the range of methods for agrarian expropriation. Panatela was one of the strongest communities in terms of land access and control of the process of privatization in the 1870s, yet between 1893 and 1898 the government forced the communities to divide Panatela's "large lots" into individual private plots, "scientifically" measured and mapped at the communities' expense.[72] Considerable discontent raged within the community;

Papantecos revolted on at least two occasions in the 1890s, and local officials had to import federal troops and *rurales* so that the land division could proceed.[73] Villagers began to lose ownership of the lands once they received individual private titles. Before 1896 individuals could buy "shares" of a *condueñazgo*, but the sale had to be approved by the community according to the *condueñazgo* regulations. Before 1896 villagers alienated only seven percent of the land, but between 1896 and the end of the Porfiriato thirty-one percent found its way into the hands of private investors, especially the non-Indian merchants in Papantla.[74] Papantla was relatively fortunate. Large numbers of peasants retained control of their lands, and landlords tended to rent the property they accumulated to peasant villagers. Other communities in the region were not so fortunate.

Temapache presents an interesting case where members of the community allied with powerful outsiders to dispossess other members of the community. After having defeated the attempt by *mestizo* residents to divide their land in 1868, the *condueños* held their property without further conflicts until the 1890s. At that time, the community elected a young "clever" villager, Julio González, as administrator. González used his post to become municipal president, and combining the advantages of both posts he began to create a "division within the *condueños*" by rewarding his followers and embezzling *condueñazgo* income from timber sales for himself. In 1901 the community elected a new administration, but González refused to turn over the books and papers from his administration and began to use police to persecute the administrator-elect and his followers. González then proceeded to carry out a division of land into individual plots in 1904. Villagers opposed to González protested the move and refused to accept the new land titles. González called in the rural police to persecute the village opposition, forcing many to flee, leaving their fields untilled. The municipal president, with the assistance of a local judge, then proceeded to declare the lands of his opponents vacant, ripe for distribution to his followers.[75] Thus, an ambitious peasant used the liberal land laws to dispossess his fellow co-owners and transform himself from a peasant who tilled the land into a landlord with political ambitions.

The people of Espinal had defended their claim to lands during all of the nineteenth century, but when their property caught the eye of Díaz's father-in-law they soon suffered expropriation. Manuel Romero Rubio had an interest in developing the oil deposits that reportedly were to be found under lands owned by the municipality. Local officials carried out the expropriation by means of a forced sale at a price set by Romero Rubio. In 1892, he offered to buy 400 hectares of the land for 2,000 pesos. The town council declared that the land in question had a value of 5,000 pesos, but the *jefe político* forced them to accept Romero Rubio's offer when he appeared before the municipal council, accompanied by a contingent of rural police, and ordered the town to accept Romero's price.[76] After the sale, the state government pressured the town to proceed with the division of communal lands into individual plots, in spite of protests that the surveyor sent to do the work was incompetent.[77]

Political intervention also weighed heavily on the indigenous peasants of Texcatepec. Like Papantla, Texcatepec had divided its land into five large lots organized as *condueñazgos* in 1884. In 1891, the municipal secretary, Conrado Hernández, with the assistance of the *jefe político*, began the process of dividing communal property. Hernández included many of his employees on his private ranch in the list of villagers with rights to the land, an action that the community protested vigorously. Hernández used rural police to violently suppress discontent within the town. Villagers claimed that the division into private plots never really occurred and that officials had created notary documents to make it seem as if there had been a division. In 1892, Hernández imposed a head tax on the pretext of putting a telephone in the town, but after several years he called an assembly and, in the presence of his uncle Miguel Hernández acting as notary, returned five pesos to each resident, telling them that he was returning the telephone tax while he told his uncle, the notary, that he was "buying" their land rights. Afterward, using these sale titles, Hernández and other officials began to demand rent and labor services from Texcatepecanos. The *jefe político*, Leonardo Chagoya, made his task easier when he ordered that the surrounding municipalities absorb the municipality of Texcatepec, removing local authority from the reach of the villagers. The Indians never accepted the claims of ownership, and after a long court battle, punctuated by threats and assassinations, Hernández returned part of the lands he "owned" to the residents. Later, Texcatepec became a center of revolutionary activity in 1910–1920.[78]

These four cases indicate that political manipulations were central to understanding how villagers lost control of communal lands in the last years of the Porfiriato. Arbitrary action by *jefes políticos* and municipal officials are central to these accounts. Villagers did not go quietly: land grabbers resorted to rural police, the federal army, and political assassinations to enforce the expropriations. The liberal legislation served as only a backdrop to the use of power. The roots of the peasantry's dispossession emerged from the autocratic use of power in the Porfiriato, power unavailable to earlier officials. Part of the impulse toward the disenfranchisement of peasants came from within the peasant community itself, as in the case of Temapache. The inequality that characterized Indian communities of the early republic continued, fortified by the liberal reform and the Porfiriato. While villages were not egalitarian before the liberal laws, communal ownership offered some limits to the amount of land that any one villager could control. Private property made it possible for ambitious local officials to expel members of the community and occupy their land.

Conclusion

Peasants were central to the political events of the nineteenth century. The view that peasants lived unaware of the political events around them is erroneous.[79] Nor can one say that the Liberal reforms resulted in the immediate loss of lands for the peasantry. The assumption that peasant interests naturally conflicted with the liberal project originates from the tendency to look back from the perspective of the Porfiriato and assume that the numerous expropriations that occurred began with the Constitution of 1857. The process of land alienation in the Porfiriato proceeded slowly. Only after the demobilization of the national guard and the strengthening of the national state did peasant producers lose land to large-scale agriculture and political hacks.

Recently, Daniel Nugent has noted that "we must discover the manner and the degree to which 'external forces' ... themselves were shaped by the actions of people in the countryside thereby restoring the peasantry to their place in world history."[80] While Nugent refers to the impact of international capitalism on the countryside, the statement is equally relevant to the initiatives of the liberal state. Peasants manipulated the state to ensure their survival even in the difficult times of the Porfiriato. Indeed, the experience of the liberal wars informed the actions of the peasant revolutionaries of 1910.[81] Local political power, especially before 1880, rested on a negotiated series of relations between peasants and *jefes políticos*, judges, and municipalities. In the political turmoil of the nineteenth century, peasants enjoyed a unique ability to re-negotiate local power relations. The need to mobilize support led liberals to reinterpret their own laws to the benefit of the villagers.

The experience of the late nineteenth century should also serve as a warning to those who would like to apply facile liberal solutions of individual ownership and competition to rural villages. These villages do not exist in a political vacuum. While peasants certainly understood the value of the land (even in its commodified form), that did not necessarily protect their ownership. As the Porfirian system became more closed, peasants lost the political clout that ultimately protected their property rights. Liberal economic reforms in the context of autocratic, closed political systems such as those in rural Mexico tend to benefit the petty autocrats who dominate local politics. Today one may once again observe a counter-discourse emerging from Chiapas peasants who question the wisdom of private property in a world of *caciques*.

Notes

1. Moisés González Navarro, "Tenencia de la tierra y población agrícola (1877–1960)," in *Historia Mexicana* 19:1 (1969): 62, for example, states that the privatization law of June 25, 1856, was the culmination of the hacienda's attack against indigenous lands. Other works take similar positions; see Gerrit Huizer, *La lucha campesina en México* (México, D.F., 1982); Jean Meyer, *Problemas campesinos y revueltas agraria (1821–1910)* (México, D.F., 1973), pp. 68–71, 116–18; and T. G. Powell, "Los liberales, el campesinado indígena y los problemas agrarios durante la Reforma," *Historia Mexicana* 24:1 (1972); and John Tutino, *From Insurrection to Revolution in Mexico: Social Bases of Agrarian Violence, 1750–1940* (Princeton, 1986), p. 259.

2. Florencia E. Mallon, "The Conflictual Construction of Community: Gender, Ethnicity and Hegemony in the Sierra Norte de Puebla," unpublished paper (Madison, May 1990); Guy P. C. Thomson, "Agrarian Conflict in the Municipality of Cuetzalán (Sierra de Puebla): The Rise and Fall of 'Pala' Agustín Dieguillo," *Hispanic American Historical Review* 71:2 (1991), 208–9. Andrés Lira González, *Comunidades indígenas frente a la ciudad de México: Tenochtitlan y Tlateloco, sus pueblos y barrios, 1812–1919* (Zamora, 1983), also notes that liberal lawyers in Mexico City won influence in the wealthier Indian towns of Mexico City, where the *sujetos* challenged conservative governments' attempt to reestablish the colonial order of land administration. The classic work of Reyes Heroles noted that elements of liberal discourse called for the amelioration of the "Indian problem." Leading politicians, such as Ponciano Arriaga, used these ideas on the local level to win adherents and build political loyalty to the liberal faction. The reader is cautioned not to confuse the radical liberalism of the nineteenth century with the "social liberalism" that Carlos Salinas de Gortari recently promoted to ameliorate, or, as some would say, disguise the harsher elements of his economic project.

3. See the case of the *sujeto*, Huacango, Chicontepec, where the village rejected a map due to defects. Archivo de la Comisión Agraria Mixta, Xalapa, Veracruz, exp. 68, f. 2 "resolución"; see also exp. 268 (hereafter cited as ACAM).

4. ACAM, exp. 88, f. 576; exp. 61, f. 165, 241. Robert J. Knowlton, "La división de las tierras de los pueblos durante el siglo XIX: El caso de Michoacán," *Historia Mexicana* 40 (1990), 9–11, documents similar problems with the division of communal land in Sahuayo, Michoacán.

5. ACAM, exp. 61, f. 241. The division into individual lots "*fue apócrifo*" [was apocryphal] according to the agrarian reform officials.

6. The most important law on the state level made no distinction between "lands obtained by viceregal grants and land they had bought in common and possessed pro-indiviso." Gobierno del estado de Veracruz, *Colección de leyes, decretos y circulares de Veracruz* (hereafter cited as *CLEV*) (Xalapa, 1900), 1869:238.

7. In 1880 the lands of Coahuitlán were divided into three large lots; unfortunately, the deeds only specify the amounts of land for two of the three lots, and the figure presented here only consists of these two lots.

8. The lands of Tihuatlán were divided into five *condueñazgos* in 1874; the figure presented here only represents the land of one of these lots, that of San Miguel Mecatepec.

9. This amount corresponds to the land belonging to the *sujeto* of Tzicatlán of Zontecometlán.

10. Includes the land belonging to the *sujeto* of Tres Cruces only.

11. ACAM, exp. 341.

12. ACAM, exp. 619.

13. Eduardo Fages, "Noticias estadísticas sobre el departamento de Tuxpan," in *Boletín de la sociedad mexicana de geografía y estadísticas*, (1856), 4:242; Manuel Fernando Soto, *Noticias estadísticas de la Huasteca y parte de la Sierra Alta formados en el año de 1853* (México, D.F., 1869), p. 148.

14. ACAM, exp. 1235 and 1183. *Condueñazgos* were "co-ownerships" set up to accommodate many owners on one piece of property. Indigenous villagers used them to hold private property but exploit the land with a communal style of tenancy. They were also called "agrarian societies." For more, see Frans J. Schryer, *The Rancheros of Pisaflores: The History of a Peasant Bourgeoisie in Twentieth-Century Mexico* (Toronto, 1980), pp. 25–26; Frans J. Schryer, *Ethnicity and Class Conflict in Rural Mexico* (Princeton, 1990); Antonio Escobar Ohmstede, "Los Condueñazgos indígenas en las Huastecas hidalguense y veracruzana: ¿Defensa del espacio comunal?" in *Indio, nación y comunidad en el México del siglo XIX*, ed. Antonio Escobar Ohmstede (México, D.F., 1993).

15. ACAM, exp. 42, fs. 64–67. The tenacity of the peasant invaders was difficult to overcome even when the law supported the rights of the landlord. For example, in 1875 the *jefe político* of Papantla declared that the villagers did not own the land, but as a concession he gave the *espinaltecos* eight years to leave the estate. But when the time expired the villagers did not respect the decision and the legal battle resumed. See foja 62.

16. ACAM, exp. 619.

17. Manuel Fernando Soto, *Noticias*, p. 248; Moisés González Navarro, "Las Guerras de Castas," *Historia Mexicana* 26:1, no. 101 (1977), 79.

18. According to the study of "*afectabilidad*" carried out by the agrarian

reform secretariat, the largest property in the area was relatively small, 978.66 hectares. The second largest estate was only 227.9 hectares. ACAM, exp. 2073. The situation was very different from that which Soto described in 1853, when the entire municipality was in the hands of two estates. Soto, *Noticias*, p. 147.

19. See Charles Gibson, *The Aztecs under Spanish Rule: A History of the Indians of the Valley of Mexico, 1519–1810* (Stanford, 1964), chap. 8. Government documents commonly referred to local town councils as "*repúblicas de indios*" or simply as the "*república*" of such and such town; likewise, town officials were collectively known as "*oficiales de república*."

20. See Rina Ortiz Peralta, "Inexistentes por decreto: Disposiciones legislativas sobre los pueblos de indios en el siglo XIX. El caso de Hidalgo," in Escobar Ohmstede, *Indio, Nación y Comunidad* (México, D.F., 1993), pp. 160–68. Gonzalo Aguirre Beltrán, *Formas de gobierno indígena* (México, D.F., 1953), pp. 58–60.

21. The works of Von Metz and Thomson have been critical in pointing out the importance of this issue for political conflict in the nineteenth century. Brigida Von Metz, *Pueblos de Indios, mulatos y mestizos, 1770–1870: Los campesinos y transformaciones proto-industriales en el poniente de Morelos* (México, D.F., 1988), pp. 66, 83.

22. Powell, "Los liberales," 655–56.

23. Examples of rental contracts indicate that royal officials benefited from low rents on community land. See the 1814 rental contract of subdelegado Gómez Escalante of a property belonging to the comunidad de Yahualica, Archivo Judicial de Huejutla, legajo 1814 (hereafter cited as AJH). For examples from the national period, in Zacualtipan during 1835 and 1836, the town council rented several *ranchos* to members of some of the leading families of the region, including the *jefe político* Juan Andrade, for a period of nine years at minuscule rates. Biblioteca del Congreso del Estado de Mexico (henceforth cited as BCEM) 1842/386/123/1–42. See also the rent contracts for Yahualica, AJH, legajo 1852 f. 1.

24. AJH legajo 1856–57, various; the two largest beneficiaries were Pedro Hernández, who received title to land valued at 3,000 pesos; and Gabriel Careta, who claimed three properties worth 2,557 pesos.

25. Powell, "Los liberales," 659.

26. "The interests of the pueblos . . . were enmeshed with those of the clergy, on the one hand, and those of the renters of land on the other. The general administration established by the government [of Santa Ana] assured the priests of the parcialidades the regular payment of their fees and guaranteed the renters their pasture lands." Lira González, *Comunidades*, p. 224. Conservative attitudes ultimately aimed at pleasing the clergy and private interests rather than the community.

27. The law referred to is that of February 9, 1825. BCEM 1842/93/118/2v.

28. Ibid., f. 3, 3v, 9. Furthermore, they note that even those who held larger portions of the communal properties held them in many different small plots, somewhat like the open-field system familiar to European history.

29. Ibid., f. 9.

30. Ibid., f. 3v–4.

31. "Pues cada ayuntamiento a su vez ha dispuesto arbitrariamente de las tierras dandoles a quienes han querido los capitulares, y con muy pocas excepciones han sacado estos gran partido adjudicandoselas as' mismos." Ibid.

32. BCEM 1842/97/118/5.

33. Ibid., 6v.

34. The town council stated that five of the sixteen petitioners were not residents of Temazola and that one of them was "a schoolboy." BCEM 1842/97/118/10v. The charge of seduction was an extremely frequent explanation given by officials during this period to explain discontent. Unfortunately, it is not known how the state government decided in this case since the file is not complete.

35. Thomson, "Agrarian Conflict," describes a similar situation in Cuetzalán.

36. Carmen Blázquez Domínguez, ed., *Estado de Veracruz: Informes de sus gobernadores, 1826–1986* (hereafter cited as *Informes*) (Xalapa, 1986), 1:433.

37. Ibid., 5:2294.

38. See the reports of governors Alatorre in 1867, Hernández y Hernández in 1869, Castillo in 1882, and Cortes y Frías in 1884, in ibid., 2:644, 665, and 4:2089, 2234. Fraser describes the liberals' (both Juaristas and Porfiristas) drive to eliminate traditional forms of tenancy, even if this process resulted in the concentration of lands in the hands of large *latifundistas*. Donald J. Fraser, "La política de desamortización en las comunidades indígenas, 1856–1872," *Historia Mexicana* 21:4, no. 84 (1972).

39. Manuel Fernando Soto, *El nuevo estado, necesidad de formarlo inmediatamente con los distritictos de Tuxpan, Tampico de Veracruz, Tancanhuitz, Huejutla y el sur de Tamaulipas* (México, D.F.,1856), p. 61.

40. Sergio Florescano Mayet, "El proceso de destrucción de la propiedad comunal de la tierra y las rebeliones indígenas en Veracruz, 1826–1910," *La Palabra y el Hombre*, Nueva época, 52 (1984), 7–9; for the texts of the laws of 1826 and the Ley Lerdo see: *CLEV*, 1855–56:287–88.

41. Knowlton, "La división," 6; Tutino, *From Insurrection to Revolution*, p. 257; Meyer, *Problemas*, p. 117.

42. A cabinet minister of the state of Mexico cited the "constant lawsuits" of communities as a rationale for eliminating the traditional tenure system. Pascual González Fuentes, *Memoria de las secretarias de Relaciones y Guerra, Justicia, Negocios Eclesiasticos e Instrucción Pública del gobierno del estado de México. Leida a la honorable legislatura en las sesiones de los dias 1 y 2 de mayo de 1849 por el secretario de esos ramos C. Lic. Pascual González Fuentes* (Toluca, 1849), p. 14.

43. See the law of April 4, 1856, *CLEV*, 1855–56:226–45.

44. *CLEV*, 1869:236.

45. *Informes*, 1:489, reports that the division of communal lands had begun in the department of Orizaba.

46. Ibid., 4:2089.

47. Archivo General de la Nación (hereafter cited as AGN), Ramo Junta Protectora de las Clases Menesterosas, V/6/49–50.

48. *Informes*, 5:2303. Apolinar Castillo had the same complaint: "the last extension of two years granted in June of 1880 has ended in the same month of this year, and in the same way as other periods, the division and distribution of community lands remains pending." Ibid., 4:2089.

49. On reviewing the notary archives of Papantla, I found that the laws of disentailment and nationalization of church goods were put into effect almost immediately insofar as they affected urban and rural properties of the church. At the same time, no one made any claim against the communal lands as per the law of June 25, 1856; Archivo Notorial de Papantla, no. 1, legajos de los años de 1856–1869.

50. When the government divided the communal lands of the region into private lots in the 1890s, it occurred under the state legislation calling for the division of land among community members rather than the Lerdo law. See ACAM, 14. Knowlton has noted that in Michoacán a similar process occurred. Local officials left the 1856 law in limbo while they applied state laws specifying division of land among the villagers. See Knowlton, "La división," 24.

51. ACAM, exp. 280.

52. Ibid., and ACAM, exp. 80. The Indians declared that the usurpers "would make them feel the oppression of corveé labor . . . and impede them from cutting wood in their forests to build their houses." The notary commented "that these consequences they presume, as if they were currently experiencing them."

53. Ignacio Toledano, a noted liberal and one of the arbiters who defended the Indian community of Temapache in 1868, also signed the final decision in favor of the Chicontepec peasants. The status of *tierras de repartimiento* under the law was uncertain. The liberals only specifically exempted *ejidos* from the reform legislation, and Miguel Lerdo urged peasants to use the law to privatize *repartimiento* land as well. Powell, "Los liberales," 657–58.

54. Velasco Toro has noted that the process of forming *condueñazgos* was a common tactic in the region used to resist the policy of land division. José Velasco Toro, "Indigenismo y rebelión totonaca en Papantla, 1885–96," in *América Indígena* 39:1 (1979), 87.

55. The state government did not lightly accede to the formation of large lots: "the government was not in favor of this class of land division at the beginning, because it implied the creation of many communities and was

fertile ground for discord and abuses . . . : questions that provoked conflicts with evil results. But . . . the infinite difficulties that appear when we attempt to execute the law have convinced the very government of the imperious necessity that some municipalities have for the division of land into large lots." *Informes*, 4:289.

56. Throughout the judicial documents, legal categories that the Constitution of 1824 had formally extinguished continued in use. Thus the Indians and *mestizos* describe themselves as belonging to distinct *repúblicas*, a term referring to the colonial system of governments that recognized caste distinctions as a basis for citizenship.

57. ACAM, exp. 341, f. 36.

58. Muñoz had occupied several local positions, finally arriving at the post of *jefe político* and *coronel* of the national guard. In 1854 he participated in the agitation against Santa Anna, and the embattled president considered him dangerous enough to have him exiled from Papantla. During the French Intervention he served with General Ignacio de Alatorre in the region.

59. Gorrochotegui wrote, "Although I belong to the class of *de razón* of Temapache and I contribute to the community expenses I am assigned, I will not deny that the majority of those who are members of the corporation (*gremio*) called *de razón* have never cared to comply with the duties compacted with the natives, these offers have always been disregarded by the *de razón* community." ACAM, 341, f. 97. Gorrochotegui later bought several shares in the *condueñazgo* and his son was elected administrator in the 1870s. Residents remembered him as an honest administrator. ACAM, exp. 341, "Acta de Información testimonial . . . " f. 1.

60. *Informes*, 4:2234.

61. Marco Bellingeri and Isabel Gil Sánchez, "Las estructuras agrarias," in *México en el Siglo XIX (1821–1910): Historia económica y de la estructura social*, ed. Ciro Cardoso (México, D.F., 1980), p. 98. See also John Coatsworth, "Obstacles to Economic Growth in Nineteenth Century Mexico," *American Historical Review* 83 (February 1978), 80–100, which also documents the weak economic performance of the Mexican economy before the Porfiriato. See John H. Coatsworth, "Los orígenes del autoritarismo moderno en México," in *Orígenes del autoritarismo en América Latina*, ed. Leopoldo Allub (México, D.F., 1983), p. 209–10, for a discussion of the effects of independence on the landed elite. For a view which suggests that the economy began to recover as early as the 1850s, see Margaret Chowning, "The Contours of the Post 1810 Depression in Mexico: A Reappraisal from a Regional Perspective," *Latin American Research Review* 27:2 (1992).

62. Francisco López Cámera, *La estructura económica y social de México en la época de la reforma* (México, D.F., 1967), p. 28.

63. Doris Ladd notes that the Mexican nobility found it increasingly difficult to extract benefits from their lands due to peasant land invasions and

litigation; see Doris M. Ladd, *The Mexican Nobility at Independence, 1780–1826* (Austin, 1976), p. 159.

64. Fages, "Noticias," 264.

65. Archivo Judicial del Estado de Puebla, 1849 packet, expediente titled "Lista de causas pendientes en el departamento de Tuxpan."

66. ACAM, exp. 341. See the parallels with Cuetzalán in the 1860s and 1870s, in Thomson, "Agrarian Conflict," 222, 239, 252–53.

67. Ibid., n. 47.

68. Tiburcio wrote that when the conspirators approached Lázaro Muñoz, who had served as the liberal *jefe político* before the Austrians took the town, Muñoz called them disorderly. See Simon Tiburcio, "Recuerdos de mi vida [en] la época del llamado Imperio y apuntes para la historia militar del cantón de Papantla" (unpublished manuscript).

69. Cited in Fraser, "La política," 628.

70. One excellent example of how liberals exploited these local divisions occurred during the French Intervention in Huautla. In 1864, as a result of a cease-fire between the local liberal forces and the French, the French army evacuated the town of Huautla. The municipal authorities immediately called on the Indian population to have them clean out the marketplace that the French had used as a stable. The liberal guerrillero Néstor Aguirre and his armed followers arrived and interrupted the cleanup. Aguirre horrified the *alcalde* when he ordered the Indians home and declared "que no lo hiciera los indios sino los de razón sin ninguna excepción espresandose más y más contra nosotros" [that the Indians did not do it, rather the (people) of reason (who,) without an exception, expressed themselves more and more against us]. The *alcalde* wrote his superior to plead for the return of the French and to complain about being abandoned. AGN Gobernación 1126/1/2.

71. For examples of such notarized regulations from the towns of Zozocoalco and Coxquihui, see ARPP Papantla 1882/15/f. 27–30, 1882/17, 18/34–40.

72. See ACAM, 14; Victoria Chenaut and Luis María Gatti, *La costa totonaca: questiones regionales II* (Mexico City, 1987), pp. 78–83; José Velasco Toro, "La política desamortizadora y sus afectos en la región de Papantla, Ver.," *Anuario* 72 (1989), 146–61.

73. For accounts of the revolts, see Isabel Kelly and Angel Palerm, *The Tajin Totonac* (Washington, 1950), p. 54, n. 88. Archivo Porfirio Diaz, Universidad de las Americas, roll 338 LV 003972, 003834, 003605, 003399.

74. See Velasco Toro, "La política," 153.

75. This account is derived from ACAM, 341, "Acta de Información testimonial." Tuxpan offers another case where local merchants and speculators bought out the *acciones* of *mestizo* small farmers who originally participated in the land purchase in 1846. When the land was divided in 1897 only 272 individuals benefited, while 583 had participated in the original pur-

chase. The 1897 land division was very un-egalitarian: while some individuals received lots in excess of a thousand hectares, others received only twelve hectares. ACAM exp. 619, "solicitud," and "Escritura de división de Asunción y Santiago de la Peña, October 18, 1897."

76. The *jefe político* called a session of the municipal council and, with rural police at his back, told the council they would be arrested if they did not comply. ACAM, exp. 42, f. 2–3, 19, 22, 26.

77. ACAM, exp. 42, f. 128–29v.

78. Summarized from ACAM, exp. 61, especially f. 39–48 and ACAM, exp. 88, f. 50 and passim. Notary documents describing sales where dozens of villagers all sell their lands to one individual on the same day and for the same price appear in the record, providing a strong indication that the sales were suspicious. For example, on December 16, 1895, Hernández supposedly bought seventy plots of land from their owners for five pesos each. ACAM, exp. 88, f. 71–77; ACAM, exp. 61, unnumbered folios.

79. Powell suggests that peasants in the 1850s were not even aware of the fact that the viceregal government had been replaced by a republic. "Los liberales," p. 658.

80. Daniel Nugent, "Rural Revolt in Mexico, Mexican Nationalism and the State and Forms of U.S. Intervention," in *Rural Revolt in Mexico and U.S. Intervention*, ed. Daniel Nugent (San Diego, 1988), p. 15.

4
Liberal Modernization and Religious Corporate Property in Nineteenth-Century Guatemala
Hubert Miller

Throughout the colonial era, the Spanish monarchy and the Catholic church were inseparable allies in the work of colonization and Christianization carried out by Spain's New World inhabitants. The alliance's deeply rooted tradition dated back to the days of early Christianity in Spain, when Pope Nicholas II in the sixth century granted royal patronage to a ruler in the Iberian peninsula. Over the centuries, especially during the long years of the *reconquista*, it developed into the more commonly known *patronato real*, which contained papal concessions to Iberian rulers. In the course of time, these grants became very extensive and gave the monarch much power over the church. For example, the *patronato real* granted the right to nominate ecclesiastical officials, to create new dioceses and determine their boundaries, to approve the promulgation of papal bulls, to remove a bishop who disobeyed civil orders, to grant permission for erecting monasteries and hospitals, and to collect tithes, known as the *diezmo*. In return for these concessions, the church could expect protection and financial support in carrying out its mission.[1]

There was considerable debate whether the papal grants of ecclesiastical powers to the monarchs were pure concessions or rights inherent in sovereignty. The "canonist" school argued in favor of the papacy, claiming that the grants of power were privileges that were rescindable and nontransferable. On the other hand, the "regalists," who wanted to increase monarchical power, contended that ecclesiastical powers contained in the *patronato real* were inherent in sovereignty and therefore transferable to the new republics.[2]

Although the "canonists" and "regalists" carried on a long debate over the origin of the royal patronage, there was no debate about the Spanish monarchs enjoying the patronage in their New World kingdoms. Shortly after the arrival of Christopher Columbus, in 1494, Pope Alexander VI extended the patronage to this area. The action was seconded by his successor,

Pope Julius II, in 1508.[3] Just as in the Crusades against the Moslems in Spain, now the Spanish rulers enjoyed the patronage to carry out their colonization and Christianization of New World Indians. In short, the state saw the church as its indispensable partner in the training and formation of moral and loyal citizens for the crown. The church, in turn, looked to the state for protection and financial support in carrying out its mission. It was inconceivable to either power that their missions could be achieved without mutual support. Thus, in the creation of good government in the Indies the church was an indispensable ally.

The legacy of the *patronato real* carried over into the national period, where it faced a challenge from the rising tide of nineteenth-century liberalism. No longer did the new governments see the church as an indispensable ally of the state in achieving good government, but rather the liberal governments saw the church as an obstacle to progress and the achievement of a modern state. It is the purpose of this essay to examine the factors that contributed to this change and to the establishment of an adversarial relationship between the two powers as the liberal ideology gained ascendancy in the nineteenth century. Especially helpful is a study of the liberal ideology and policies in the area of religious corporate holdings, which were crucial to meeting liberal goals of progress and modernization.

Liberal ideology, an heir of the Enlightenment, stressed in varying degrees individual liberties such as freedom of speech, press, and religion and property rights. Also part of the ideology was a republican form of government unencumbered by corporate privileges, a laissez-faire economic policy, and land reforms. Along with these goals, the liberals wanted a secular state to achieve modernization. No longer could the allegiance to the state be shared with other corporations, be they church, university, or Indian community. Seeking implementation of these goals, liberals were on a collision route with the church. Modernization and secularization goals limited the traditional role of the church in developing good moral citizens. Working to achieve these goals, the liberals wanted to abolish ecclesiastical privileges, or *fueros*, and undertake land reforms directed at religious corporate holdings.[4]

The Latin American liberals did not have to look far for models in carrying out their program. The Bourbons working in the spirit of the Enlightenment provided initial models for church reforms, such as the expulsion of the Society of Jesus in 1767 and the expropriation of its property. Like liberals of a later date, they saw the Society as a threat to the state with its control of education and vast economic resources. Even Bourbon paternalism served as a model for "transitory dictatorship" sanctioned by Guatemalan liberals in 1876.[5]

The Bourbon legacy of enlightened reform also was evident in the Spanish Constitution of 1812, which served as a guide for subsequent Latin American constitutions, including Guatemala. According to Ralph Lee Woodward, "the Bourbon policies laid the foundation for the development of the liberal-capitalist state that would eventually be associated with the Liberal party in Guatemala from 1871–1944."[6] Essential to this Bourbon legacy was the need for a change of the traditional role played by the church.

The Central American independence, on September 15, 1821, was essentially a conservative pronouncement, which retained much of the colonial heritage. The fact that Captain General Gavino Gaínza was selected as head of the provisional government confirmed the fact that the independence leaders envisioned few changes. Particularly pertinent was the declaration of independence of September 15, 1821, which gave official recognition to the Catholic church.[7] Furthermore, some thirteen clergymen signed the document, with the exception of Archbishop Ramón Casaus y Toreres—behavior that led to his expulsion a few years later and raised doubts in the minds of civil authorities about ecclesiastical leaders' loyalty to the new government.[8]

The conservatives in control of the independence movement achieved another victory when the Gaínza provisional government annexed itself to the Mexican empire of Agustín de Iturbide on January 5, 1822. For the church, it guaranteed protection under the emperor's Plan de Iguala, which called for the preservation of the Roman Catholic religion and ecclesiastical *fueros*.[9]

The annexation was short-lived, however, when Iturbide met his downfall in March of the following year. Again the Central American provinces called, on July 1, for a second and absolute independence, which reconfirmed the first act of independence from Spain. As before, the Roman Catholic religion was proclaimed the official and exclusive belief.[10] In effect, from the first act of independence of 1821 to the one of 1823, the colonial status of the church had remained unchanged—a policy in keeping with conservative interests who wished to retain colonial institutions. In the case of the church, it was an assurance that its corporate interests, including property, were well protected.

Ending the ties with Mexico afforded the liberal faction its first opportunity to offer a reform program. The liberals controlled the constituent assembly that reconvened on June 24, 1823. The first action of the assembly was the already noted declaration of independence on July 1, followed by the formation of a six-man government *junta* headed by Padre José Matías Delgado, a liberal from El Salvador. The assembly's major task was to draft a constitution for a confederation of Central American states, which consisted of Guatemala, El Salvador, Honduras, Nicaragua, and Costa Rica.[11] The Constitution was ready for promulgation by November 1824 and was ratified by the Central American provinces the following January. The liberals scored another victory with the election of Manuel José Arce, a moderate liberal from Honduras, as first president of the Central American confederation.

During the drafting of the Constitution, the constituent assembly took a number of actions affecting the government's relations with the Catholic church. One such action was a law requiring all clergy to take an oath of loyalty to the new government. The assembly's action was spurred on by the fact that in 1824 a number of clergymen refused to take the oath of loyalty to the new government, but the cases were few and easily resolved, with the clerics either leaving the country or eventually taking the oath. The archbishop himself had opposed the original act of independence, but by this time he recognized the reality of independence. In fact, he thought the government was overly suspicious about clerical loyalty.[12]

An initial liberal effort at modernization was the constituent assembly's action in September 1823 to reduce the number of religious holidays. The action was intended to assure a more productive labor force and to reduce alcoholic consumption associated with these religious festivities. On the other hand, the liberals, like their conservative counterparts, did not hesitate in 1824 to claim the *patronato real* to restrict pastoral-letter publications and confirm ecclesiastical appointments.[13] Neither did the liberal-controlled assembly wish to do away with an officially recognized church, as became evident in its Constitution of 1824. Again, Catholicism was declared the official religion, but the Constitution allowed limited toleration for non-Catholic sects.[14]

The new government, elected under the Constitution of 1824, enabled the liberals to push more reform with Arce in the presidential seat and Mariano Gálvez, an ardent liberal from Guatemala, serving as president of the newly elected confederate congress. The legislature's initial efforts in undoing colonial legacies and in modernizing included the reduction of ecclesiastical tithing by one-half. Hitting at the power of religious orders, the legislature no longer permitted the promise of obedience by religious members to their authorities in Spain and required a minimum age of twenty-three to enter religious life.[15]

The liberal reforms were short-lived. By 1826, Arce had second thoughts about the reforms, which he felt had caused much divisiveness, especially in the attacks on religious orders and in acts that undermined religious traditions, such as those that reduced religious holidays. With the president's change of heart, the conservatives gained the upper hand in the assembly and set about to repeal the laws and remove restrictions on religious orders.[16]

The conservative control ended abruptly in April 1829, when Francisco Morazán, a radical liberal from Honduras, and his army gained control of the confederation government and installed José Francisco Barrundia as provisional president. Within three months, Barrundia ordered the expulsion of Archbishop Casuas y Torres and some 289 religious members of the Franciscans, Dominicans, and Recollects on the grounds that they were involved in a plot against the government.[17] Although there was no evidence for such a conspiracy, his suspicions appeared to rest mostly on the fact that the archbishop and the religious members were native Spaniards. A more plausible explanation is the government's financial need for the religious corporate holdings, which immediately were turned over to the national treasury to be used for governmental operations.[18]

The confederate congress quickly approved Barrundia's actions against the prelate and the religious orders. The movable goods of the expelled orders were ordered sold in public auction, except gold and silver items, which were turned over to poor parishes. The monastery libraries served as the beginning for the development of public libraries. Rural religious corporate holdings were either rented or sold. The income from the properties was modest; for instance, the Dominican *finca* "San Jerónimo," consisting of 473 *caballerías*, brought the highest price of 253,526 pesos. The next highest was 28,075 pesos, for the sale of "Palencia," also a Dominican *finca* of 97 *caballerías*. The income from these properties and others fell far short of meeting governmental expenditures on education and indebtedness.[19]

The congress continued its liberal-reform work with the election of Morazán in 1830 as president. From 1831 to 1833, it abolished church tithes, prohibited the promulgation of papal edicts without government authorization, proclaimed religious toleration, and recognized civil marriage and divorce. At the same time, the lawmakers continued recognizing Catholicism as the official religion and insisted on the right of the royal patronage.[20] By the end of the decade, the Morazán government had initiated a reform that was intent on destroying the political and economic power of the church—destruction that the liberal reformers deemed necessary to achieve economic development and modernization. For instance, limited religious toleration, as well as civil marriage and divorce, was intended to create an atmosphere attractive for immigration. According to liberal thinkers, immigration from Europe and the United States was indispensable in improving labor productivity, particularly in Guatemala, where the Indian population constituted a vast majority. Both liberals and conservatives saw the indigenous people as backward, viewing their customs and values as a drag on economic productivity and an obstacle to modernization. They hoped to utilize the labor of industrious and educated immigrants, who, in turn, served as model workers for the native people.[21]

Enactment of liberal reforms at the confederate level did not mean implementation or similar action at the provincial or state level. First of all, article 10 in the Constitution of 1824 declared each state "to be free and independent in its government and interior administration," a provision that the states interpreted as granting sovereignty.[22] Added to the strong sense of state sovereignty was geographic isolation, which made communication and implementation of confederate mandates difficult. Finally, the central government's inability to collect revenue weakened its ability to exert its authority over the states. In short, any implementation of confederate reforms at the local level was mainly dependent on the goodwill of the state authorities.[23] Such was the case in Guatemala, where Gálvez served as governor from 1831 to 1838. Not only did he support the reform measures of confederate authorities, but he and his liberal cohorts pushed their own reforms.

Prior to the Gálvez governorship, the Guatemalan assembly had enacted laws touching on religious property. For instance, in December 1829 the assembly ordered that certain clerical stipends and levies be used for support of the national University of San Carlos, which served as the university for all of the Central American provinces during the colonial period. No longer were priests allowed to collect fees for the administration of the sacraments. Instead, the legislature directed that income from pious funds of suppressed religious orders and voluntary contributions be used for compensating these services.[24]

A key plank in the liberal program was public education. Therefore, monasteries of banished religious orders were converted into primary schools. The national university received the Dominican monastery and the books of the suppressed religious orders. The Franciscan monastery became a house of correction, subsidized by income from the Franciscan corporate holdings.[25]

The suppressed religious orders had been traditional providers of education, but under the Gálvez government the state pushed a policy of secularization and modernization of the entire educational system. On March 1, 1832, the Guatemalan legislature passed a law calling for revamping education from the primary level to the university and for the introduction of the Lancastrian system as a method of combating illiteracy. The law gave the state the prime responsibility for education rather than the church, as was the case during the colonial period. Education was public and free, but private schools, such as seminaries for the priesthood, continued to function. Education was highly centralized under the newly created Academy of Studies, and the curriculum reflected the eighteenth-century Enlightenment with its stress on scientific and useful studies. The teaching of religion, both at primary and secondary levels, was still part of the official curriculum, as were theology courses in the university. The power of the Academy over all levels of education was very much in evidence in the fact that it had the final decision-making power in matters of instruction and texts. Furthermore, it had the power to authorize the conferral of all degrees, including those in the ecclesiastical sciences.[26]

The liberal modernization efforts did not always meet with much popular approval. First of all, church officials saw the state as a usurper of its property as well as of education, traditionally the church's dominion. The faithful felt their religion and customs were threatened by the reduction of religious holidays and the prohibition of religious processions. The liberal laws called for recognition of civil marriage and divorce, which, popularly dubbed "Ley de perro," aroused further opposition.[27] Neither did the Gálvez government help its cause of modernizing the judicial system when, in 1837, it introduced trial by jury—a practice that ran counter both to Indian and Spanish customs.[28] The antiliberal sentiment galvanized with the arrival of a cholera epidemic at the beginning of 1837. Unfortunately, the government's efforts to stem the epidemic led to rumors among the people that civil officials were poisoning the waters—a rumor that the local pastors encouraged. As a result, the discontented masses became a ready tool for the newly rising *caudillo*, Rafael Carrera, seeking control of the state government in eastern Guatemala. He possessed charismatic leadership traits and was able to convert untrained peasants into an effective guerrilla army. Calling for an end to liberal reforms, he led his army to Guatemala City and forced the resignation of Gálvez in January 1838. His cause was aided greatly by conservatives and an anti-Gálvez liberal faction led by Barrundia, who saw him as a convenient tool to remove Gálvez. Morazán, who was suppressing a rebellion in El Salvador at the time of Carrera's uprising, returned to Guatemala to crush the rebellion. He had some initial successes, but after a series of encounters, Carrera with his guerrilla tactics defeated Morazán decisively on March 18, 1840.[29] The defeat consolidated conservative control in Guatemala and signaled the end of the Central American confederation, which for all practical purposes had ceased to exist by the late 1830s.

The conservative break with liberal policies started on a moderate and cautious note. Provisional President Mariano Rivera Paz, appointed by Carrera in 1838, immediately suspended liberal laws of civil marriage and divorce, reducing religious holidays and limitations on taking religious vows. Conservative measures reinstated included the *diezmo* and the ecclesiastical *fuero* exempting clergymen from civil trials.[30]

A number of liberal reforms were retained. For instance, the corporate holdings of suppressed religious orders, especially in rural areas, were not returned, although the suppressed orders were reestablished.[31] The one exception was the *finca* of "Palencia," which Carrera returned to the Dominicans in 1848, on the condition that the *finca* was not to be sold or rented and that the rights of the families living on the hacienda would be protected. According to David McCreery, "none of the orders ever regained even the limited position in agriculture they had enjoyed before 1829."[32] Another liberal legacy that continued under conservative rule was recognition of the Catholic religion as the official one, but with religious toleration for all sects.[33]

The conservatives climaxed their undoing of the liberal program with the Constitution of 1851, which for all practical purposes restored the Catholic church to its privileged colonial status, along with the state's claim to the exercise of the *patronato real*. In a concordat with the Vatican the following year, the pope recognized the government's right to the patronage. In return, the state recognized the Catholic church as the official religion, agreed to collect the *diezmo* and recognized the right of religious corporations to hold property—all of which were provided for in the Constitution of 1851. The Vatican agreed with the Carrera government in not requiring expropriated religious property under liberal regimes to be returned, but it did insist that the government promise not to repeat the action in the future.[34] The end result was the normalization of church–state relations until the liberals regained control in 1871.

The liberals returned to power in June 30, 1871, with the overthrow of Vicente Cerna, Carrera's successor. Miguel García Granados, a moderate liberal who had been forced into exile in Mexico by Cerna, became provisional president. His proclamation of May 8, in keeping with his philosophy of moderation, called for an end to dictatorship, a new constitution, freedom of the press, tax reforms, expanding educational opportunities, and abolishing liquor monopolies.[35] The radical direction of the liberal revolution did not become evident until after the liberal wing headed by Justo Rufino Barrios gained control.

Barrios was a colleague in arms of García Granados, whom he accompanied from exile in Mexico to overthrow Cerna. Barrios, a well-to-do rancher and coffee planter from western Guatemala, represented the growing prominence of the coffee industry and the resentment of the landed elite in western Guatemala against the conservative and liberal elites in the capital. In sharp contrast to García Granados, he was not guided by philosophical considerations but, rather, by pragmatic ones. He was an aggressive leader who pushed radical liberalism in a dictatorial fashion, which he deemed essential to prevent a repetition of what the conservatives under Carrera had done to the liberal governments of Morazán and Gálvez. Shortly after the fall of Guatemala City to the liberals, Barrios opted to take command of the military forces in Quezaltenango—a position from which he was able to force García Granados to accept more radical measures, as happened when he expelled the Jesuits from that city. According to the liberals it was a sign of things to come—namely, modernization—and the Jesuits served as a convenient target to launch their program. The liberals claimed that the Jesuits and the Catholic church in general were the chief obstacles to the development of a modern state.[36] The changing of the guard became complete when Barrios took over as elected president in June 1873.

The magic slogan of the new liberals in the 1870s was order and progress. They were realists and pragmatists who saw Barrios's aggressive leadership as essential in carrying out their goals of progress. Being realists, the liberals of the 1870s were convinced that their country was unprepared for a republican form of government, and so they spoke in terms of "transitory dictatorship." The political realism of the new reformers helps to explain García Granados's unsuccessful efforts in drafting a constitution during his provisional presidency, as he had promised. In fact, a new constitution did not materialize until 1879, and even then it ended by being a document tailored for a dictatorship.[37]

Liberal ideology, in keeping with Positivism and the tenets of the day, argued that order was indispensable for progress. Their models for order and progress were North Atlantic nations, such as England and the United States. The arrival of the new age of progress and modernization was well exemplified by an anecdote of a threshing machine arriving in the little town of Tecpán—an event accompanied by festivities usually reserved for the welcoming of dignitaries.[38] Another example of the coming of modernization was a *hoja suelta*, during the Barrios administration, depicting a train crashing into a church with the monks, in their religious paraphernalia and carrying items for worship, scattering in all directions. The broadside cartoon was, for the new breed of liberals, a revealing representation of the Catholic church standing in the way of progress and modernization.[39]

More specifically, the new government pushed coffee production, which during the previous conservative government had already been promoted by means of government subsidies and tax exemptions.[40] Increased coffee production was imperative for Guatemala to enter the world market, for its aniline industry collapsed shortly after the mid-eighteenth century. Coffee required an infrastructure that the conservative governments failed to deliver—a failure that contributed to their overthrow in 1871. Therefore, the first order of business was construction of roads, railroads, and telegraphs. In addition, coffee required a labor force, which the Barrios government supplied by means of forced-labor legislation. Also essential to the modernization program was credit availability and land reform that placed land into industrious hands and thereby increased its productivity, especially land devoted to coffee production.[41]

No modernization for the liberals of the 1870s was complete without a complete revamping of the educational system, which had to have a foundation of Positivism, namely, a curriculum that was scientific and useful.[42] In all these areas, the government played the central role, such as the creation of a *ministerio de fomento* to modernize the economy and setting up a secularized system of education completely controlled by the government. In both instances, the Barrios liberals were on a collision course with the Catholic church and with religious congregations who had substantial corporate holdings and were in charge of education.

The initial conflict between the church and the liberal government, as already noted, took place in Quezaltenango, where Barrios during the provisional presidency of García Granados served as military commander of the western highlands, known as Los Altos. The anticlerical *El Malacate*, under the editorship of Andrés Telléz, with close ties to Barrios, unleashed vitriolic attacks against the Jesuits in Quezaltenango, who were in charge of a parish church and a school. Expecting to halt the attacks, the Jesuits sought help from the city *cabildo*, but to no avail. The council members agreed with *El Malacate* and questioned the right of the Jesuits to be in the country because their re-entry was due solely to President Carrera's decree in 1851. Accusing the Society of offering a sterile education and exploiting persons in Los Altos, the council on August 12, 1871 ordered their expulsion from the district—an order carried out by Barrios.

With the expulsion, the city took control of the Jesuit *colegio* and introduced a curriculum of useful subjects. Religion was no longer a part of the curriculum because the council members considered such instruction the responsibility of parents. The *cabildo* urged the García Granados government to adopt a similar secularized system of education in keeping with nineteenth-century ideas.[43]

The expulsion action received the endorsement of *El Malacate*, which saw the Society as an obstacle to progress.[44] The exploitation reference in the expulsion act referred, in all probability, to the Jesuits acting as a credit agency in the absence of banks. Due to political instability and bad harvests in 1871, planters and ranchers found it difficult to pay off their obligations and accused the Society of practicing usury.[45]

The fortune of the Jesuits did not change when they arrived in the capital. Immediately, they faced anti-Jesuit propaganda, which prompted Archbishop Bernardo Piñol y Aycinena to urge García Granados to end the anti-Jesuit broadside attacks and assure him that the Jesuits would not suffer the same fate in the capital. The prelate received no specific response from the provisional president.[46] The evasiveness of García Granados can be explained by his reluctance to limit freedom of the press—a freedom he had decreed shortly after taking office. Equally important was the political situation of not clashing with Barrios and thereby creating a split in the liberal ranks, as had happened in the overthrow of Gálvez.

In the battle of the broadsides in the capital, the Jesuits found some defenders, who praised their educational work and considered their expulsion from Quezaltenango a violation of their guaranteed rights. The defenders also rejected the charges of the anti-Jesuit writers, who claimed that members were supporting conservative rebellions against the liberal government, especially the ongoing rebellion in eastern Guatemala, known as the Oriente.[47] It was this area that had strongly supported Carrera in his defeat of the Gálvez and Morazán governments. According to Padre Rafael Pérez, a member of the expelled Jesuits, prominent residents in the capital gathered sixty-five hundred signatures in the city and the neighboring towns to combat the anti-Jesuit propaganda.[48] Despite this support and the urging of the ecclesiastical *cabildo* to end the attacks, there was no letup in sight. Joining in the attacks were "patriotic clubs" in Guatemala City and nearby Antigua, along with persons closely associated with Barrios, such as Marco A. Soto, Ramón Rosa and Manuel Ubico, all of whom served in Barrios's cabinet after 1873. Their anti-Jesuit campaign, along with the broadside writers, accused the Society of amassing wealth, perverting youth, and inciting rebellions. The campaign reached its climax with the call for the expulsion of the Jesuits from the entire republic.[49]

It did not take long for the anti-Jesuit campaign to achieve success. Bowing to the pressure of the radical liberal wing, García Granados let out the word that he had decided to expel the Society.[50] The expulsion became a reality on September 3, when seventy Jesuits left their Colegio de Tridentino in the city for the port of San José.[51] It was not until after their departure that the provisional president offered reasons for his action, which were essentially the same as those stated in the anti-Jesuit broadsides and those of the Quezaltenango *cabildo* the previous month.[52]

The following spring Barrios, who briefly served as interim president during the absence of García Granados, ordered the nationalization of the Society's property. The decrees, dated May 24, 1872, ordered that the Jesuit properties be nationalized and sold at public auctions. The income was to serve public needs and compensate the government for expenses incurred in expelling the Jesuits. The only rural property mentioned in the decrees was the *finca* "Las Nubes" near the capital, which the Society had received from Archbishop Francisco de Paula García Peláez after their return in 1851. Income from the *finca* was intended to support the Jesuit administration of the church of La Merced in the capital.[53] Father Rafael Pérez, one of the expelled Jesuits, noted the existence of another small *finca*, called San José and located near Quezaltenango. The Society had used income from this holding to support their parish church and *colegio* in that city.[54] The fact that the Jesuits had been in the country only some twenty years was hardly enough time to acquire extensive holdings. The claim that the government intended to use these properties for the public good, such as education, did not always hold true. There is ample evidence to suggest that some of these holdings ended up in the hands of Barrios's friends.[55] Nonetheless, there can be no doubt about the fact that with the expulsion of the Jesuits, leadership was passing from the moderate García Granados to Barrios, who had the support of the radical liberals.[56]

The expulsion of the Jesuits carried serious consequences for Archbishop Piñol y Aycinena, who continued to insist that the provisional president explain his rationale for the course of action in this matter. After their expulsion from the country, his demands for an explanation intensified in his pastoral letter of August 16. He protested the government's action and held the civil authorities, not the Jesuits, responsible for the Oriente rebellions. He refused to honor the provisional president's request to issue a pastoral urging the faithful to avoid violence. He felt that to do so could be interpreted as approving the expulsion. He further reminded the civil authorities that the ecclesiastical curia approved of his behavior.[57] The government's reaction to the prelate's pastoral quickly resulted in his expulsion as well as that of Auxiliary Bishop Mariano Ortiz Urrutia on the grounds that both failed to calm the faithful and thereby aided the rebel cause. Additional accusations included the prelate's refusal to remove pastors implicated in rebellious activities and replace them with government-approved curates, which civil authorities claimed they had the right to do according to the Concordat of 1852.[58] The expulsion decree cited no specific cases of pastoral involvement in rebel activities; in fact, evidence suggests that clerical rebel activities were not a serious problem.[59] Replacing the exiled archbishop was the apostolic administrator, Padre Francisco Espinosa y Palacios.

Another bone of contention between the church and state leaders involved the *diezmo*, which was a ten-percent tax on an individual's income collected by the state for support of the church. Although agreed upon in the Concordat of 1852, the state in December 1871 proposed to substitute a fixed subsidy of 24,000 pesos for the *diezmo*. The church authorities objected, claiming the subsidy was inadequate and Vatican approval was needed to make the change. The ecclesiastical leaders further feared that the fixed subsidy could make the church too dependent on the state.[60] Marco Aurelio Soto, minister of ecclesiastical affairs for García Granados, considered Vatican approval a mere formality and insisted on implementing the change as of January 1. He argued that the public clamor demanded it because it was an unfair tax and difficult to collect.[61] The Vatican's response in May temporarily agreed with the change, pending further negotiations. The final decision was to suspend the *diezmo* indefinitely.[62]

The fixed subsidy did not always meet full approval in liberal ranks. A case in point was *El Malacate*, which claimed that the clergy were already too wealthy and therefore saw no need for a fixed state subsidy. Rather, it was the periodical's contention that the subsidy was needed to retire the public debt. It did admit that the subsidy of 4,000 pesos stipulated in the Concordat of 1852 was in order.[63] The periodical's thinking reflects liberal pragmatism in the sense that whereas the ultimate goal was U.S.–style separation of church and state, realistically in Guatemala more time was needed to wean the church from government support. This thinking was reiterated in *El Malacate's* attacks on the congregation of St. Philip Neri, which it accused of exploiting renters on the congregation's hacienda. It went on to demand that all religious property be disentailed and returned to the people. Again, it allowed for state subsidies to religious communities and at the same time called for separation of church and state. In an effort to reconcile the two opposing positions, the editor, Andrés Telléz, pointed to the Mexican Constitution of 1857 as a model. The paper's attacks on religious corporate holdings frequently ended up condemning religious orders as hypocrites, promoters of ignorance, and exploiters of people, and it was the paper's intention to free the country from the "brutal domination" of Catholicism.[64]

Anticlerical attacks on religious corporate holdings, calls for banishment of the Society of Jesus, and the abolition of the *diezmo* contributed to church officials' growing apprehensions about the security of religious property in general. In a confidential memorandum of February 1, 1872, the ecclesiastical *cabildo* drafted plans to convert the cathedral property to private accounts and to place all income not needed for urgent necessities into European accounts.[65] It was only a matter of months before church officials realized their worst fears, when Barrios became interim president while García Granados led an invasion into Honduras to prevent Guatemalan conservatives from using the neighboring republic as a place of refuge.

True to his reputation as a man of action, Barrios on May 24 made the expulsion of Jesuits official and declared their property nationalized. Three days later he decreed the dissolution of the congregation of St. Philip Neri and the nationalization of their property. He justified the action on the grounds that with only one or two members the congregation could no longer serve the public. According to the decree, all the nationalized property of the congregation was placed in the office of Administrado General de Rentas to await later instruction for final disposition. The decree did not nationalize sacred objects used for worship, but ordered that these be delivered to the archdiocese.[66] Included in the rural holdings of the congregation was the *finca* "Incienso," whose estimated value did not exceed 25,000 pesos.[67] Ownership of the *finca* had been in litigation ever since the colonial period, and Barrios insisted that the matter be settled as soon as possible. A settlement was reached on a portion of the rural property, which immediately was sold. The government hoped that income from the sale would help reduce government debt, but the income was minimal. Yet Barrios scored political points by making the land available for sale.[68] In addition to the *finca*, the congregation owned the Escuela de Cristo in the center of the capitol. This prize real estate ended up in the hands of Francisco de Lainfiesta, a close associate of Barrios.[69]

Two weeks after suppressing the congregation of St. Philip Neri, on June 7, Barrios disbanded all male religious communities—three days before García Granados returned from Honduras. The decree permitted the religious members to remain in the country, but only as secular clergymen. The churches of the congregations were converted into parish churches and their libraries given to the university. According to the interim president, the action was necessary because religious associations rejected democratic principles. Their properties, the liberal argument maintained, were in "manos muertas" [dead hands] and therefore an obstacle to economic development.[70] The apostolic administrator, Padre Espinosa, immediately protested the government's action, to which Soto, who was minister of foreign affairs at the time, replied that social, political, and economic expediency made it imperative for the government to act.[71]

Disbanding the male religious communities was immediately followed by taking an inventory of their properties. For instance, the Franciscan inventory lists the Church of San Francisco and the adjoining monastery, both urban properties, and no rural holdings.[72] The Dominicans reported having a church and a monastery in the capital and the hacienda "Palencia."[73] A third example is the case of the Capuchins in Antigua, who reported two churches, Belén and Beatas, and a monastery in that city, but no rural properties.[74] The decree disbanding the male religious orders gave no specific instructions for the disposition of monasteries and rural properties, except for ordering that these be utilized to support "free public instruction."[75] More detailed and specific instructions came with the Barrios decree of August 27, 1873, that nationalized and consolidated all religious properties. At this point, it is significant to point out that the inventories listed no extensive rural properties, despite the liberal propaganda that claimed massive holdings.[76]

García Granados, who again resumed his presidential duties on June 10, 1873, made no effort to abrogate the actions of his comrade in arms, despite his stated philosophy of moderation and nonradical action.[77] In fact, two days after reassuming the presidency, García Granados ordered that in each one of the abandoned monasteries of the Capuchins, Recollects, Dominicans, and Bethlemitas in Antigua there be established a free public school.[78] Taking over the church-operated schools offered the liberals the opportunity to introduce their educational reform. García Granados took the first step toward educational reform with the creation of a ministry of public education on August 14, 1872. Essentially, the break with the conservative system of education, as spelled out in the Ley de Pavón of 1852, was making education purely a state function, thereby denying the local pastor a voice in elementary education.[79] The liberal philosophy of education was spelled out clearly by José M. Samoyoa, the minister of education of Barrios, in December 1874. The minister's report for revamping the system at all levels called for secularization, centralization of administration, and courses in Positivism. The stress on teaching empirical and useful subjects was deemed essential for economic development. The by-product of this focus was the elimination of studies that failed to meet empirical criteria. In short, liberal arts did not fare well in this type of curriculum. Neither did religious studies, which at the primary and secondary levels were replaced by a rational code of ethics called morality and urbanity. At the university level it meant doing away with ecclesiastical sciences.[80]

The liberals in their reform efforts to modernize education and convert religious corporate holdings into more productive channels received support from two foreign publications reprinted in Guatemala in 1872. The first one, a short pamphlet addressed to the French revolutionary assembly, was by a French author named Francois Laurent who argued that the state with its unlimited sovereignty can expropriate religious corporate property when it no longer serves the common good. Unlike the true existence of an individual, a corporation is a "fictitious" one, owing its existence to the state. Therefore, a legislature can dissolve the corporation when the public good requires it. Not only has the church failed in its mission of charity, but its ever-increasing wealth has become an obstacle to economic development. Even where it has offered charity, it has helped to create a clan of beggars and vagabonds. In short, it no longer served the common good. His ultimate fear was that the church had become too independent because of its wealth.[81]

Reprinted in the same year as the Laurent publication was one by José María Luis Mora of Mexico, who in 1833 played a key role in the Valentín Gómez Farías administration's efforts to bring about Mexican church reforms. In his dissertation on religious corporate holdings, he set out three areas to be studied: 1) the origin and nature of ecclesiastical goods, 2) the governmental right to regulate these holdings, and 3) the determination of rightful disposition of these goods. Under the first category, he considered the church as a "mystical body" entitled to receive goods for its sustenance and the promotion of the faith. As a political association, the church could acquire other types of goods such as livestock and estates, but here it fell into the second category, namely, where property was subject to state regulation. In Laurent's thinking this category was his fictitious entity. Looking at the history of Christianity, Mora concluded that the church was essentially a mystical body up to 325 A.D. under the emperor Constantine. He cited the early Christian fathers like St. Ambrose, who condemned church wealth as inimical to its spiritual mission. With the coming of an official status under Constantine, the church became also a political association and accumulated vast amounts of property that he described as dead or unproductive wealth serving no useful purpose. Therefore in keeping with his third category, the state had the right to limit property acquisitions by the church or religious corporations for the common good.

Mora, like many of his fellow liberals, was realistic in admitting that an immediate return to the early days of Christianity, when the church was purely dependent on voluntary contributions, was unrealistic. Although he recognized the ideal of separation of church and state, he believed that for the time being the church needed to enjoy a state subsidy as practiced under the *patronato real*. To do otherwise could endanger the very existence of the church. The final advice of Mora as well as of Laurent was to urge the liberals to educate the citizenry in these matters in order to bring about a true separation between the two entities so that each could fulfill its true mission.[82] The publication of the two works in Guatemala was an effort on the part of the liberals to propagandize for their religious-reform programs.

Ever since the liberal takeover in 1871 the anticlerical broadsides had been educating the citizenry about the evils associated with religious corporate wealth. Barrios, as interim president, had implemented many of the liberal aspirations with his suppression of male religious congregations and the nationalization of their property, but there still remained the property of the church in general, namely, cathedral and parish properties, endowments, and various funds. Another unresolved question was the status of female religious communities. All of these matters and more were addressed by Barrios after he became president on June 3, 1873.

Within a month of taking office, Barrios ordered the expulsion of the apostolic administrator, Padre Espinosa, whom he accused of failing to cooperate with the government, namely, of refusing to remove pastors in rebellious areas and replace them with ones more to the government's liking. Neither did the president appreciate the apostolic administrator's continuous protests against the religious-reform decrees, but the most serious charge was the allegation that Espinosa was supporting rebel activities in the Oriente through his relative, Enrique Palacios, who was a key political leader in the previous conservative government and after 1871, while in exile, worked for the overthrow of the liberal government.[83] The expulsion of the religious head resulted in the selection of Padre Francisco W. Taracena by the ecclesiastical curia as apostolic administrator.

Less than a month after taking over the duties of apostolic administrator, Taracena was confronted with Barrios's nationalization and consolidation decree of August 27, which included all religious property. The decree called for setting up municipal commissions to carry it out and created a special treasury to administer and invest the property. Compensations were promised when in order. Subsequent decrees instructed the commissions to hold public auctions to dispose of the properties. On the same date of the nationalization and consolidation decree, Barrios ordered the creation of a Banco Agricola Hipotecario to administer and invest the income from the nationalized properties in agricultural pursuits.[84]

The decree was very specific in describing property to be nationalized, which included real estate, movable property, livestock, rent and interest income, legacies, properties belonging to churches, monasteries, convents, religious brotherhoods, parish *cofradías* or confraternities, hospitals, orphanages, hospices, schools, and houses for spiritual exercises.[85] Only religious property directly devoted to religious purposes escaped nationalization, namely, churches and pastoral residences.

The *considerando* reflected liberal rationale. First, there was the urgent necessity to prevent religious funds from falling into the hands of rebellious factions.[86] Second, expropriation of the property was essential to promote economic development and prosperity—a goal unattainable as long as the properties remained in "dead hands." In the words of the decree, "The existence of property in 'dead hands' withdraws considerable capital from commerce, agriculture and industry and takes out of circulation territorial property, fettering it perpetually on certain bodies and families, who possess it in an exclusive manner." In short, the property must be placed into hands "of active and industrious proprietors, who make it produce and increase the public wealth."[87] Finally, the government justified its actions in terms of Mora's thinking. Like the Mexican thinker, it argued that religious corporations were "moral institutions" that owed their existence to civil law. Therefore, a civil authority could regulate these associations and their properties to promote the common good.[88]

In carrying out the intent of the common good, both the García Granados and Barrios governments converted many of the monasteries into public schools. For instance, García Granados, on October 18, 1872, ordered the establishment of five primary schools in the expropriated monasteries of the Franciscans, Dominicans, and the Recollects.[89] A few months later, on January 2, 1873, the provisional president modified the order by setting up a military college in the Recollect monastery, which became the Escuela Politécnica.[90] Another example was the Barrios decree of February 25, 1874, ordering that the Jesuit Colegio Tridentino become part of the university, which later housed the law school. The same decree made the major seminary of the Vincentions into a public normal school to train teachers for primary instruction.[91]

In setting up the Banco Agricola Hipotecario in 1873, Barrios hoped to use it as a depository for income from the sale of religious property and as a credit agency for agricultural development. Already noted was the fact that religious rural holdings were very limited and produced only a modest income. More income was realized from the sale of urban religious holdings, but here again the income fell far short of liberal expectations. According to Herrick's study, the estimated sum of two million pesos was available to capitalize the Banco Nacional, which had replaced the Banco Agricola Hipotecario in 1874. Admitting that information on the sales of religious properties was incomplete, Herrick calculated that sales from 1872 to 1883 amounted to only 92,845 pesos. Furthermore, from this amount must be subtracted 33,709 pesos, which were debts owed to the church. Although the net income was small, Herrick concluded that expropriated religious property was an important source for capitalizing the Banco Nacional. In addition, he pointed to the government's use of religious landholdings to stimulate the cultivation of special crops and religious urban facilities to offer social services.[92]

Barrios's actions received endorsements from liberal pamphleteers, who were constantly urging the government to take radical measures against religious corporations. One such pamphleteer, whose work appeared shortly after Barrios issued his decree, claimed that the church gained much of its property by promoting religious superstitions and threatening the faithful with hell. Although the church received property for charitable purposes, in the end it failed to fulfill its mission and, as a result, became unduly wealthy. The amassing of wealth had even drawn the criticism of popes, saints, and Protestant reformers. The author concluded that because the church failed in its mission of charity, the state therefore had the duty to take over the funds and administer them in accordance with the wishes of the donors. The net effect of Catholic charity had been the worsening of socioeconomic conditions by destroying a person's initiative. This result, according to the writer, was far from the minds of the donors when they made the contributions, and so it became imperative for the state to take over all religious holdings to end the decadence and impoverishment of society.[93] Whether the rationale came from official or unofficial sources, the justification for expropriation of these goods centered on economic development and modernization. In the case of the liberal broadsides, the justification carried a strong dose of anticlericalism to make the message more effective.

The ecclesiastical *cabildo* immediately, on September 10, protested the decree of nationalization and consolidation. The church authorities declared the decree null and void without consulting the Holy See. They counseled the clergy and members of religious communities not to give any moral consent and to offer verbal protest upon the implementation of the decree.[94]

The nationalization of religious corporate holdings carried immediate implications for female religious associations, who had not suffered suppression when Barrios dissolved the male religious orders in 1872. In her letter of September 4, 1873, Madre Encarnación, the superioress of the Bethlemitas in Quezaltenango, was the first nun to voice concern about the decree of expropriation being applied to the nuns. Her fears were well founded because the community rented a house that belonged to a *confradía*, which had been nationalized by the Barrios decree. She reported that the community's temporary residence was the house of a local pastor, but this was due to be sold in the very near future.[95] Although this is the only letter on record in the archdiocesan archives expressing concern over the properties of nuns, other communities of nuns must have seen the handwriting on the wall. The decree of August 27 included all religious corporate properties without exception, and its implementation in regard to female religious communities became a reality when Barrios decreed the dissolution of female religious communities.

Beginning February 9, 1874, Barrios issued a series of decrees that culminated in the suppression of female religious associations. His first action was to concentrate all nuns in the capital in one convent—a move that he ordered to be completed within eighteen days. At the same time, he prohibited the taking of religious vows and offered a monthly pension of twenty pesos for any nun who wished to leave the religious life. The reasons for his actions were similar to those given for disbanding male religious communities, namely, "to remove a social and economic obstacle." In addition, he found perpetual vows to be a renunciation of individual liberty and moral suicide not to be tolerated by society.[96] Voicing their approval of the president's action were liberal editorials, which in stronger anticlerical terms condemned religious life as a product of the Middle Ages and not in keeping with the simple faith of the early Christians. Like Mora, the editor of *El Guatemalteco* argued that religious associations were dependent on the authorization of civil laws and so could be revoked when the public good demanded it. Finally, from a social and economic viewpoint, the editor described religious life as unproductive slavery, lacking initiative and accumulating wealth in "dead hands."[97] In short, religious life, male or female, was not in keeping with the nineteenth-century liberal goals of modernization and economic development.

Efforts to concentrate 126 nuns from five religious communities into one convent proved impractical. First of all, the selected Convent of Santa Clara was not large enough, and second, each community practiced its own rules of community life. In the case of the Carmelites, it was a contemplative life, whereas the other communities were active outside the convent wall. Barrios added to the difficulties by insisting that civil officials must conduct periodic checks on sanitary conditions—an order that the apostolic administration immediately condemned as a violation of the cloistered convent life. Padre Taracena's protest of the president's action went unheeded as the president, on March 5, ordered the extinction of female relogus communities. He contended that the nuns could serve mankind better in a secular status with their ministries to the sick, the destitute, and orphans.[98] The March 5 presidential decree was a logical conclusion following the dissolution of male religious orders and nationalization of all religious corporate properties. At the same time, it was in keeping with the liberal goal of modernization.

In carrying out the mission of modernization, the government followed the pattern it had established in disposing of male religious properties in the capitol. The convents, schools, and charitable institutions of the religious sisters were converted into facilities providing various state social and educational services. The chart below provides examples of the conversion of these facilities into state use.[99]

Suppression of religious communities and nationalization of their properties had all been accomplished by means of presidential decrees. During the provisional presidency of Garciá Granados, there were two unsuccessful attempts to write a constitution, as had been promised when the liberals took power in 1871. Barrios made a third attempt in 1876, but again the

Table 4.1: Conversion of Religious Facilities

Nuns Facilities	State Use
Convent of Belén	Boy's Normal Training School
Academy of the Sisters of Notre Dame	Girls' Secondary School
Convent of Santa Teresa	Women's Prison
Convent of Santa Clara	Reformatory
Ursuline Academy	Military Hospital
Capuchin Convent	Insane Asylum
Third Order of St. Francis Chapel[100]	Telegraph Office

effort was fruitless. In fact, it was the constituent assembly's decision to operate under a "transitory dictatorship," which the liberals deemed essential for making their reforms lasting.[101] It was not until 1879 that the liberals fulfilled their promise of giving the country a constitution.

On November 9, 1878, Barrios called for the election of a constituent assembly to draft a constitution, which began its work the following March 15. The two articles of pertinence to religious corporate holdings were 21 and 25. The former called for the "absolute prohibition" of *vinculaciones*, or entailment of religious corporate holdings. The second one prohibited the establishment of any type of monastic institution.[102] The assembly's deliberations started in March and concluded the following December. Not surprisingly, much discussion centered on constitutional provisions relating to church–state issues. The chief spokesman for the liberals, who were in control of the assembly, was Lorenzo Montúfar, the architect of the newly drafted document. He spoke eloquently in defense of the proposed constitution, as was the case in defending articles 21 and 25, which outlawed the existence of religious associations and corporate religious property, or *vinculaciones*. In his remarks, frequently interspersed with biting anticlerical comments, he noted that monastic institutions did not come into existence until the fourth century, during the reign of the emperor Constantine. Therefore, using the Mora thesis, the state had the sovereign right to recognize the creation of these institutions and by the same token retained the right to dissolve them when necessary. He buttressed his rationale by reminding his audience that popes had already dissolved religious societies, as had been the case with the Jesuits in the eighteenth century. The major thrust of his remarks was a reiteration of liberal ideology, which considered monastic wealth as unproductive and devoted to charity, which fostered vagrancy and laziness. He concluded that the state could not tolerate the "exotic growth" of these institutions in the nineteenth century.[103] Despite the urging of Padre Angel

Arroyo, a moderate liberal clerical delegate, to leave the door open for the possible reestablishment of monastic institutions, the articles were overwhelmingly approved by the assembly.[104] In effect, the constituent assembly ended up constitutionalizing previous presidential decrees. To have acted otherwise could have meant censuring the conduct of Barrios.

The constituent convention in 1879 afforded the liberals a convenient opportunity once more to reiterate liberal ideology on church–state matters. At the same time, the liberal thesis of economic development and modernization served as a guiding spirit for the new document. For instance, articles 16, 20, and 21 guaranteed protection of property rights, with the exception of religious corporate holdings, which were "absolutely prohibited." Article 20 also permitted the chief executive to grant concessions for the establishment of new industries.[105] Another example included the lenient requirements for foreigners to become citizens. Article 10 permitted a foreigner to accept a government position, and merely by accepting automatically became a citizen.[106] The liberals saw immigration as an essential tool to use in attracting needed skills for a modernized state. Their thinking on immigration was little different from that of contemporary Mexico, Argentina, or the United States. Well could Herrick conclude that the liberal thesis of economic development reached its apogee in the Constitution of 1879, with its defense of property rights, concessions to the business sector, and lenient citizenship requirements for foreigners. In short, it was "most favorable to entrepeneurs."[107] The deliberations made it clear that the liberals had achieved their goals and the Constitution symbolized their success. Essentially, their goals called for economic development, secularization, and modernization. In reaching their objectives, they developed a state-controlled and secularized system of education. By dissolving religious congregations and *vinculaciones,* they terminated religious corporate holdings, which they saw as obstacles to economic development and modernization.

The achievement of modernization goals was greatly aided by an atmosphere of anticlericalism. It is not easy to determine the exact degree of influence that anticlericalism played in promoting the liberal program, but there is no denying that anticlerical propaganda was effective in lessening traditional respect for the church and its ministers.

A by-product of the church's weakened political and economic status was the loss of its traditional role of helping the state develop good, moral, and loyal citizens, as was the case under the colonial *patronato real* and the national conservative governments. The loss, plus a politically and economically weak institution in a secularized society, was a legacy carried into the twentieth century. Although the current Guatemalan Constitution no longer contains the anticlerical provisions of the one of 1879, the liberal legacy still remains a challenge for the Guatemalan Catholic church today.

Notes

1. J. Lloyd Mecham, *Church and State in Latin America* (Chapel Hill, 1966), pp. 3–10; and Mary P. Holleran, *Church and State in Guatemala* (New York, 1949), pp. 15–17 and 27.
2. Mecham, *Church and State*, pp. 3–4; and J. Lloyd Mecham, "The Papacy and Spanish-American Independence," *The Hispanic American Historical Review* 9 (May 1929), 154–75.
3. Mecham, *Church and State*, pp. 11–18.
4. Charles A. Hale, *Mexican Liberalism in the Age of Mora, 1821–1853* (New Haven and London, 1968), p. 39.
5. Jorge Mario García Laguardia, *La reforma liberal en Guatemala* (Guatemala, 1972), pp. 20–21. For a more detailed examination of the enlightened Bourbon legacy, see his *Orígenes de la democracia constitucional en Centro América* (San José, 1971), pp. 17–98.
6. Ralph Lee Woodward, Jr., "Changes in Nineteenth-Century Guatemalan State and Its Indian Policies," in *Guatemalan Indians and the State: 1540–1988*, ed. Carol A. Smith (Austin, 1990), p. 52.
7. Acta de la Independencia, cited in Jorge Luján Muñoz, *La independencia y la anexión de Centroamérica a México* (Guatemala, 1982), pp. 133–37.
8. Holleran, *Church and State in Guatemala*, pp. 67–68.
9. Mecham, *Church and State*, p. 341.
10. Holleran, *Church and State in Guatemala*, p. 70.
11. Chiapas, which was part of the Central American provinces during the colonial era, opted to remain with Mexico after the downfall of Agustin de Iturbide.
12. Holleran, *Church and State in Guatemala*, pp. 77–83.
13. Mecham, *Church and State*, p. 310.
14. Ibid.
15. Ibid., pp. 310–11.
16. Holleran, *Church and State in Guatemala*, p. 91.
17. Mecham, *Church and State*, p. 314.
18. Holleran, *Church and State in Guatemala*, pp. 93, 99, 101, and 104–5.
19. David Vela, *Barrundia ante el espejo de su tiempo* (Guatemala, 1956), 1:197–98; Lorenzo Montúfar y Rivera, *Reseña histórica de Centro-América* (Guatemala, 1878), 1:241–46; and David McCreery, *Rural Guatemala, 1760–1940* (Stanford, 1994), p. 77. A *caballería* is equivalent to 105.75 acres.
20. *Recopilación de las leyes de Guatemala* (Guatemala, 1872), 3:260, 276, and 294.

21. For a more extended analysis of liberal immigration policy, see William J. Griffith, *Empires in the Wilderness* (Chapel Hill, 1965), pp. 5–31.

22. Franklin D. Parker, *The Central American Republics* (London, New York, and Toronto, 1971), p. 78.

23. For a summation of factors that disunited the provinces, see José Mata Gavidia, *Anotaciones de historia patria centroamericana* (Guatemala, 1953), pp. 337–41.

24. *Colección de los decretos y de las órdenes mas interesantes que obtuvieron la sanción, emitidas por la Segunda Legislatura del Estado de Guatemala* (Guatemala, 1830), pp. 27–28.

25. Ibid., pp. 28 and 42–47.

26. Hubert J. Miller, *La iglesia católica y el estado en Guatemala, 1871–1885* (Guatemala, 1976), pp. 29–33. For the complete text for the creation of the Academy of Studies, see Antonia Batres Jauregui, *El Dr. Mariano Gálvez y su época*, 2d ed. (Guatemala, 1957), pp. 85–125.

27. Holleran, *Church and State in Guatemala*, pp. 120–23.

28. Batres Jauregui, *El Dr. Mariano Gálvez*, pp. 48–49.

29. For an extended examination of the factors that contributed to the populist uprising under Rafael Carrera, see Pedro Tobar Cruz. "Los montañeses" (Licentiate thesis in history, Universidad de San Carlos de Guatemala, 1958).

30. Holleran, *Church and State in Guatemala*, pp. 125–27; and *Recopilación de las leyes de Guatemala*, 3:262 and 297.

31. Holleran, *Church and State in Guatemala*, p. 128.

32. McCreery, *Rural Guatemala*, pp. 77–78.

33. *Recopilación de leyes de Guatemala*, 3:262 and 297.

34. Holleran, *Church and State in Guatemala*, pp. 125–46; Miller, *La iglesia católica*, pp. 36–54; and José Rodríguez Cerna, *Pactos con países europeos y asiáticos* (Guatemala, 1944), pp. 250–55.

35. Adrián Vidaurre, *La constitución de Guatemala* (Guatemala, n.d.), p. 41; and José Santacruz Noriega, *Gobierno del Capitán General D. Miguel García Granados* (Guatemala, 1979) 3:56–58 and 99.

36. Hubert J. Miller, "Expulsion of the Jesuits from Guatemala in 1871," *Catholic Historical Review* 54 (January 1969), 636–54.

37. García Laguardia, *La reforma liberal*, pp. 235–58.

38. David McCreery, *Development and the State in Reforma Guatemala, 1871–1885* (Athens, 1983), p. 1.

39. García Laguardia, *La reforma liberal*, p. 222.

40. Marco Antonio Villamar C., *Apuntes sobre la reforma liberal*, Investigación para la Docena No. 5 (Guatemala, 1977), pp. 10–11; and Ralph Lee Woodward, Jr., *Class Privilege and Economic Development: The Consulado de Comercio of Guatemala* (Chapel Hill, 1966), pp. 50–51.

41. Enrique Dussel et al., *Historia general de la iglesia en América Latina* (Salamanca, 1985), 6:286. For a detailed study of liberal ideology and pro-

grams for economic development, see McCreery, *Development and the State*, and his "Coffee and Class: The Structure of Development in Liberal Guatemala," *Hispanic American Historical Review* 56 (August 1976), 438–60. Also valuable is Thomas R. Herrick, *Desarrollo económico y político de Guatemala durante el período de Justo Rufino Barrios, 1871–1885* (Guatemala, 1974).

42. Hubert J. Miller, "Positivism and Educational Reforms in Guatemala, 1871–1885," *A Journal of Church and State* 8 (Spring 1966), 241–63.

43. Casimiro D. Rubio, *Geografía del General Justo Rufino Barrios, reformador de Guatemala* (Guatemala, 1935), pp. 132–34; Paul Burgess, *Justo Rufino Barrios* (Guatemala, 1972), pp. 135–38; and *Boletín Oficial* (Guatemala), July 23, 1872, 6.

44. *El Malacate* (San Marcos, Guatemala), November 7, 1871, 2–3.

45. Santacruz Noriega, *Gobierno*, p. 105.

46. Archivo Histórico Arquidiocesano, "Francisco de Paula de García Peláez," (hereafter cited as AHA), 1871, doc. 427; Miguel Angel García, *Diccionario histórico encyclopedico de la República de El Salvador* (San Salvador, 1935), p. 428; and Rafael Pérez, *La Compañía de Jesús en Colombia y Centro América después de su restauración* (Balladolid, 1898), 3:177.

47. Gilberto Valenzuela, comp., *Colección de hojas sueltas publicadas en los años de 1871–1873*, vol. 6 (Guatemala, Biblioteca Nacional), August 11, 19 and 20, 1871. The *hojas sueltas* are not paginated but arranged in chronological order.

48. Pérez, *La Compañía de Jesús en Colombia*, pp. 185–88.

49. Valenzuela, *Colección*, vol. 6, August 26, 1871, and November 2, 1871; Pérez, *La Compañía de Jesús en Colombia*, p. 191; García, *Diccionario*, 2:425; and Santiago Malaina, *La Compañía de Jesús en El Salvador, C.A. desde 1864 a 1872* (San Salvador, 1939), p. 54.

50. Pérez, *La Compañía de Jesús en Colombia*, pp. 194–95, and *La Revolución de 1871, sus promesas y el modo de cumplirlas* (Guatemala, 1894), p. 7.

51. Pérez, *La Compañía de Jesús en Colombia*, pp. 197–206; and Rubio, *Geografía*, p. 183.

52. Valenzuela, *Colección*, vol. 6 September 5, 1871.

53. *Recopilación de las leyes emitidas por la República de Guatemala, desde el 3 de junio de 1871, en que el Ejército Libertador al mando de los Generales Don Miguel García Granados y Don J. Rufino Barrios desconoció la administración de Don Vicente Cerna* (Guatemala, 1874), 1:89–90; *Boletín Oficial*, December 6, 1871, 1; and Pérez, *La Compañía de Jesús en Colombia*, p. 102.

54. Pérez, *La Compañía de Jesús en Colombia*, p. 102.

55. Miller, *La iglesia católica*, pp. 114–15.

56. Pérez, *La Compañía de Jesús en Colombia*, pp. 183–84.

57. Bernardo Piñol y Aycinena, *Círcular del arzobispo de Guatemala, al clero y a todos los fieles de la arquidiócesis* (San Salvador, 1872), pp. 1–3. It

was not unusual to reprint a protest of this nature later in another Central American republic so as to have a wider audience.

58. *Recopilación de las leyes emitidas*
59. Miller, *La iglesia católica*, pp. 121–22.
60. AHA, 1871, doc. 704.
61. Ibid.; and *Recopilación de las leyes emitidas*, 1:70–71.
62. AHA, 1871, doc. 704, and 1872, doc. 424.
63. *El Malacate*, January 5, 1872, 4.
64. Ibid., January 15, 1872, 3; February 17, 1872, 2–3; March 2, 1872, 2; and March 9, 1872, 1–3.
65. AHA, 1872, doc. 78.
66. *Recopilación de las leyes emitidas*, 1:89–91.
67. AHA, 1872, doc. 287.
68. José Santacruz Noriega, *Barrios el pacificador* (Guatemala, 1983), pp. 89–91.
69. Miller, *La iglesia católica*, p. 115.
70. AHA, 1872, doc. 281; *Recopilación de las leyes emitidas*, 1:101–2; and Valenzuela, *Colección*, vol. 6, June 7, 1872.
71. AHA, 1872, doc. 287.
72. Ibid.
73. Ibid.
74. Ibid.
75. *Recopilación de las leyes emitidas*, 1:101.
76. The Barrios decree of August 27, 1873, will be treated later. The liberal contention of vast religious rural properties in 1871 is still accepted without question by Thomas R. Herrick in his study of economic and political development of Guatemala, 1871–1885; see Herrick, *Desarrollo económico y político*. A more realistic picture of religious rural holdings is available in the well documented and detailed study of rural Guatemala, 1760-1940, by David McCreery; see McCreery, *Rural Guatemala*, pp. 76–77.
77. Miguel García Granados, *Memorias del General Miguel García Granados* (Guatemala, 1952), 2:279.
78. *Recopilación de las leyes emitidas*, 1:106–7. After the devastating earthquake of 1773 in Antigua, the colonial capital was transferred to present-day Guatemala City. The relocation caused many of the religious orders to abandon their monasteries in Antigua, except for the Capuchins. The Recollects were a reformed order of Franciscans dating back to the sixteenth century. The Bethlemitas were of Guatemalan origin, founded by Hermano Pedro de Betancourt in the late 1600s to do convalescent hospital work.
79. Ibid., pp. 115–16.
80. Miller, "Positivism and Educational Reforms," pp. 251–63; and Jesús Amurrio Gonzáles, *El positivismo en Guatemala* (Guatemala, 1970), pp. 61–91.

81. Francois Laurent, *Secularización de la iglesia* (Guatemala, 1872), pp. 8–25.

82. José Maria Luis Mora, *Disertación sobre bienes eclesiásticos* (Guatemala, 1872), pp. 5–83; and Hale, *Mexican Liberalism*, pp. 133–35.

83. *Recopilación de las leyes emitidas*, 1:184–85.

84. Ibid., pp. 193–96.

85. Ibid.; and Santacruz Noriega, *Barrios el pacificador*, p. 109.

86. *Recopilación de las leyes emitidas*, 1:192; and Dussel et al., *Historia general*, 290.

87. Ibid.

88. Ibid.

89. Ibid., pp. 127–28.

90. Ibid., pp. 135 and 141–54.

91. *Recopilación de las leyes emitidas por el gobierno democrático* (Guatemala, 1876), 2:22–23.

92. Herrick, *Desarrollo económico y político*, pp. 228–31. The liberal government recognized church debts dating back to the previous conservative regime.

93. *Párrafos de un buen libro, los bienses de la iglesia* (Guatemala, 1874), pp. 3–40.

94. AHA, 1873, docs. 495, 703, 705, and 718.

95. Ibid., docs. 495, 703, 705. and 718.

96. *Recopilación de las leyes emitadas por el gobierno democrático*, pp. 13–14.

97. *El Guatemalteco*, February 17, 1874, February 1 and 21, 1874, 1–2.

98. For a step-by-step account of disbanding female religious communities in 1874, see Miller, *La iglesia católica*, pp. 267–88.

99. *Recopilación de las leyes emitidas por el gobierno democrático*, 2:13–14, 125–28, and 155; *Recopilación de las leyes emitidas por el gobierno democrático de las República de Guatemala desde el 3 de junio de 1871, hasta el 30 de junio de 1881* (Guatemala, 1881), pp. 145–46; and Holleran, *Church and State in Guatemala*, pp. 183–84 and 199–200.

100. AHA, 1874, doc. 407. The Third Order of St. Francis was a lay group, following the rule of St. Francis of Assisi. Their property, along with that of the nuns, was nationalized by the Barrios decree of February 9, 1874.

101. Garciá Laguardia, *La reforma liberal*, pp. 249–51.

102. Secretariá de Instrucción Pública, *Ley constitutiva de la República de Guatemala decretada por la asemblea constituyente en 11 de diciembre de 1879* (Guatemala, 1899), pp. 9–10.

103. *Diario de sesiones de la asamblea constituyente de 1879* (Guatemala, 1899), pp. 9–10.

104. For further study of church–state issues in the constituent assembly of 1879, see Miller, *La iglesia católica*, pp. 430–50. The Sisters of Charity who worked in the hospital in the capital were never suppressed by the Bar-

rios decrees. Padre Arroyo saw their continued existence as a potential opening for the reestablishment of other religious associations. The fact that the sisters took yearly promises rather than perpetual vows served as a rationale for not including them among the traditional monastic institutions. More compelling than this technicality were their needed nursing skills.

    105. Secretariá de Instrucción Pública, *Ley constitutiva*, pp. 8–9.

    106. Ibid., 6.

5
Liberalism and Indian Communities in Peru, 1821–1920
Nils Jacobsen

During the first century after independence, liberalism provided the most influential set of ideas for integrating the members of historic ethnic Andean corporate groups into the newly proclaimed Peruvian nation as autonomous proprietors or industrious workers. Yet by the 1920s and 1930s most commentators felt that this project had failed. Indian peasants, it was said, had lost much of their land to seignorial *latifundia* in the highlands or capitalist plantations on the coast; their labor was exploited through force and a myriad of ruses by landholders as well as local and central government authorities. But even within the remaining communities, liberalism had failed: Pro-Indian writers such as Hildebrando Castro Pozo, Luis Valcarcel, and José Carlos Mariátegui all rejoiced in their conviction that communal property or usufruct of land had remained the undergirding of Indian peasant solidarity. Liberalism thus stood doubly indicted: Not only had it failed to transform the Indian *comunero* into an enterprising yeoman farmer or industrious worker; its preaching had been responsible for an actual deterioration in the lives of Peru's Indian majority population over the already bad situation of the Spanish colonial regime.[1]

But was this really an adequate portrayal of the nation's Indian community peasants one hundred years after independence? In their indictment of liberalism, had the *indigenista* authors considered the tremendous variation of the communities' resources, cultural characteristics and political clout between sierra, Amazon basin, and coast, between north, center, and south of Peru? Moreover, was liberalism really to blame for whatever situation the Peruvian peasantry faced a century after independence? Many observers have stressed the country's strong tradition of liberal economic policies, at least since the 1850s. But that finding is largely based on trade and investment policies.[2] In fact, it is difficult to find liberal anticommunity campaigns by the Peruvian central government comparable in strength and duration to those waged in Mexico during the Reforma and the Porfiriato, in Guatemala since the presidency of Rufino Barrios (1872–1885), and in Bolivia between the rule of Mariano Melgarejo (1864–1871) and Bautista Saavedra (1920–1925).[3] In Peru the elite sectors most directly interested in taking control of Indian communal resources—land, labor, and agricultural commodities—were the large landholders, traders, and authorities in the districts and provinces of the highlands, where most communities were located. In the halls of power in Lima their influence was not paramount, having to contend with *hacendados* and merchants from the coast, military *caudillos*, and urban professionals, who did not always share the same ideological perspective or interests vis-à-vis "the Indian problem." Peru's dominant classes were splintered sectorally, regionally, and ideologically, and the *gamonales*, the rural bosses from the highlands, had no automatic lock on decisions by the executive or Congress.

Since the days of John Locke, Baron de Montesquieu, and Adam Smith, liberalism, as theory and as political movement, has assumed a bewildering array of guises, both as a doctrine of emancipation and one of justifying a given status quo. Yet in its core "liberalism has been a theory and a movement of *reform* to advance *individual liberties* in the horizon of *uncertainty*," as Ralf Dahrendorf recently wrote.[4] A notion of property, in which the totality of rights over a resource, including those of disposition, are invested in individual persons, was constitutive for classical liberalism; it viewed private property as a powerful tool to liberate the individual and civil society as a whole from the fetters of the absolutist state and from stifling "irrational" traditions.[5] But even during the age of classical liberal doctrine, the first half of the nineteenth century, a tension had begun to develop between those writers—such as Jean Baptiste Say and David Ricardo—who viewed private property primarily as the precondition for creating effective markets, and those—such as Sismonde de Sismondi—who, continuing a moral "statecraft" tradition, stressed the need for a broad distribution of property and emphasized its civic function of fostering an engaged, virtuous citizenry.

These tensions in nineteenth-century liberal thought surfaced in contemporary debates over the Indian community. For the Bolivian case, they have been masterfully portrayed by Erick Langer. Until the early 1860s, those politicians and intellectuals in the *altiplano* republic who favored a broad distribution of communal lands between indigenous peasants maintained the upper hand in the deliberations of congresses and governments. Before 1880 attempts to abolish the Indian community by law failed in Bolivia, in part because of the continued fiscal importance of head taxes (successor taxes to colonial *tributo*) levied and collected through the communities, and in part because the state did not have the administrative capacity and the repressive force to intervene massively in the property regime of the Indian communities. Only between 1880 and the Federal War of 1899 did a social Darwinist, positivist interpretation of liberalism become dominant in Bolivia. Now the state put its repressive force fully in the service of transferring communal lands to the "capitalist," the owner of large haciendas, declared economically superior to the Indian peasant smallholder.[6]

To understand the impact of liberalism on Peru's Indian communities, we need to look beyond the laws and decrees emanating from Lima. Liberal ideas could be employed by actors on various levels of the country's power structure, from the central government apparatus to regional courts and prefectures, to the local authorities and rural elites. It could even be embraced by Indian community peasants themselves. The strength and role of liberalism in the transformation of Andean peasant communities ultimately depended on local constellations of power, social structure, and the specific mechanisms by which communities were integrated into broader economic circuits.

This chapter seeks to link national debates about the Indian community among politicians and intellectuals with what actually happened on the ground, in a number of Peruvian regions with different economic and social structures. It focuses on the issue of how liberalism may have affected communal property regimes, but also considers taxation and Indian peasant labor, as these issues were inextricably linked. The essay is divided into two main parts: "Emancipatory Liberalism and Fiscal Conservatism, 1821–1854"; "Liberalism Unbound and the Invisible Community, 1854–1879." In the conclusion I will consider the paradoxical rise, during the half-century following the War of the Pacific, of new protectionist and corporatist ideas just when market influences on freeholder peasants were intensifying.

Emancipatory Liberalism and Fiscal Conservatism, 1821–1854

When José de San Martín, the Argentine general leading the patriot forces against the colonial regime in the Andes, assumed power over Peru's fledgling autonomous state in mid-1821, he found Indian communities in a state of flux. Uncertainty about their relation to state and society was greater than at any time since the early decades after Spanish conquest. Habsburg rule in the Andes (1532–1700) had dismantled the statewide organization of the Inca polity, and had deeply affected the resources, institutions, and cultural practices of the overwhelming majority of Andean people who derived their livelihood from the land. While traditions varied between regions and specific ethnic groups, Andean notions of land were organized around two guiding principles: 1) Access to land, livestock, and other resources was mediated through kinship groups (*ayllus*), which based their claim to the use of specific territories on legendary ancestors elevated to the status of cultural heroes or deities; 2) Usufruct rights to land of individuals, lineages, *ayllus*, and more encompassing ethnic groups were established by contributing labor and exchanging it both among the families of the *ayllus* and with higher-level units. Reciprocal labor exchanges tied the lineages of *ayllus* with a complex web of moieties, sister *ayllus*, larger ethnic state structures, and ultimately the pan-Andean administrative and ceremonial net created and dominated by the Incas. These exchanges gave definition to the identity of social groups and their rights to specific resources, such as land, mineral deposits, or water.[7]

To the Spanish colonial administrators, the notion of rights to resources through labor and kinship, extending outward from a mythic lineage ancestor to ever larger nested groups, was not fully comprehensible.[8] The Habsburgs viewed the conquered Andean peoples as their vassals. Vassalage was expressed through their duty to pay tribute—first in labor and commodities, increasingly in money—and provide corvee labor services (*mita*). The Andean territories were considered crown lands (*tierras realengas*), which could be disposed of in various ways reflecting the complex Spanish property notions of the sixteenth century, a mix of Roman law, legal precepts developed during the *reconquista*, and localized Iberian common law practices.[9] While Spanish colonists and Andean lords (*señores naturales*) could receive land grants (*mercedes*) in fee simple, and municipalities were granted commons (*ejidos* or *dehesas*) with clearly defined property rights and borders, communities were granted usufruct of the land they occupied, partly in recognition of their "historical titles," and partly because unassigned crown lands (*baldíos*) were considered the possessions of those who worked them. The Andean peasants' obligations toward the crown were once again mediated through the communities, and thus in principle the crown sought to guarantee the lands worked by them. During the Habsburg era the major impact on communal lands was probably not exerted by the corporate colonial order that the crown sought to establish, but through economic displacements that followed from the commercial interests of the settlers and from massive population loss. Although crown officials tried to inscribe communities into tribute records according to Spanish notions of territoriality and property, during the seventeenth century many communities, at least in the southern highlands, had managed to reconstruct the Andean linkage between territoriality, kinship, and ethnicity.[10] The Habsburg regime in the Andes had neither the power to erase completely Andean notions of managing land resources, nor did the contemporary Spanish concepts unequivocally favor individual property.[11]

It was during the Bourbon era (1700–1808), and particularly during the reign of Charles III (1759–1788), that the notion of communal property or usufruct to land came under attack. Seeking to increase crown revenues and production in the colonies, reformist Bourbon bureaucrats began to apply enlightened notions to Peru's agrarian structure, after they had begun to do so in Spain itself.[12] "Historical titles" to community lands were not recognized any more, and between the 1750s and 1780s the sale of "excess" community lands to private persons was made easier. The position of the *kurakas*, village headmen, and Andean nobles, who had continued to play a vital role during the Habsburg era in the reproduction of ethnic cohesion, was undermined as they slowly lost their key tribute-collection function to appointed crown officers. Yet the Bourbons never dared to apply the proto-liberal reforms of corporate landholding—undertaken in Spain between the 1750s and 1790s—to the Andean communities. This reticence had both fiscal reasons—the need of cooperation of communal authorities in the collection of increasing tribute payments—and political reasons—the fear of de stabilizing the crown's control over the Andean countryside, a powerful concern in the aftermath of the Túpac Amaru rebellion of 1780–1781.[13] The liberal Cortés at Cádiz came closest to dissolving the compact between crown and Indian communities when, in 1812, it abolished tribute and *mita*, a measure immediately reversed upon the return of Ferdinand VII to the throne in 1814.

The earliest measures concerning the Indian peasant that were proclaimed by the authorities of the independent Peruvian state expressed their view of what kind of nation Peru should be. Whatever grievances and resentments had driven the creole leaders into the insurgency against Spain, clearly group interests would not do as the basis of legitimacy for the new nation. In their discourse, in laws and constitutional declarations, they proclaimed universal principles as legitimization for destroying the colonial order and establishing a new nation, so that all ethnic and social groups might recognize the new republican order.[14] Indians, vassals of the king of Castile by conquest, were the crucial group symbolizing the injustice of the Spanish regime. Within weeks after declaring independence, José de San Martín decreed, on August 27 and 28, 1821, that henceforth Indians were citizens of the nation and were to be known as *"peruanos."* Tribute was abolished, and it remained strictly forbidden to subject the former Indians to any type of involuntary servitude. Such colonial practices were denounced as "crimes against nature and liberty" through which Spanish "tyranny" brought about the "moral degradation" of the Indians.[15]

Clearly, the language of these decrees derived from enlightened and liberal thought. By stressing the civil rights of citizens, the principle of equality before the law, and, as the preamble to one of the decrees stated, the reestablishment of "reason and justice," San Martín and his followers proclaimed their vision for Peru's future political order, based on universal principles rather than corporate historical privileges. Beyond their pragmatic goal of attracting the Indian peasantry to the patriot cause in the escalating civil war against the royalists, the decrees had profound implications for the reform of Peru's agrarian structure. By abolishing tribute San Martín removed a key pillar of the colonial link between crown and Indian community: If the state relinquished interest in the community as a source of revenue, then in the future it would have no reason to protect and guarantee its internal social and agrarian order. Abolition of tribute was thus a prerequisite for disestablishing common usufruct of land in the *ayllus*.[16]

In the comparative perspective of Europe, San Martín's abolition of servitude should have formed the capstone of liberal agrarian reform. For there agrarian reform laws between the 1770s (Denmark) and 1861 (Russia) sought to terminate the feudal order on the land by disentangling the servile obligations and privileges of labor tenants on manorial estates, through quitrents, division of lands between tenants and owners, and compensation payments to the estate owners through agrarian debt funds.[17] But San Martín's fledgling administration did not attempt to undo the manorial estate;[18] abolition of servile obligations without compensation to the *hacendados* and without dividing the lands to which labor tenants held usufruct rights was bound to remain a dead letter. This was to be true for more than a century of Peru's agrarian legislation, and only the Agrarian Reform of 1969 undertook Draconian measures to undo the Andean manorial estate, when it was already in a process of internal decomposition. Thus, for the first century after independence the privately held Andean hacienda was largely excluded from agrarian reform legislation—forming an expanding manorial reserve, with attention exclusively focused on the Indian community, state lands, and the land or encumbrances on land held by various institutions of the Catholic church.[19]

The reform measures that were to provide the legal basis for property in the Indian communities for the entire first century after independence were proclaimed in the brief span of four years between 1824 and 1828, when the majority of Peru's founding fathers were still persuaded that a virtuous republican legislation would suffice to overcome the nation's colonial heritage. In April of 1824, soon after Simón Bolívar assumed supreme power of Peru's independent state, in desperate straights due to the deadlocked struggle against the royalist forces, he decreed a major revamping of the country's rural property regime. All state lands were to be sold for one-third below their assessed value. State-owned haciendas were to be sold by lots so that new settlements could be founded on them. The land actually in possession of Indians was excluded from this sale; it would become the present tenants' property without any restrictions on its subsequent sale. The decree treated *"tierras de comunidad"* separately. They were to be parceled out, also in fee simple, in proportion to the size of benefiting families to all those Indians who had no other land; remaining community lands were to be sold just as other state-owned lands. To prepare for the distribution and sale of state lands, *visitadores* (land judges) were to be appointed in each province. The preamble to the decree left no doubt as to Bolívar's motivations: The government desperately needed funds to "bring to its conclusion the present struggle against Spanish domination"; Peru's agriculture was in a state of decay largely because much land was in precarious possession or rental.[20]

Bolívar aimed at the creation of a broad class of Indian yeoman smallholders with unlimited property rights to a plot of land. As seen in the introduction, enlightened and liberal writers considered property unencumbered by liens, owned by individuals rather than by corporate groups (such as the church, municipalities, or communities), freely alienable and inheritable, as crucial for increased production and general economic progress. Bolívar embraced a special brand of liberal doctrine, stressing the benefits of a broad distribution of property, seen as prerequisite to the formation of an industrious and informed citizenry. He envisioned the creation of a socially democratic republic, in which corporate or ethnic privileges had no place, and which needed to be politically authoritarian in order to avoid the danger of anarchy arising from social inclusion.

Perhaps the most significant aspect of Bolívar's decree is its differentiation between the lands actually in possession of individual Indian families (article 2), and "community lands" (article 3). It assumed that a significant number of Indian peasants precariously held state lands without being subject to a communal regimen. These could include lands held by *kurakas*, as well as lands on which Indian peasants were squatting—for example, crown lands in dispute between communities and estate owners. For such lands, already in possession of individual peasant families, the decree merely improved the present holders' tenure from precarious possession to fee simple.

The decree of April 1824 was the most liberal of Bolívar's land laws, as it placed no restrictions on the sale of the lands that Indian peasants were to receive in fee simple. But it is uncertain whether this decree found much immediate application, as great parts of the highlands remained under royalist control. When Bolívar traveled through the southern highlands in mid-1825, after the defeat of the Spanish forces at Ayacucho, he proclaimed a series of decrees aimed at the Indian communities that in several ways took up the more cautious Bourbon statist type of reformism. One of the decrees of July 4, 1825, specified that *tierras de oficio*, community lands granted to *caciques* and tax collectors in compensation for their services, were to be included in the general distribution of community lands. Yet the *caciques de sangre*, the descendants of Andean nobility, were to retain the lands they had received "in distribution."[21] At the same time, *caciques* without any other land were to be included in the general distribution of community lands in such a way that for each family member they would receive five *topos* of land while Indian commoners would receive only one or two *topos*. Finally, the decree stipulated that no Indian could sell any of the land received in fee simple before 1850.[22] While favoring *caciques* one last time, based on their social position rather than on privileges stemming from their office, Bolívar proceeded on the very same day (July 4, 1825) to extinguish the title of *cacique* altogether.[23]

The dilution of liberal contents in the agrarian legislation became more marked during the following year. Because of mounting fiscal pressure, in August 1826 the Bolívarian council of government, in which Bourbon reformists such as Hipólito Unanue and José de Larrea y Loredo figured prominently, reintroduced Indian tribute under the euphemistic denomination of *contribución de indígenas*, a measure that replicated most of the modalities of its predecessor tax. The inevitable consequence for the agrarian program followed on the heels, when in December 1826 Bolívar instructed provincial authorities to prefer *originarios*, who paid the full rate of the *contribución de indígenas*, to *forasteros* in the distribution of community lands.[24]

As things stood by December of 1826, the Bolívarians had removed any legally fixed privileges from Indian communities, but had recognized existing stratification based on social prestige and wealth, ratifying the claims of former *caciques* and *originarios* to communal lands. Having understood the scarcity of communal lands in many regions of the country, they once again stressed the Bourbon practice of distributing strictly limited amounts of communal lands in a manner reaffirming social hierarchies within the communities, albeit with the decisive difference that the plots now were to be held in fee simple. Moreover, by imposing a twenty-five-year prohibition on the sale of any land granted to Indians in fee simple, the Bolívarians now had taken back the key liberal property concept of unfettered circulation. Apprehensive about Indian peasants' capacity to compete with powerful provincial elites in the ideally envisioned free market, the Bolívarians had sacrificed the notion of free circulation in order to safeguard the goal of a broad distribution of productive land.[25] But in so doing and by introducing the *contribución de indígenas*, they had also taken the first steps toward reconverting the *"peruanos"* back into an ethnically defined corporate group, requiring special protection.²⁶

Bolívar's agrarian-reform program floundered out in the provinces, where it required the loyal cooperation of land commissions to oversee the distribution of community lands "with impartiality and justice." During 1826 and 1827 numerous complaints must have been filed against these provincial commissions, some of which failed to undertake the measurement and registration of community lands, while others committed the "most pernicious abuse" of unjustly granting land titles to their favorites. The Council of Government sent repeated circulars to the prefects in the departments, admonishing them to the strictest application of the laws of 1824 and 1825, and admonishing the land commissioners not to "grant property titles ... and even less to distribute lands or grant land by *composición*; they are merely empowered to inform [the supreme government]."²⁷ The circulars also underlined that the commissioners were not supposed to undertake a "general remeasurement of the land" that might "disturb the Indian proprietors in their peaceful possession." The government merely wished that, "respecting the actual possession [of land] of the *peruanos* [that is, Indians], the lands not currently occupied be distributed according to the decrees of His Excellency the Liberator." This should be a "simple operation, very easy to carry out."²⁸ In contrast to the decrees themselves, this language suggests that all community lands currently in possession of Indian peasants were to become their property automatically (prior to the measurement of communal lands) and that only the *sobrantes*, community or state lands not presently occupied, were to be included in the distribution. But it was far from clear which lands could be considered *sobrantes*, and it was in this kind of imprecision that disputes and abuses could arise on the local level. As the upshot of these conflicts, and perhaps also as a rebuke to the Bolivarians who had become highly unpopular, the newly elected Constituent Congress resolved on August 3, 1827, that "any sale of community land" should be suspended for the time being until the land commissions had presented their reports.²⁹

Nevertheless, on March 27, 1828, the Constituent Congress passed a new land law. It again declared Indians, but now also *mestizos*, to be proprietors of the lands that they presently occupied on the basis of the periodic distributions of communal lands, or—in the case of land outside the communities as defined by the Bourbon authorities—"without contradiction," that is, without other claimants coming forth to dispute their possession. Landless Indians and *mestizos* were to receive allotments from the remaining state lands once the newly created departmental assemblies (Juntas Departamentales) had provided information on their extent. Should there be any lands left after this operation, they were to be assigned to pay for schools in the *"pueblos"* where they were located. This law provided no limitation on the sale of land assigned in fee simple to Indians and *mestizos*.[30]

The land law of 1828 became the cornerstone of how the national government, the courts, and notaries throughout Peru treated land in the Indian communities until the early twentieth century. The trend from the first Bolívarian law of 1824 to this last of the major agrarian reform laws of the 1820s was to downplay sale, parcelization, and distribution of community or other state lands. What mattered most now was the conversion of the precarious titles of Indians and *mestizos* to what, until now, were considered state lands into full property. Rather than a redistribution of land, this law primarily aimed at improved tenures for those previously in possession—from usufruct of state lands to fee simple. What had emerged in the 1828 legislature, then, appears to be a pragmatic compromise between Bolívar's social liberal vision and the reasserting of corporate hierarchical notions. The sanctity of property was one liberal precept that rapidly entered even the canon of conservative social thinkers.[31] Declaring the Indian community peasants to be property owners, on the one hand, might be viewed as a rather conservative measure, merely designed to increase agricultural productivity in the cheapest way possible. On the other hand, as we shall see, conferring the title of proprietors on Indian peasants until the 1870s never lost a politically emancipatory aspect. Since property ownership and citizenship were viewed as closely related, declaring Indians to be proprietors also sent a political message: Indians were to be citizens with equal rights. In the following decades government decrees made clear that proprietorship entailed citizenship, or that those deemed to be citizens ought to have the possibility to become proprietors.[32] Yet by 1828 these notions had been newly merged with a corporate, caste image of society. For reasons of fiscal necessity, the state was going to collect a head tax—the *contribución de indígenas*—which treated the Indian peasants once again as a corporate caste group, with profound implications for the relationship between the state authorities and the communities.

This curious balance between liberal and conservative corporatist elements in the approach toward Indians and their communities finds apt expression in a pamphlet by Pedro de Rojas y Briones, published in 1828.[33] The author, an aging miner and deputy from the northern sierra, outlined a number of "practical" projects to stimulate the languishing economy of the republic, which he had unsuccessfully introduced in the Constituent Congress, ranging from a development bank for the mining sector to artificial clouds to protect crops in the fields from frost. A man of strong conservative instincts and an abiding respect for ancient institutions "because their very survival stamps them as good," Rojas loathed any economic policy that strengthened the position of foreign businessmen vis-à-vis the native sons, especially concerning the ownership of mines and agricultural estates.[34] He considered it "degrading for our nation, composed of no more than 1,200,000 persons, that two thirds of these find themselves inactive and without properties in which to work, when before conquest [that is, in the Inca empire] more than eight million people were employed without suffering want." The "best way" Rojas knew to overcome Peru's economic problems and to "increase our wealth,"

> consists in establishing our principal alliance with the Indians, the greatest treasure which Peru has; let us gain their confidence of which to date we have been deprived because of their mistreatment, although the tree of our liberty has been irrigated with their blood: with their sweat and drudgery the fields are cultivated and the mines worked, and, in the last analysis, they have always provided us with all kinds of comforts. And what has that most noble nation, the legitimate heirs of the realms of the great Manco-Capac, received in return? . . . [Nothing other than what donkeys are given:] . . . they are driven with a whip to eat from the worst pasture.

Rojas was worried that the *patria*, whose tree of liberty still had shallow roots, might one day have to rely on the "Indian caste" for its defense, and the Indians might not be willing to sacrifice their blood, if they had received nothing in return and possessed no properties to defend. "If we want mining and agriculture to flourish to an immeasurable degree, let us provide extensive properties to the Indians in these two branches." The Indians would become "our" [that is, the Peruvian creoles'] loyal friends, both out of gratitude and self-interest. The state would gain greatly, because Indians, as property owners, could marry their children to spouses of other ethnic groups and in time "all would be reduced to the white caste." As property owners they could afford to give education to their children in all the sciences and present "us" with a multitude of superior talents obscured so far by oppression. Instead of treating Indians like slaves, Peruvian entrepreneurs would profit much more if they formed companies with Indians, both in agriculture and in mining, because "he who works with mercenaries" loses time, faces labor shortages and theft.[35]

Potential property owners and talented, industrious citizens, the Indians were yet to be considered as a separate "nation" or "caste," who—supreme irony—could serve "our nation" [that of the Peruvian creoles] best by disappearing through a process of whitening! Such ambiguity between the virtues of spreading individual property and the reaffirmation of socio-ethnic hierarchies largely remained intact in state policies toward Indian communities until the 1850s. The national government did not wish communal land—conceived of as the land of individual peasant proprietors—to pass to proprietors outside of the communities (hence non-Indians) because of the revenue loss that would entail. In 1847 Finance Minister Manuel del Río even called for the passage of a law prohibiting Indians to sell their land to non-Indians.[36] When local authorities or provincial subprefects wanted to appropriate Indian community land for public purposes (such as financing schools), something unproblematic under the colonial notion of *tierras realengas*, the central government repeatedly disallowed it, at times expressly referring to the "complete property" that individual Indian peasants now enjoyed over their land through the law of March 31, 1828.[37] A liberal notion of private property was here used to protect peasant community lands for the purely fiscal-utilitarian maintenance of an Indian caste.

Indeed, until the 1850s losses of community land appear to have been quite limited in various regions of Peru. Most elite-controlled agricultural and livestock enterprises were in crisis, on the coast as much as in the sierra, greatly diminishing the interest of *hacendados* in increasing their domain. Land values and rents remained depressed, commercial circuits—especially in southern and far-northern Peru—were disrupted, and the cost of transportation had increased.[38] Prepared to absorb declining commodity prices and rising costs by relying on family and communal labor, Indian peasant enterprises often seem to have fared better in this difficult commercial environment.[39]

Whatever happened out in the provinces was only indirectly the consequence of laws and decrees promulgated in Lima, as the power of the incipient nation-state remained tenuous until late in the nineteenth century. The effect of the new republican legal and political frame was perhaps strongest on those lands most easily identified with a corporate land regime: estates belonging to religious orders, as well as community lands rented to creoles and *mestizos* under the aegis of the Caja de Censos. By a decree of 1826, male religious orders with less than eight resident friars were disbanded and their estates granted to worthy patriot officers of the wars of independence, or sold off to creoles below market price.[40] Ownership of community lands administered by the Caja de Censos, from the rental income of which communities defrayed some of their taxes and fees, were transferred to the departmental Sociedades de Beneficiencia Pública (which took over the administration of hospitals, asylums, and cemeteries), or passed into possession of the renters, as the state became increasingly lax in collecting lease fees.[41]

In the southern sierra, especially the departments of Cuzco and Puno, with a high percentage of Indian population and perhaps the strongest communal tradition, three trends characterized communities during the early decades of the republic: a consolidation of their land base, conflicts with a newly emerging local elite over power and resources, and early signs of a shifting notion of land within the communities themselves.

In both departments "the community manages to break, in its own favor, the rural equilibrium maintained with the hacienda during the colonial period." Put more modestly, the expansion of haciendas onto community lands was halted in many provinces.[42] Lands on which *forasteros* and poor *originarios* were squatting and which, since the mid-eighteenth century, had been disputed with *caciques* and *recaudadores de tributo*, with the church and with owners of private estates, became the undisputed property of the peasant families in possession at the moment of the reform laws of 1824–28. Subsequent transactions over these lands routinely referred to the 1828 law as basis of the owner's legal title.[43] Concerns about the scarcity of land for Indian peasants, so frequent in the administrative and judicial documentation around 1780, temporarily diminished. The combination of their own struggles and the reform legislation of the 1820s had broadened the space of peasant land and allowed the consolidation of communities on a broader basis.

The major challenge to Indian communities in Cuzco and Puno during the early post-independence decades arose from the new layers of local and provincial officeholders created by the republican state. There has been a lively debate among historians recently as to how strong these groups had become by midcentury and how much damage they had inflicted on peasant communities by then.[44] Certainly, the relationship established between district governors, tax collectors, justices of the peace, provincial subprefects, and judges of first instance, on the one hand, and Indian communities or individual peasant families, on the other, were central both for building a republican state and for the entrenchment of local and provincial elites that by the late nineteenth century became reviled as *gamonales*. This broadening layer of local and provincial representatives of the central state sought to bully, cajole, or force peasant communities to pay a maximum amount of taxes and fees, render labor services for public and private purposes, and relinquish control over certain communal lands. But often these authorities still lacked the power to force their will on the communities. As administrations changed frequently and had become politicized, communities could negotiate and appeal to rival authorities. While one finds evidence for abusive local authorities during this time, reports by subprefects and governors exasperated about their powerlessness vis-à-vis the communities are no less frequent.[45]

Peasants appear to have pitched their discourse according to the audience and issue at hand. In disputes over land with owners of estates, adjudicated through courts, justices of the peace, or notaries, they stressed their title rights, as individual proprietors, derived from the 1828 legislation. In matters of taxation, however, they defended land as vital for the whole community's ability to maintain its livelihood and pay *contribución de indígenas*. Most communities in Cuzco and Puno lost little land between independence and 1850.

Inside the communities of the southern sierra the early republican regime and its ambiguous reform legislation of the 1820s fostered increasingly differentiated local practices. In many communities of Puno, where livestock herders during the 1830s became integrated into the wool-export funnel, communal administration of lands was largely reduced to the scant crop lands worked through communal rotation (*lihua* plots). Family descent groups within the communities, kin groups of up to ten households, shared usufruct of pastures while treating the same land as private property in terms of inheritance and at times for sale or lease. Still, whole communities rallied to defend lands that they considered part of their territory against neighboring communities or private landholders.[46] In Cuzco's upland provinces, such as Canas, issues of family inheritance of land were also becoming more important by the 1840s.[47] Yet at least in the cereal-growing regions of Cuzco, such as the province of Anta, most plots continued to be redistributed annually by the communal authorities, even if families retained the same plots year after year.[48] And throughout Puno and Cuzco departments, community peasants continued to think that their rights to lands, even to those considered family property, were somehow reaffirmed and strengthened by rendering *servicios personales* and participating in the *cargo* system, the communal offices and services supervised and exploited by local authorities.[49] But this was hardly a reaffirmation of the "colonial compact" between community and state, whereby rights to land were guaranteed to Andean *ayllus* in exchange for accepting their vassalage to the king, expressed through tribute payment and *mita* labor. Rather, it affirmed the embeddedness of their lands, even if viewed as family property, within ethnic communities that the Andeans themselves still considered as distinct (although not categorically separate) from the Hispanic realm.[50]

The agrarian structure of the central Peruvian department of Junin had been unusual even during the colonial period. While some livestock estates had developed in the *puna* regions, the fertile bottomlands of the Mantaro Valley dedicated to producing corn and wheat were largely controlled by smallholders and peasant communities. This did not change in the aftermath of the agrarian reform legislation of the 1820s. Peasants from the valley were actively participating in a regional market economy by selling cereals and livestock products in Lima and the nearby mining districts, by plying the roads as muleteers or by working in the mines during the agricultural off-season. As the regional economy flourished between the late 1830s and 1870s, so did the majority of peasant households. Before the War of the Pacific (1879–1884), students of the region agree, peasants lost little land.[51]

Yet the insertion of the peasants into thriving regional trading circuits, together with the republic's new fiscal and agrarian policies, initiated rather deep changes in the very nature of the communities. Ethnic cohesion diminished. In- and out-migration, as well as the purchase and sale of parcels of land, became frequent, all pointing to heightened social mobility. Community peasant families who received title to their land through the 1820s agrarian reform were viewed—for tax purposes at least—as *castas* (people of mixed racial descent). And new collection mechanisms for the *contribución de indígenas*—switching from collective to individual responsibility for its payment—diminished the power of the communal authorities.[52]

By the mid-nineteenth century the ethnic corporate community of the colonial era was being replaced in the Mantaro Valley with a "new type of rural community based on the voluntary association of peasant families."[53] In this favored Andean ecological space the liberal planks of the post-independence policies functioned as a permissive frame for the gradual dissolution of the corporate Indian peasant community, a process whose roots were to be sought in more gradual economic, cultural, and social processes. Moreover, many community peasant families seem to have embraced the broadening options for redefining their individual and group identity offered by the republican order. Certainly, these effects of the agrarian and fiscal reforms of the 1820s did not as yet lead to rapidly accelerating encroachments upon their resources.[54]

On the north coast Indian communities at the moment of independence were concentrated close to the ocean, in the lower part of the short river valleys emerging from the Andes, where access to water was scant. In the vast province of Piura (elevated to the rank of department in 1861), haciendas raising goats and cattle, and producing cereals and a few other crops for regional markets, occupied the plains of the Rio Chira and the upper run of the Rio Piura, where water for irrigation was relatively plentiful. But the plains surrounding the lower run of the Rio Piura, below the provincial capital, where the river frequently dried out, were occupied by the enormous Indian communities of Catacaos and Sechura. Here, a surprisingly dense population—with over sixty percent of the province's total population as late as 1876—was eking out a living by a complex adaptation to the difficult environment. In years of plentiful water native varieties of cotton, as well as maize and legumes, were planted in the floodplains and the few fields that could still be reached by the remnants of pre-Hispanic irrigation canals. In years when the river remained dry below Piura agriculture was reduced to planting garden plots irrigated from hand-carried well water and utilizing the oasis patches of pasture and tamarind trees in the *despoblado* (the arid plain south of the river valley imperceptibly passing into the Sechura Desert) for tending a few goats. Fishing, the sale of salt, working as muleteers, and a wide variety of artisanal activities—especially spinning, weaving, and hatmaking—assumed strategic importance for the livelihood of the Catacaos and Sechuranos.[55]

Early republican legislation here did not immediately threaten the continued control of the communities and their Indian residents over resources. But it did exacerbate and accelerate internal economic differentiation as well as the development of a more fluid notion of community. Buying and selling of parcels of land became more frequent, as did conflicts over inheritance. It was increasingly less clear what lands belonged to the community, and precisely what this signified in terms of individual families' rights to the land. Declaring specific parcels of land to be communal property was becoming a ploy in the struggle over land between various families.[56] In 1838 the Catacaos lost a court case that forbade them to dislodge old *mestizo* residents within the geographic space of the community, probably the remaining former labor tenants of an hacienda that had passed into control of lineages of communal families. The judge considered not allowing the *mestizos* to hold title to the lands they presently possessed as a breach of the agrarian reform law of 1828, which had expressly included *mestizos*. Establishing differences "between the sons of one people, brothers and compatriots," differences "unknown to the laws and repugnant to reason," would "tend to subvert the social order."[57] Clearly, the judge of Piura had a rather different understanding of Peru's social order than the elite in Cuzco and Puno, for whom these differences remained highly significant.

In the 1838 court case, the Catacaos identified themselves as "the community of Catacaos, and thus the municipality." In 1868, Congress acceded to the petition of the community's officers and elevated it to the rank of "city," with important fiscal, electoral, and administrative consequences.[58] Notions of republican citizenship mattered greatly to these "Indian community peasants." Yet during the whole of the nineteenth century the citizens of Catacaos and Sechura continued to insist on their identity as members of Indian communities, still marked through ethnic dress and ceremonial practices, although no longer through use of their ancestral Tallan language. By the mid-nineteenth century Catacaos and Sechura were becoming rural Peruvian towns, with their municipal institutions, urban professionals, and incipient citizens' associations, which insisted upon their ethnic indigenous status as a matter of pride, control over resources, and power for native family lineages.

Liberalism Unbound and the Invisible Community, 1854–1879

The quarter-century between the early 1850s and the mid-1870s in Peru, as in most Latin American countries, represented the high-water mark for liberalism, due especially to three domestic and external constellations: 1) The rise of free-trade policies among the major industrializing powers of the North Atlantic region, symbolized by Great Britain's repeal of the corn laws in 1846, helped persuade politicians, merchants, and growing numbers of regional *hacendado* groups in Peru to embrace such policies as well, especially as they increasingly reaped benefits from selling products to European export merchants established in the port cities; 2) the spectacular boom of guano exports between 1847 and 1873 led to a fivefold increase of state revenues, tempting governments to lower or abolish other tax income,[59] and it also helped to set the stage for broadening discussions about the relation between the state and society; and 3) the European revolutionary cycle of 1848–49, its liberal and democratic impulses and its authoritarian-repressive aftermaths, inspired radical, reformist, and authoritarian intellectuals to seek the incorporation of European political ideas into the Peruvian polity.[60]

While many Peruvian writers and politicians during this quarter-century of liberalism's heyday proudly identified their ideas as liberal, only a small coterie of ideologues, such as José and Pedro Gálvez, Mariano Amezaga, and José Simeón Tejeda, identified themselves as Liberals with a capital *L*; a Liberal Party of any consequence only emerged in the early years of the twentieth century. Most influential figures espoused liberal ideas in a complex amalgam with authoritarian, corporatist, or racist ideas. This was the era in which the Indian community nearly disappeared from public discourse, and some politicians even attempted to outlaw the institution altogether. When people discussed the Indian at all, as during the mid-1850s and between 1866 and the early 1870s, the debate focused on a stereotyped individual, and whether he was a proprietor or a worker, a distinction of far-reaching political consequence. Politicians and essayists were concerned about how best to integrate him into the republican order, for which most now considered the community merely as a deleterious remnant.

Peru's first civil code, promulgated on Independence Day, July 28, 1852, did not mention the Indian community at all. Its aims were to strengthen and extend a finely woven net of legal norms over all types of property and all contractual obligations; put differently, the code was to strengthen guarantees for property and contracts. While the conservative commission that drew up the code sought to retain many strictures over the economic behavior of citizens, it included liberal provisions that aimed at broadening the circulation and distribution of landed property, through equal inheritance among all heirs at law and the disamortization of church property.[61] Writing early in the twentieth century, the conservative intellectual Francisco García Calderón claimed that these provisions of the Civil Code signified, "in the political realm, the condemnation of any oligarchy, of any latifundia aristocracy, in the social order the ascent of the bourgeoisie and of mestizaje." The Civil Code, in his view, had distributed private wealth broadly and given a boost to small property.[62]

But the effects of the Civil Code were quite distinct from its presumed liberal intent. It was characterized by juridical formalism, favoring complex proofs of property rights, which placed poor and illiterate litigants at an automatic disadvantage. Indeed, over the next eighty years these formalistic legal figures became important tools used by ruthless *gamonales* for grabbing land from community peasants.[63] Moreover, the Civil Code completely neglected to consider and regulate the vast area of customary practices inside the peasant communities. Like a huge blank spot on a map, the legislators, fascinated by the rationalistic figures of Napoleonic law, were silent about that parallel "configuration of rights and obligations regulating the rural world," which continued to shape the Indians' "personal relations, their systems of communal property, their regime of inheritance and the nature of their conventions."[64] In the words of Jorge Basadre, by the 1850s the Indian community had become "a submerged juridical patrimony, alive in the soul and customs of the peasants, although invisible and strange to the formal mentality of legislators, magistrates and authorities."[65]

This did not mean the abolition of the Indian community by the Peruvian legislators, in contrast to what happened in Mexico, where during the Wars of the Reform Liberals applied the 1856 Ley Lerdo by confiscating and auctioning off community lands not registered by the peasants as individual property. Yet the gap between the formalistic liberal notion of private property espoused by the Civil Code and the variegated communitarian practices of Peru's Indian peasants opened the door to a prolonged debate as to whether the latter really were proprietors of their land and enjoyed the corresponding protection of the law. In 1858, for example, the mayor of Cuzco, Francisco Garmendia, sought clarification from the government in Lima as to whether the Indian community peasants in his province were to be considered as property owners and thus had the right to participate in popular elections. His doubts arose because the community peasants "have not considered themselves as such [as property owners, that is] but as mere holders of usufruct rights; none of them has been able to sell their plots, nor have they passed them to their heirs . . . ; rather they have routinely given the plots to others in new communal distributions." These doubts were reinforced by the fact that since the abolition of the *contribución de indígenas* in 1854, the Indians did not pay taxes on their land any longer.[66] The lawyer for the ministry of government, the doctrinaire Liberal José Simeón Tejeda, brushed Garmendia's doubts aside and reminded the mayor of the proprietary rights that the Indians had gained over their lands by the law of March 31, 1828: "The fact that the Indians until today have not put the full title to their lands into practice . . . in no way argues against the law, because facts do not destroy rights." The "abuses" committed by tax collectors, *caciques*, and *revisitadores* in carrying out redistributions of communal lands "cannot serve as precedents against the laws."[67]

Ironically, Garmendia's doubts about the status of Indian peasants as proprietors had been reinforced by the abolition of *contribución de indígenas* by Ramón Castilla on July 5, 1854. The measure had immediate political goals, as Castilla hoped to attract the support of Indians in the popular revolution against the corrupt government of José Rufino Echenique. But it symbolically marked the erstwhile end to the government's treatment of the Indian as member of a corporate group. The decree aimed at "putting into practice the rights of liberty, equality and property" guaranteed in the Constitution.[68] But for Mayor Garmendia property—one of the sources of production, along with capital, labor, and industrial skills—was only recognizable as such if taxes were paid on it.[69] Most Indian smallholders were exempt from paying property tax, as their holdings were said to produce rents below the minimum assessment. This was the ideological construct by which Garmendia had taken the abolition of *contribución de indígenas* to weaken the status of the Indians as proprietors of their community lands.

Within a year after abolishing the *contribución de indígenas*, the administration of President Ramón Castilla sought to introduce a new head tax labeled *contribución personal*, but the attempt failed after heated political debate. The government installed a commission, chaired by the conservative Felipe Pardo y Aliaga, with the charge to overhaul the entire system of direct taxation. The commission argued that the nation urgently needed new direct taxes, much diminished through the abolition of the *contribución de indígenas*. Even with the bountiful revenues from guano sales, government budgets contained deficits now, and everybody anticipated that "this income [from guano sales] will disappear in a very few years." "Woe to the Republic if once this happens the means to face national expenditures are not well entrenched!"[70]

The centerpiece of the new tax scheme was to be a *contribución personal* levied on all male heads of households. In contrast to the abolished *contribución de indígenas*, this was to be a tax on work, on "the product of personal labor." Theoretically it eschewed any racial classification, and the commissioners expressly called for "banning from our official language the repugnant denomination of indígenas and castas." The tax was to be calculated at the rate of six daily wages of two reales per year (for a total of 1.5 pesos), in those provinces where standard wage rates were below four reales, and of six daily wages of four reales per year (for a total of three pesos) where standard wages lay above four reales. The commissioners justified their plan as a measure of equity. In their conception every source of income should be taxed separately. Besides the taxes on property and on industrial production already on the books, it was fair to tax the fruits of labor. Yet this presumed measure of tax equity aimed specifically at the Indians. Since the abolition of *contribución de indígenas*, the commissioners argued, Indians were not contributing anything to the revenues of the nation, and "equality of rights with all the inhabitants also necessarily presupposes equality of obligations."[71] This proposal, then, arose from the same conception of the Indian that prompted Garmendia's query of 1858: The Indian community peasant was not a property owner, but a worker, and the only way to integrate him into the national polity was as such.[72]

By the mid-1860s such ideas had become fairly common, buttressed by the recent spread of the doctrines of classical economics and modern racism.[73] In 1867 an anonymous pamphlet writer seeking to explain the causes of the Bustamante Rebellion (1866–1868) in the Peruvian *altiplano* suggested that it was due to the impoverishment of the highlands, which he claimed to have begun in 1854 with the abolition of *contribución de indígenas*. Because the Indian race was naturally lazy and frugal, and the land in Peru was very fertile, the Indian peasant only needed to work a fraction of his time for subsistence. Since the Incas, the land worked by the Indians had always been viewed as state lands for which they needed to pay rent, either in the form of labor or of a monetary tribute. It was through this rent-paying mechanism that the Indian was forced to work more than was necessary for subsistence. The abolition of *contribución de indígenas* had thus led to the diminution of labor power in the highlands, causing a reduction in production, skyrocketing prices for agricultural goods, and a crisis for many estates. In order to overcome this presumed crisis *contribución personal* urgently needed to be introduced. In fact the Indians themselves were clamoring for it, the author claimed, because they viewed the head tax as "rent for a parcel of land, which they owned neither before nor after the conquista."[74] This and other similar pamphlets utterly misconstrued the economic development of Peruvian agriculture from the mid-1850s to the mid-1860s, characterized by rapid growth in many regions of the coast and the highlands. More importantly for the purposes of the issues of this essay, they completely ignored the agrarian-reform legislation of the 1820s, which had made the Indian peasant a proprietor of the land he worked.[75] In effect such ideas represented an updating, in the language of liberal political economy and modern racism, of colonial notions about crown-sanctioned tribute and labor extraction from the Indian community in exchange for guaranteed usufruct of land.[76]

The *contribución personal* was finally introduced in 1866, abolished in 1867, reintroduced by various governments between 1879 and 1885, and abolished for good by the Congress of 1895, although it lingered in various departments and provinces at least until 1900.[77] Even if certain groups of Andean peasants continued to insist on some form of reciprocity between labor and tax obligations in exchange for state guarantees on the possession of communal lands, the *contribución personal* was sufficiently unpopular to figure as the major cause of the two largest "Indian rebellions" during the second half of the nineteenth century, the Bustamante Rebellion of 1866–1868, and the Atusparia Rebellion of 1885.[78]

But liberalism also influenced the ideas of those who rejected the *contribución personal* and the reduction of the Indian peasant to "worker." Santiago Tavara, a prominent liberal supporter of Castilla's revolution of 1854, was outraged when a year later his *caudillo* sought to reintroduce the head tax, now in the guise of a tax on labor. "A social question of general and profound influence for our society has been reduced . . . to a fiscal issue." "The reestablishment of the head tax is unjust, antisocial, impolitic, anti-economic and inefficient." It would lead, Tavara wrote, to renewed abuses by the collectors and would hit the poorest members of society, who only had their labor power to sell, much harder than those with property and capital. The abolition of *contribución de indígenas* had amounted to the emancipation of the Indian from servility; it made him "an independent man." Reimposing it now under a different guise would stamp the Indian as a useless proletarian. The way to overcome any fiscal shortfalls in Távara's view was to strengthen the property taxes, to form precise cadastres of real estate, and accurate, up-to-date registers of all the professions and businesses. Most Indians would continue to be exempt from paying property tax, because of what Távara presumed to be the minimal size of their landholdings. But he had little doubt that to integrate the Indian into the polity, to overcome all his supposed vices accumulated through centuries of servility, it was necessary to treat him as a citizen equal to those who held property.[79]

A decade later Juan Bustamante outlined a vision of an integrated Peruvian *mestizo* nation in which the property and personal rights of each individual Indian would be guaranteed by a just state. A self-educated *mestizo* businessman, world traveler, writer, and politician from the southern highland department of Puno, Bustamante had fought for years to relieve the plight of Indian community peasants and estate *colonos*. In 1867, he made himself spokesman of the Indian community peasants from the *altiplano* who were protesting against the reimposed *contribución personal* and abuses by local authorities, protests that were read as an "Indian rebellion" or "caste war" by the majority of the regional Hispanicized elite pursuing political goals opposed to those of Bustamante. In August of 1867, he founded the "Sociedad Amiga de los Indios," a milestone in the history of Peru's pro-Indian rights movements, and also for the unfolding of the country's civil society.

Bustamante's conception of the place of the Indian in the Peruvian polity was anchored in the abstract liberalism of the 1820s Bolívarian reform legislation. It seemed scandalous to him that the equality of citizen rights, which then had been bestowed upon the Indian, continued to be flouted by governors, priests, justices of the peace, military commanders, and *hacendados*. The life of Indian peasants and estate *colonos* had in his view changed little from their deplorable state under the Spanish tyranny. A manifesto that the directorate of the Sociedad Amiga de los Indios addressed to Peru's Indian peasantry listed eight frequent abuses against which they should be on their guard. One concerned the issue of property:

> Nobody can take away from you that which you own individually or collectively, nor force you to sell, for a price you do not agree to, your house, your livestock, your wool or any of the articles that you weave or otherwise produce with your hands, or which you make your lands produce by sowing, cultivating and harvesting; anybody who tries to take these goods from you at a price which you do not agree to, commits a crime against your freedom and property, against whom you have the right to defend yourself with all [legal] means.[80]

Like all Peruvian writers and politicians of the mid-nineteenth century, Bustamante was concerned with the Indian as an individual citizen, not with the community. But in stressing the importance of property rights, Bustamante pragmatically included "collective" landholdings, underscoring both his familiarity with the southern sierra's communities and the sincerity of his paternalist concerns for the Indians' rights.

Bustamante's agenda was twofold. In order to achieve the transformation of the Indians into productive citizens, he stressed both the need for society to enforce rigorously their equal rights, trampled upon to date, and the need for the Indians to assimilate to what Bustamante saw as the standards of enlightened society: they needed to learn Spanish, send their children to school, adopt European garb, and improve their hygiene. Yet what was novel in Bustamante's approach was that he placed this transformation within civil society. The transformation was to come about through voluntary efforts within civil society, through exhortation of the Indians by members of the Sociedad Amiga de los Indios and other well-meaning citizens. For Bustamante, the ownership of property was an unconditional basis of Indian citizenship.

But this kind of association between citizens' rights and voluntary liberalism remained highly fragile when applied to the Indian. Only a few months after Juan Bustamante was brutally executed in early January 1868 following the defeat of his peasant troops, Miguel Zavala, founding member of the Sociedad Amiga de los Indios, published a legislative project that purported to push the same Indian-rights agenda. Yet Zavala reverted to proposing a heavy-handed authoritarian state institution to guide the Indian in achieving the transformation into productive citizen. In his view, the originally vigorous and intelligent Indian had become a dim-witted, lazy brute through four-and-a-half centuries of "benevolent tutelary despotism" of the Incas and through three centuries of "slavery" under the Spaniards. In establishing the republic, Peru's founding fathers followed ill-considered radical democratic, egalitarian ideas when they bestowed the full civil and political rights on the Indians, which redounded to the Indians' own disadvantage as they did not understand these rights and could not use them. From the application of the democratic "principle of majorities" thus resulted "the humiliating and ridiculous absurdity that the Sovereignty of Peru was placed in the hands of an idiot race of proletarians, given that this race [the Indians] formed the overwhelming majority." But in spite of these citizens rights, and in spite of having been granted a number of "privileges, such as complete property rights and the abolition of *contribución de indígenas*, "in fact the Indian is the same Pariah" because these laws fell into disuse.[81] Since Indians were naturally lazy, their absolute freedom meant a reduction in their work, which hurt the interests of both the private landlords and the nation. Thus it was not surprising that local authorities colluded with the *hacendados* in committing a "crime of oppression and tyranny" against the Indians by forcing them to work for the *hacendados*, in violation of the "aborigines' rights and guarantees."

The only way to stop these abuses in Zavala's mind was the appointment of a "Protector of Indians" in every province. He would be responsible for the kind of dual agenda outlined by the Sociedad Amiga de los Indios: rooting out the abuses against Indians "regarding diminution of his freedom, mistreatment of his person, violence or fraud in contracts, usurpation of his properties, or fraudulent compensation of his labor" committed by *hacendados*, local authorities, priests, or anybody else. Contracts involving goods valued at over eighty soles—primarily land—would be valid only if signed by the Protector. At the same time the Protector was to civilize the Indians, by checking on the hygiene and decency in every peasant hut, by registering all seven- to twelve-year-old Indian children for school attendance, and by enforcing a proposed labor decree, through which any Indian deemed vagrant could be arrested and put to forced labor for one to four days. But it was to be strictly prohibited to force Indians to work for others "when they have their own work on their property, exercise any industry or dedicate themselves to domestic occupations."[82]

Zavala justified the urgency of such Draconian interventionist measures through an evolutionary scheme that was liberal only on the surface. Society was ascending from despotism to freedom, as from childhood to adulthood. Peru's Indians were still like children, and thus it was to their own benefit to have their freedom restricted. Freedom, in any case, "ceases where it does not correspond to rational goals." Indians still needed to be taught that work was a "natural law," an existential condition imposed by the "Supreme Creator." Once Indians had been brought to moral adulthood they could be released into the full freedom of civil society and Peru's national polity.[83]

Zavala's plan, then, was to root out abuses and forced labor arbitrarily imposed upon Indians by powerful individuals through a state-imposed regime of tutelage and forced labor: "driving out the devil with Satan," as the German saying goes. In the name of Indian protection, he proposed a state intervention that moved in the same direction as the liberal Guatemalan regime's *mandamiento* decrees of the 1870s, which aimed at supplying labor for the burgeoning coffee estates.[84] Zavala's was the project in Peru's core liberal era (1850–1879) that most explicitly called for tutelage of the Indians, a notion that would gain broad currency during the early twentieth century. Significantly, it was not approved in 1868. Yet it vividly demonstrates how liberal precepts of property rights and individual responsibility were often coupled to, indeed subverted by, updated authoritarian colonial notions of Indian separateness, dependency, and limited rights.[85]

But in all the public debates about the Indian during the liberal era, during the mid-1850s, and between 1866 and the mid-1870s, the community was nearly totally absent, at best mentioned as an obstacle to the development of an industrious citizenry. In another pro-Indian rights project introduced in Congress in September of 1868 by Pio Benigno Meza, senator and wealthy large landholder from Cuzco, *ayllus* and *parcialidades*, "to which the Indians were subjected under the dependency of the so-called caciques, curacas, mandones and segundos," were not to be recognized anymore.[86] This project seems to have been voted down. But in 1876 the administration of Manuel Pardo, credited recently by scholars as putting forth the most serious developmentalist project of the era, issued a decree reaffirming the law of March 1828 about full property rights of the community peasants. But it added the new twist that communities could not intervene in the sale of land by any of its members.[87] The Indian community was here viewed as an institute of force, indeed often as nothing but a ploy by local or provincial bosses to exploit the peasants' labor or land.[88] Those few writers who, like Zavala, continued to proclaim the need to protect the Indian, even at the height of liberalism's influence, did not think of the community as the appropriate institution, now doubly tainted as the residue of a detested ethnic identity and an artificial construct of illegitimate dependency and exploitation. If the liberal vision allowed any institutional protection at all, it was to be proffered by the modern nation-state in favor of the individual Indian, a ward in training for citizenship. But at the height of liberalism the call for Indian protection was rather insignificant, a distant echo of the colonial past, or the first whispers of modern state-sponsored *indigenismo*.

More important was the debate between viewing the Indian as a mere worker, without property and with limited citizen's rights, or as a proprietor of a plot of land in the community, endowed with full rights of Peruvian citizenship. Clearly those who saw the Indian peasant as a proprietor with full citizens' rights were in the minority. Given the preponderance of an updated authoritarian vision of the Indian peasant as an unproductive worker with diminished capacities, requiring some type of coercion to be valuable for the nation, it is surprising how little legislation was passed during the three decades of liberalism's heyday that was positively damaging to the interests of the Indian peasantry.

On the ground, in the various districts and provinces across Peru, the fate of the community seems to have varied greatly during the third quarter of the nineteenth century. In the Peruvian *altiplano*, some peasant communities lost lands to expanding or newly founded haciendas. By that time a new republican provincial elite had emerged in the region, composed of families who profited from the exportation of wools and the consolidation of positions of authority due to enhanced state revenues. These commercial and politico-administrative developments allowed a few dozen families to integrate peasants into client networks based on trade and credit advances. Inside many communities the language and practice of private property began to take hold, as the frequency of sales and mortgage contracts, as well as litigation over land, increased and a small number of peasants habitually paid property tax on their *estancias*. Yet Indian peasants differentiated between the right to transfer land—where liberal notions of individual rights were applied—and the practices attached to the use of land, where the communities or, more often, family descent groups still played a preponderant role. Thus one finds documents that speak of the same plots of land as both, *tierras del común* and private property of certain individuals. Conflicts within and between peasant families of one community, often resulting in litigation, arose from this ambiguity. In order to strengthen the practice of common usufruct of land, some descent groups registered the family *estancia* as joint property of all heirs in the tax rolls. Corrupt or clientelistic justices of the peace, professional judges of first instance in the provincial capitals, district governors, and provincial subprefects did little to help establish property legislation as an unambiguous and impartial arbiter of practice. The laws instead became tools, and the courts became arenas in the contests for power between various *gamonal* factions.[89]

In the uplands of the department of Cuzco, adjacent to the *altiplano*, the rising demand for wool during the third quarter of the nineteenth century translated into a period of economic and demographic growth and social differentiation within the peasant communities.[90] The conflicts over resources generated by external demand were similar to those in Puno. Yet until late in the nineteenth century they were often played out inside the peasant communities. The newly emerging stratum of large landholders, the *mistis*, often came from families of affluent community peasants who had done well in the wool trade. As late as the 1870s, twenty years after the abolition of the *contribución de indígenas*, many communities had officers called *caciques recaudadores*, responsible for the collection of various taxes and fees, who often received community pasture lands considered vacant by the provincial authorities. Community lands continued to be viewed as in some way under the control of the state. Only Congress's swift abrogation of the new *contribución personal* in early 1867, during the mounting peasant protest movements in Huancané and La Mar provinces, led to a major campaign to inscribe lands of community peasants in the property tax rolls: In Canas province the number of inscribed peasants jumped from 51 in 1850 to 1,390 in 1871 and 2,035 in 1877, only to fall to 217 in 1888, after the renewed introduction of *contribución personal* in 1885. In 1892 numerous peasants from a community in Yauri district protested the inclusion of their lands in the property tax lists on the grounds that they only held "community lands."

Even though many of the protesters operated flourishing family livestock enterprises, the peasants in Canas, as elsewhere in Cuzco, continued to invoke the notion of communal property in defense of their resources.

During the late 1850s, even before the first shot had been fired in the U.S. Civil War, British merchants were prospecting for new regions to supply cotton for the mighty textile mills of Manchester. In Peru they set their sights on the vast plains surrounding the Piura and Chira rivers on the north coast. During the last four decades of the nineteenth century cotton production in the department of Piura surged, and the region supplied more than 50 percent of Peru's total cotton production until 1894.[91] But this commercial takeoff of a hitherto rather sleepy region brought with it changes in its agrarian structure, intensifying social and political conflicts. The arena for these struggles was the territories of the Indian communities of the lower Piura, especially Catacaos, where the land was deemed especially good for cotton cultivation. The issue that triggered the conflict was access to water, and the construction of irrigation canals, without which cotton production could not be expanded significantly. The conflict first erupted in the 1860s, when powerful *hacendado* families from the Upper Piura Valley appropriated more and more water to turn their semiarid pastures into cotton fields and members of the departmental elite proposed a vast system of canals. But until the late 1880s these elite projects largely failed, because they were unable to draw labor away from the communities of the lower Piura and lacked the land most appropriate for cotton cultivation, which was still controlled by the Catacaos and Sechuranos. Much of the early expansion of cotton cultivation was undertaken by lower Piura's community peasants, increasing plantings of their hardy perennial variety of cotton, which they sold to the merchants and owners of cotton gins.[92]

The proposal of a dam and irrigation canals in the Piura River Valley by members of the department's large landholding elite in 1866 mobilized the Indian communities/towns of Catacaos and Sechura. The dam was to be constructed above the city of Piura, and the proponents demanded a fifty-year privilege prohibiting any other irrigation project along the river, and the right to charge users for the water from their irrigation canals.[93] The project infuriated the communities of the Lower Piura. In their letters of protest and petitions to higher authorities, they stressed that this was an attack on ancient rights of "the community of proprietary natives," on the water and lands of "the one single family which we, the Catacaos, are." They were peaceful proprietors, the leaders of Catacaos pointed out, whose labors benefited the well-being of the entire department, while the proponents of the irrigation were mere speculators who despised "the indigenous farmer who disembowels the earth with his sweat and drudgery to provide sustenance and life to all classes of society." Prophetically, they declared that after losing control over their water they would lose control over their land; they would be converted from proprietors into peons, forced into "mendicancy and sloth."[94]

The municipal council of the province of Piura, far from representing the department's *hacendados*, cited the "great public displeasure" which the proposed dam and irrigation scheme had caused "in the masses." It chastised the cynicism with which its proponents had petitioned the government for a privilege that was only the Indian communities' right to grant as legal owners of the water and lands in question.[95] The authorities of Catacaos declared that even without long-promised government aid the whole community was resolved to carry out its own irrigation project, "for the progress of our agriculture," "to fulfill the duties which the Nation imposes on us."[96]

Immediately after defeating the *hacendados'* project, the municipality and Indian community of Catacaos began to work on its own irrigation project, without any help from the government. On Independence Day, July 28, 1867, the mayor called the citizens together in the plaza. After the ringing of the bells, and the singing of the national anthem, the fifty-three male community members present solemnly signed a declaration pledging to rebuild the pre-Hispanic irrigation canal Tacalá. As "native owners of the valley of Catacaos" they had an indisputable right to carry out this irrigation project, and thus "to enjoy the goods which our freedom and political emancipation entail." A *juez divisor de tierras* was to be named for the project, who would assign parcels of the hitherto undivided community land—the arid pastures to be irrigated now—to all the community members, including those not presently living in Catacaos. The municipality would present "a certificate confirming property" to every community member receiving a plot of irrigation land. Every male adult member of the community had to contribute three days of labor for the opening of the canals; failure to do so would forfeit one's right to a parcel of land. It was strictly forbidden to gather in the *chicherias* (pubs) during the days when communal work on the canal was carried out. Elaborate regulations were drawn up governing the assembly of the workers in the various sectors of Catacaos, as well as "the mathematical measurement" of the land to be distributed. A Sociedad de Agricultura was founded, which was to be in charge of all matters relating to land and water in the community.

The purpose of the communal irrigation project was twofold. It would allow the community members to put more land—now only used to graze a few goats and cattle—into lucrative production of cotton, thus contributing to Catacaos' well-being. But at the same time it was viewed as a defensive measure: by putting the vacant and arid communal lands into regular cotton production in the form of individual family-farm property, the community hoped to block the attempts by wealthy and powerful outsiders to appropriate lands inside the communal domain. Thus the July 28 declaration and the regulations of the Sociedad de Agricultura emphasized the obligation of every community member receiving a parcel of land to cultivate it annually; failure to do so gave the Sociedad de Agricultura the right to rent out the plot to a third person.[97]

The municipality of the province of Piura and the Prado administration in Lima welcomed the project of the Catacaos. On August 19, 1867, after enthusiastic addresses by their own mayor, the parish priest, the subprefect, and the mayor of Piura, all exalting the "heroic and patriotic efforts" of the Indian community, an estimated two thousand community peasants began the labors of refurbishing their old Tacalá canal.[98] Catacaos never completed the reconstruction of the Tacalá, but the community built various smaller irrigation canals until the late 1880s.

In 1891 all communal irrigation projects of the preceding quarter-century in Catacaos and Sechura were destroyed as a result of major floods caused by a "Niño," which changed the course of the Piura River and forced many community peasants to abandon their native territory. From then on all irrigation projects were carried out by powerful entrepreneurs and the Peruvian government. In the 1870s entrepreneurs began to acquire parcels of land in Catacaos, which were expanded more rapidly in the 1890s and the first decade of the new century. With the completion of new irrigation projects controlled by outsiders, such plots were consolidated into haciendas of forty to one thousand hectares, dedicated to the cultivation of more productive, but ecologically problematic varieties of cotton. While most new *hacendados* came from families of Piura's emerging elite or immigrants such as the Hilbcks or the Romeros, some in fact came from within the community of Catacaos, such as the Yarlequés. By 1914 the small native farmers of Catacaos were reduced to less than one-fourth (21.7 percent) of the expanding area of irrigated lands in their district.[99] More and more Catacaos and Sechuranos had to rely on income from fishing, crafts, trade, or working as *yanaconas* (sharecroppers) on estates throughout the department of Piura.

More than most communities in Peru, Catacaos demonstrated the contradictions, dangers, and possibilities associated with liberalism for indigenous agriculturalists during the third quarter of the nineteenth century. The leading families of Catacaos embraced the republican order from the beginning, to the point that communal (ethnic) authorities were given up in favor of municipal (republican) authorities. By the 1860s they adopted the liberal agrarian agenda by calling for the distribution of the remaining communal lands in fee simple to all members of the community when irrigation was to convert those lands from pastures into cotton fields. As a vehicle for this project, they introduced another important innovation that expressed the associational, civil-society notions of liberalism: in all matters concerning land the community constituted itself as a Sociedad de Agricultura, a voluntary association of citizens tied by common interest, that is, by landownership within the boundaries of the municipality and community of Catacaos. Clearly, the affluent and educated communal elite embraced key tenets of liberalism. Yet they steadfastly insisted upon being members of an Indian community when it came to matters concerning the integrity of the communal domain—conceived of as a separate space reserved for the native sons and daughters. The Catacaos had created a complex set of institutions and identities: governed by a republican municipality, and representing their interests as property owners through a voluntary association, they defined themselves as the native people of Catacaos, with their own "Indian" myths, festivities, and customs. The leading families of Catacaos aspired to be citizens of the republic, "progressive" farmer-agriculturists and members of an Indian community at one and the same time. They also sought to keep maximum control over the domain of Catacaos. To block any critique of their defense of that domain as barbaric, or anachronistic, they adopted the discourse through which provincial and national elites hoped to integrate Indians into the nation, and they pushed for development projects that would transform the community's economy into a "modern" export-oriented economy. Indeed, the leading citizens of Catacaos had formed important alliances with certain political and social groups in Piura. In the short run, until the late 1880s, they were quite successful in keeping control of the land and water of the community in local hands. It may be that when the avalanche of modern irrigation and estate formation commenced during the 1890s the leading families of the community were in a position to benefit from the process to a greater degree than previously thought.

Conclusion: The New Corporatism and the Community of Peasant Freeholders

Let us return to the critique of liberalism which José Carlos Mariátegui formulated during the mid-1920s, more than forty years after the devastating War of the Pacific (1879–1884) had brought the liberal era of Peruvian politics to an end. "The formal liberalism of republican legislation," Mariátegui noted, "only acted against the Indian 'community.' The concept of individual property has had almost an antisocial function in the republic, because of its conflict with the existence of the 'community.'" This would have been acceptable in the framework of a vigorous capitalism, through which dispossessed communal peasants would have been forced to organize themselves as free wage laborers, Peru's true proletarians preparing to challenge the country's bourgeoisie. But here "the gradual expropriation and absorption of the 'community' by the latifundium not only plunged [the Indian] deeper into servitude, but also destroyed the economic and legal institution that helped safeguard the spirit and substance of his ancient civilization." Mariátegui based this profoundly pessimistic evaluation of liberalism's impact on Peru's agrarian structure on his understanding of the process of fundamental change of societies:

> When a people are traditionally communist, dissolving the "community" does not help to create small properties. A society cannot be transformed artificially, still less a peasant society deeply attached to its traditions and its legal institutions. Individualism has not originated in any country's constitution or civil code. It must be formed through a more complicated and spontaneous process."[100]

Mariátegui's keen observations suffer from the polarizing and essentializing vision of institutions, classes, and races typical of his era.[101] Two trends characterizing Peruvian rural society and thought during the decades leading up to the 1920s were especially responsible for shaping views of the community. In many parts of the country haciendas had just gone through a phase of unprecedented expansion. The years around World War I may be considered the high point of the Peruvian hacienda in its long trajectory since the sixteenth century. It is easy to understand why observers from that vantage point considered the Indian community in jeopardy. Second, liberalism in Peru had come under increasing attack among Peru's intellectuals and politicians—first through positivist and anarchist writers; then, after about 1910, from nationalists and *indigenistas*; and a decade later, from socialists and conservative neo-corporatists. Retreat from the influential brands of liberalism of the pre–War of the Pacific era occurred earlier and went further concerning political and social issues, but by the 1920s it had reached economic thought and policymaking.

Mariátegui overemphasized the process of land concentration in *latifundia*, its solidity and transformative power at the expense of the communities. Even by the 1920s there still were valleys and plains in districts and entire provinces of diverse ecological setting throughout Peru in which the landed estate did not predominate. Many of the haciendas newly formed since the 1880s remained rather small, a far cry from the stereotypical *"latifundium"* of the 1920s *indigenista* literature. Moreover, in many parts of the highlands new and expanded estates remained unstable. Their borders, livestock, and installations were routinely attacked by neighboring *hacendados* and communities, while the owners' power over their own labor tenants was strictly limited. Inside the estate's borders the former community peasants who had been incorporated into the estate, together with their land, often reconstituted their communal institutions.[102] To the extent that Mariátegui was correct in assuming that liberalism was artificial, alien to the thought of Peru's community peasantry, this artificiality, or lack of acceptance in the conventions, practices, and institutional arrangements of Peru's local societies affected estate owners just as much as it did the peasantry. It meant that even by 1920 they often had not reliably gained the type of well-defined dispositionary rights over their resources that liberal notions of property and contract promised. But neither could the invocation of liberal property rights, free wage labor, and freedom of contract fortify a kind of organic "feudal" order in the Andean countryside, as Mariátegui seemed to believe.

And yet Mariátegui and other *indigenista* writers of the 1920s were clearly wrong in assuming that liberalism was totally rejected by the Andean "communistic" peasantry, that a century of agrarian policies by enlightened Bourbon statemongers, by emancipatory and authoritarian liberal nation builders—not to mention nearly four centuries of sometimes lesser, sometimes greater pressures from the market—had not been, in part, assimilated into the strategies and practices of communities and individual peasant families.[103]

By the second half of the nineteenth century marked differences had emerged concerning the impact of liberalism on various regional community complexes.[104] These differences may usefully be construed as a continuous scale, with the semisedentary communities of the Amazon basin at one extreme and the large, urbanized communities of the north coast at the other. The "tribal" Indians of the Amazon rain forest were viewed as mere laborers by entrepreneurs and government agents, without any proprietary rights to the land on which they lived. While their definition as laborers echoed categories in liberal political economy, this served as elite legitimization for instrumentalizing them through utterly "illiberal"—authoritarian to terrorist—measures, reaching its most gruesome form in the natives' enslavement and extermination in the Putumayo rubber fields between the 1890s and 1910s.[105] As most elite outsiders scoffed at the applicability of notions of property and citizenship to Amazon Indians, these had little reason to embrace any part of the liberal agenda.

The situation was quite distinct for the large north coast communities. Their claims as proprietors found much support in wider regional society, and nobody doubted that at least some of their prominent members, including lawyers, doctors, and merchants, were active citizens of the republic. It is thus not surprising that the leadership in these communities combined liberal and communitarian conceptions in representing their constituents' interests before government authorities and public opinion and in adjusting the internal governance and land tenure pattern.

The cases of most highland communities lay between these two extremes, with liberal property notions gaining greater currency in some of the communities in the Central Peruvian Andes than in the South. It was these "intermediate"-type communities where limited adaptations to liberal ideas produced the greatest resilience of the communal tradition, while the extreme cases on the scale were most exposed to the danger of disappearance, through genocidal "erasure" in the case of the Amazon "tribes" and through complete assimilation in that of the north-coast communities.

Liberal ideas found varying degrees of acceptance not only between different types of communities, but also within one and the same community. Dynamic peasant families in a good position to benefit from broader monetarized trade, or with work experience and education attained outside the community, often were the first to withdraw recognition from the old communal authorities, insisting on private-property titles for the *estancia* worked by their family, as well as "free" local trade unimpeded by the authorities, be they communal officers or district governors.[106] They pushed for a more associational—less obligatory—communal organization. Conversely, old powerful family lineages, which in many communities continued until the early twentieth century to monopolize high communal offices, often insisted on longstanding corporate practices because it could enhance their family's power and material interests through alliances with Hispanicized local authorities.[107] Insistence on "traditional" forms of communal solidarity had become by the early twentieth century as politicized and mired in group interest conflicts as the open adoption of "reformist" associational notions of community.

In short, contrary to Mariátegui's assertion of an utter rejection of liberal ideas by Peru's communities, peasants often adopted certain aspects of liberal agrarian and sociopolitical notions, while rejecting others. Throughout this essay we have encountered examples from community complexes as distinct as those of the *altiplano*, the central sierra, and the north coast that illustrate a complex pattern of purposeful, piecemeal adoption and partial rejection of liberal tenets and practices. Even in the Mantaro Valley during the early twentieth century, with communities well advanced toward becoming associational organizations, some of which would take on the form of cooperatives by the 1960s, customary local corporate restrictions continued to be placed on inheritance, designed to block the transfer of peasant land to individuals outside the community.[108] Even communities where land was routinely inherited, bought, and sold and whose members predominantly produced cash crops for monetarized markets, still clung to communal solidarity, in defending the communal domain against outsiders, in common labor projects and in religious and civil celebrations reenacting long-standing local identities with distinct ethnic overtones.

There never was a close "fit" between Peruvian liberal thought and policymaking and the battering of the Andean peasant community and its resources during the century after independence. Three strands of evidence support this assertion: the comparative timing of liberalism and pressure on Indian communities, the impact of distinctly nonliberal thought and policymaking on the communities, and the strength of *structural* socioeconomic trends, especially related to the market and population growth, in exerting pressures on peasant communities.

Liberalism gained the greatest currency in Peru during the decades of the guano boom, between the 1850s and 1870s. Although most writers and politicians at the time considered the communitarian heritage of the Andean peasantry an obstacle to their goals of an integrated, modern national society, authoritarian or democratic, the central government did little—beyond the abolition of the *contribución de indígenas* and the frequent reiteration of the principle of individual title to community lands—that might have contributed to the dissolution of communities. With the partial exception of the southern highlands, communities in most regions fared relatively well during this liberal era.

Communities came under the greatest pressure from Hispanicized landholders and local officialdom between the 1890s and 1910s. In one *altiplano* province they lost between one-third and one-half of the lands they still held during the 1850s, and most of those losses occurred after the mid-1880s. The year 1893 was the last time that the national Congress passed a declaration reiterating the core liberal tenet that all community peasants were owning their lands individually in fee simple.[109] During the first decade of the twentieth century, when communities in many regions were losing more land than in any preceding decade, liberalism had ceased to be the predominant ideology guiding government policy toward the Indian peasantry. The *civilista* governments of the era stressed technical modernization of agriculture, but many in Lima felt that the "feudal" or "semifeudal" hacienda of the highlands was blocking such progress, and began—reluctantly still—to call for the protection of the communities against encroachments by neighboring haciendas.[110] When, despite such rhetoric, the government did aid and abet abuses and encroachments against communities by *gamonales* in the sierra, it did so in the name of "saving the white race" against imminent "extermination in a race war" instigated by the indigenous peasantry, or in the name of advancing "modern civilization," or, at best, in the name of an effort to have "national laws respected." Scientific racism, combined with positivist or evolutionist sociology, now occupied the center of the "hegemonic discourse" concerning "Indians" and their communities. Such notions were cited both to justify the incorporation of ever more community peasants into expanding estates, and to call for protective measures against further assaults on Andean communities. While many landholders, authorities, and intellectuals still embraced liberal trade, fiscal, and monetary policies, they increasingly called for state intervention or protection concerning Indian labor and land.[111] The type of intrusive authoritarian "protective" scheme proposed by Miguel Zavala, which had so little chance of being passed into law in 1868, became reality under President Augusto Leguía during the early 1920s in the form of his Janus-faced double project, the "National Patronage of the Indigenous Race" and *conscripción vial*, the national road-building scheme based on corvee labor that in effect largely burdened the indigenous communal peasantry.

During the past decade many historians of the Andes and of other Latin American regions have sought to move beyond purely structural socioeconomic explanations for the fate of communities since independence. They have rightly stressed the conflictive projects by local elite groups and national oligarchies of constructing power, privately and in association with the state, and how such projects interacted with those pursued by various strata of community peasants.[112] Liberalism, as ideology and government policy, is of central concern to this approach to the fate of community peasants within emerging nation-states. And yet it would be dangerous to neglect the powerful impact of structural variables, such as the market and demography, on the changing configuration of peasant communities. Over the longer run they appear to be better "predictors" of the rhythm of pressures on the resources of the communities than any specific set of ideologies and agrarian policies. The first three decades of Peru's republican era generally saw few inroads into the domain of the peasant communities, as markets for domestic and export commodities remained sluggish. Demand for a broad range of agrarian products, from cotton and wool to sugar, alcohol, and comestibles, increased considerably between the 1850s and 1870s. Yet most community complexes, in the southern and central sierra as well as on the north coast, weathered rather well the growing pressures on their land and labor by the incipient local and regional oligarchies of large landholders and state authorities. A major reason for this may have been demographic: Population growth slowed down in much of the central and southern sierra due to epidemics, and in most communities demographic pressure on the land was still sufficiently low to allow accommodation of intra-communal conflicts without dislodging the poorest families of community peasants. With the exception of sugar, much of the growing agricultural output for markets during these decades was supplied by community peasants.

Things changed after Peru recovered from the devastating economic and political crisis between 1876 and the late 1880s. Market pressures increased, even compared with the liberal-era boom, and now penetrated farther into the interior due to ongoing improvements of the transportation system. By the early years of the twentieth century demographic pressures on the communities in many regions of Peru had become so strong that increasing numbers of poor peasants were compelled to either be incorporated into estates or leave their communal territory altogether for frontier regions in the eastern Andean piedmont, for mining camps, for the flourishing export-oriented haciendas on the coast, or for the cities. Thus, between the 1890s and 1920s expanding monetary markets and rural population growth had an especially strong impact, both on the external pressures on many communities and on changes in their internal structure. Paradoxically, just when *indigenista* notions of protecting Indian communities became more influential, markets were having a stronger impact on communal land regimes.

Of course, the processes leading to these transformations were considerably more complex than suggested in these few words. The struggles between individual peasant families, communities, large landholders, traders, and government authorities were never the automatic and predetermined consequence of market and population pressures: ideologies and influence on government policies were part and parcel of the constructs of power through which various actors fought over rural land and labor. But the point is that a whole range of rather different ideologies and government policies could be harnessed for these constructions of power, while the outcome of such struggles between community peasants and various elite groups were nearly always dependent on the underlying structural conditions in which they were played out.

In Peru liberalism neither provided the magical wand through which provincial elites could turn peasant communities into *latifundia* overnight, nor was it simply an abstract, foreign ideology that had absolutely nothing to say to "communistic" Andean agriculturalists. The noted German social historian Werner Conze wrote, nearly fifty years ago, that the effects of the nineteenth-century liberal agrarian reforms in Central Europe varied from province to province, depending on particular feudal arrangements prior to the reforms, contemporary economic conjunctures, state of agricultural-production methods, location relative to large urban markets, and the existence or nonexistence of "agrarian capitalist consciousness" of peasants and large landholders alike.[113] It would be foolish to expect any greater uniformity in the effects of liberalism on the diverse and vast agrarian landscapes of the emerging Peruvian nation-state.

In 1920 the newly promulgated Constitution recognized Indian communities and declared their lands as inalienable, the first piece of republican legislation since independence to do so. In 1925 President Leguia established the mechanism by which peasants could have their communities officially recognized.[114] While during the entire first century after independence scarcely more than a dozen national laws and decrees were promulgated dealing with the Indian community, during the 1920s and 1930s a veritable flood of legislation issued forth from Congress and the executive branch of government on every conceivable aspect of communal life, from land and water issues to schools and literacy campaigns, health, communal authorities, police, taxation, labor, agricultural extension, and the livestock of the communities. The response of the Andean peasantry varied greatly. Curiously, it was the communities from the central Peruvian department of Junin, with intensive market ties to nearby Lima and the modern mining centers around La Oroya and Cerro de Pasco and with a relatively advanced land market, that availed themselves most enthusiastically of the new opportunity for state protection for their communal domains. The new corporatism did not aim at recreating the historical ethnic corporate communities of the Habsburg era. Rather, it was a different strategy for the same project pursued by Peru's nineteenth-century liberals: integrating the "Indians" as "productive citizens" into the nation-state. Many members of the country's local, provincial, or national elite sought to use the new government policies merely as a further set of tools to fortify their power over Andean peasants. Yet the community peasants themselves—in varying ways and to varying degrees—increasingly embraced the notion of a Peruvian national identity because they could interpret it to advance their own interests and goals. They used the elite's attention on "the Indian problem" to push for greater autonomy of their community, to get a school, a medical post, or a road financed through one of the multiplying state agencies dealing with rural Peru.

The liberal agrarian policies of the nineteenth century formed a crucial experience in shaping the responses of community peasants to the neo-corporatist *indigenista* policies of the 1920s and 1930s. Put differently, selected facets of liberalism became one more layer in the collective memory of groups of Andean peasants identifying themselves with changing communities. Far from predetermining the fate of the communities during the century after independence, liberalism presented both new dangers and new opportunities for the Andean peasantry. It could serve as justification for authoritarian projects to drag the denizens of corporate ethnic communities into the emerging Peruvian nation as subordinate workers, a neocolonial crutch in the strategies of rising oligarchic groups to construct and fortify their own positions of power. But it also presented the ideological and discursive tools to Andean peasants and their allies among middle-class politicians necessary to confront these challenges, which had their roots in intensifying market and demographic pressures and the growing power accumulated by elite groups in the process of constructing the nation-state. The liberal stress on property rights, citizenship, and free association allowed dynamic groups of peasants to push for recognition of their own rights before the nation's courts and other authorities, as well as the court of public opinion. Where communal institutions and culture were weak, and the obstacles to entry into national society relatively feeble—at least for the wealthier families within the communities, as on the north coast—liberalism exacerbated this weakness in conjunction with the pressures from the market. Where, on the other hand, communal institutions and the associated ethnic identity were vigorous and conflicts with emerging local elites over the resources of the communities were fierce, liberalism was instrumental in creating communities of peasant freeholders. The combination of their ancient communitarian traditions, derived both from Andean pre-Hispanic civilization and Spanish colonial corporatism, with emancipatory aspects of liberalism allowed Peru's peasant communities to confront relatively successfully the ongoing challenges of nation-state formation and capitalist market penetration. This has been a painful, slow, and contradictory process, filled with losses and victories for the Andean peasantry. But today, in 1995, many of the communities of peasant freeholders, themselves profoundly changed by accelerating transformations of Peru's agrarian landscape, stand as the victors in the centuries-old conflict with haciendas, *latifundia,* and the giant state-dominated cooperative enterprises of the 1970s. The Andean communities' creative and purposeful engagement with nineteenth-century liberalism proved a crucial historical experience for their continued vitality until today.

Notes

1. José Carlos Mariátegui, *Seven Interpretive Essays on Peruvian Reality* (1928; Austin, 1971); Luis Valcárcel, *Tempestad en los Andes* (1928; Lima, 1972); Hildebrando Castro Pozo, *Nuestra comunidad indígena*, 2d ed. (1924; Lima, 1979).

2. Paul Gootenberg, *Between Guano and Silver: Commercial Policy and the State in Post-Independence Peru* (Princeton, 1989), p. 134, where he speaks of the dominance of "exclusivist" liberalism during the guano age; Heraclio Bonilla, *Guano y burguesía* (Lima, 1974). For the presumed preponderance of "laissez-faire liberalism" during much of the century since 1890, see Rosemary Thorp and Geoffrey Bertram, *Peru 1890–1977: Growth and Policy in an Open Economy* (New York, 1978), esp. p. 323; cf. Alfonso Quiroz, *Domestic and Foreign Finance in Modern Peru, 1850–1950* (Pittsburgh, 1993), esp. chap. 6, for a positive evaluation of economic liberalism's dominance in policymaking, at least until 1919.

3. Florencia Mallon, "Indian Communities, Political Cultures, and the State, 1780–1990," *Journal of Latin American Studies* 24, quincentenary issue (Fall 1992), 35–53; David McCreery, *Rural Guatemala, 1760–1940* (Stanford, 1994), esp. chaps. 8 and 9; Erick Langer, "El liberalismo y la abolición de la comunidad indígena en el siglo XIX," *Historia y Cultura* 14 (1988), 59–95; Tristan Platt, *Estado boliviano y ayllu andino: Tierra y tributo en el Norte de Potosí* (Lima, 1982); Silvia Rivera Cusicanqui, *Oppressed but Not Defeated: Peasant Struggles among the Aymara and Qechwa in Bolivia, 1900–1980* (Geneva, 1987); Robert H. Jackson, *Regional Markets and Agrarian Transformation in Bolivia: Cochabamba, 1539–1960* (Albuquerque, 1994), chaps. 2 and 3.

4. "Liberalism," in *The New Palgrave: The Invisible Hand*, ed. John Eatwell, Murray Milgate, and Peter Newman (New York and London, 1989), p. 187 (emphasis in the original).

5. Ibid.; Alan Ryan, "Property," in Eatwell, Milgate, and Newman, *The New Palgrave*, p. 228.

6. Langer, "El liberalismo"; see also Jackson, *Regional Markets*, pp. 66–89; Platt, *Estado boliviano y ayllu andino*, pp. 73–93; Danièle Demelas, "'Darwinismo' a la criolla: el darwinismo social en Bolivia," *Historia Boliviana* 1:2 (1981), 55–82.

7. Michael E. Moseley, *The Incas and Their Ancestors: The Archaeology of Peru* (London and New York, 1992), chap. 3; Karen Spalding, *Huarochiri* (Stanford, 1984), chap. 1; Susan Ramirez, *The World Upside Down* (Stanford, forthcoming), chap. 3. There may have existed an embryonic development of proprietary rights to lands in the late pre-Hispanic period, among noble lineages associated with the Inca court. It also remains unclear to me by what conception an *ayllu* could claim rights to the same lands generation after generation.

8. Ramirez, *World Upside Down*, chap. 3; Carlos Sempat Assadourian, *Transiciones hacia el sistema colonial andino* (Lima and Mexico, 1994), chap. 3.

9. Cf. David Vassberg, *Land and Society in Golden Age Castile* (Cambridge and New York, 1984), chaps. 1 and 3.

10. Luis Miguel Glave, *Vida símbolos y batallas: Creación y recreación de la comunidad indígena, Cusco, siglos XVI–XX* (Lima, 1992), chaps. 1 and 2.

11. Vassberg, *Land and Society*, chaps. 1 and 3; Joaquin Costa y Martínez, *Colectivismo agrario en España* (1898), vols. 7 and 8 of *Obras completas*, ed. George Cheyne and Carlos Serrano (Zaragoza, 1983); Ramirez, *World Upside Down*, chap. 3.

12. Cf. Richard Herr, *Rural Change and Royal Finance in Spain at the End of the Old Regime* (Berkeley, 1989), pp. 47–77; Jean Sarrailh, *La España ilustrada de la segunda mitad del siglo XVIII* (México, D.F., 1957), pp. 565–70; Rudolf Leonhard, *Agrarpolitik und Agrarreform in Spanien unter Karl III* (München and Berlin, 1909), esp. pp. 176–235.

13. Cf. Nils Jacobsen, "Campesinos y tenencia de la tierra en el altiplano peruano en la transición de la colonia a la república," *Allpanchis* 23:37 (1991), 25–92.

14. The alternative consisted in a historicizing concept of nation, which inevitably would have pitted a Hispanic Catholic Peru, against a native Andean Peru, two mutually exclusive national projects.

15. Peru. Dirección General de Asuntos Indígenas, *Legislación Indigenista del Perú* (hereafter cited as *LIDP*) (Lima, 1948), pp. 7–8.

16. For the post-independence period the terms *ayllu* and *community* are used interchangeably in this essay, although the relation between both was more complex and the former could be contained, but did not need to be contained, in the latter.

17. For an overview see Blum, *The End of the Old Order in Rural Europe* (Princeton: Princeton University Press, 1978).

18. On the local level we know of at least one radical attempt to abolish manorial estates: In 1822 Andrés de Santa Cruz, as governor of the vast northern district of Piura, decreed the distribution of hacienda lands among their labor tenants. When the decree was revoked a little later due to intense pressure of the owners, labor tenants in two major haciendas rose in rebellion. Susana Aldana Rivera and Alejandro Diez Hurtado, *Balsillas piajeñs y algodón: Procesos históricos en Piura y Tumbes* (Piura and Lima, 1994), p. 92.

19. Cf. Mariátegui, *Seven Interpretive Essays*: "The liberalism of republican legislation was passive in its attitude toward feudal property and only took action against communal property" (p. 53).

20. *LIDP*, pp. 9–11.

21. It is unclear whether "distribution" [*repartimiento*] here refers to land distributions by the Spanish crown or by the communities, although the former seems more likely.

22. *LDIP*, pp. 14–16.

23. P. Emilio Dancuart and R. M. Rodríguez, *Anales de la hacienda pública del Perú*, 24 vols. (Lima, 1902–26), 1:272; Victor Peralta Ruiz, *En pos del tributo: Burocracia estatal, elite regional y comunidades indígenas en el Cusco rural, 1826–1854* (Cuzco, 1991), pp. 36–43.

24. Dancuart and Rodríguez, *Anales*, 1:277–78; Carlos Valdéz de la Torre, *Evolución de las comunidades de indígenas* (Lima, 1921), p. 148.

25. Jean Piel, *Capitalisme agraire au Pérou*, vol.1, *Originalité de la societé agraire peruvienne aux XIX siècle* (Paris, 1975), 1:281–82.

26. For a discussion of shifting elite terminology during the 1820s—from *"Indio"* to *"peruano"* to *"indígena"*—see Mark Thurner, "'Republicanos' and 'La Comunidad de Peruanos': Unimagined Political Communities in Postcolonial Andean Peru," *Journal of Latin American Studies* 27:2 (May 1995), 291–318, esp. 297–303.

27. *LDIP*, pp. 16–19.

28. Ibid., p. 19.

29. Ibid., p. 21.

30. Ibid., pp. 21–22; Dancuart and Rodríguez, *Anales*, 2:136; Jorge Basadre, *Historia de la República del Perú, 1822–1933*, 11 vols., 7th ed. (Lima, 1983), 1:200. Several authors (including myself) have suggested, apparently erroneously, that the assigned lands could only be sold if the owners were literate; perhaps the literacy requirement was established through subsequent decree.

31. Frank Safford, "Politics, Ideology and Society in Post-Independence Spanish America," in *Cambridge History of Latin America*, ed. Leslie Bethell, 8 vols. (Cambridge: Cambridge University Press, 1984–1995), 3:385.

32. Hamlets, communities, or villages located on the property of others, but with a sufficient population to exercise the rights "which constitute the political and municipal representation," according to a law of November 19, 1839, should be granted property rights of the land on which they are located, with compensation of former owners. For the case of the town of Chongollape, on the lands of Hacienda Tuman, dept. of La Libertad, see Juan Oviedo, ed., *Colección de leyes, decretos y ordenes publicadas en el Perú desde el año de 1821 hasta 31 de diciembre de 1859* (Lima, 1861–70), 4:297; for comunidad de Chullay, distr. Higueras, province of Huánuco, see ibid., p. 305.

33. Pedro Rojas y Briones, *Proyectos de economía política, que en favor de la República Peruana ha formado el ciudadano . . . , Diputado del soberano Congreso nombrado por la provincia de Cajamarca* (Lima, 1828).

34. Ibid., pp. 5–10.

35. Ibid., pp. 22–23.

36. *Memoria que presenta el Ministro de Hacienda al congreso de 1847* (Lima, n.d.), pp. 3–4.

37. See the cases from Conchucos (1830) and Huarochirí (1849), in Oviedo, *Colección*, 4:142–43, 295–96.

38. Nils Jacobsen, *Mirages of Transition: The Peruvian Altiplano, 1780–1930* (Berkeley and Los Angeles, 1993), chaps. 3 and 4; Manuel Burga, "El Perú central 1770–1860: Disparidades regionales y la primera crisis agrícola republicana," in *América latina en la época de Simón Bolívar*, ed. Reinhard Liehr, pp. 227–310 (Berlin, 1989); Magnus Mörner, *The Andean Past: Land, Societies and Conflicts* (New York, 1985), chap. 6; Luis Miguel Glave and María Isabel Remy, *Estructura agraria y vida rural en una región andina: Ollantaytambo entre los siglos XVI y XIX* (Cuzco, 1983), pp. 437–43, 488–89.

39. Alberto Flores Galindo, *Arequipa y el sur andino, siglo XVIII-XX* (Lima, 1977), p. 44; Jacobsen, *Mirages*, pp. 53–54.

40. Manuel Burga, *De la encomienda a la hacienda capitalista: El valle de Jequetepeque del siglo XVI al XX* (Lima, 1976), pp. 150–55.

41. Valdéz de la Torre, *Evolución*, p. 158.

42. Peralta Ruiz, *En pos del tributo*, p. 67.

43. Jacobsen, *Mirages*, p. 125.

44. Charles Walker, "Peasants, Caudillos, and the State in Peru: Cusco in the Transition from Colony to Republic, 1780–1840" (Ph.D. diss., University of Chicago, 1992), chap. 6; Christine Hünefeldt, "Poder y contribuciones: Puno, 1825–45," *Revista Andina* 7:2 (1989), 367–407; David Cahill, "Curas and Social Conflict in the Doctrinas of Cuzco, 1780–1814," *Journal of Latin American Studies* 16 (1984), 241–76; María Isabel Remy, "La sociedad local al inicio de la república: Cusco, 1824–1850," *Revista Andina* 7:2 (1988), 451–84; Peralta Ruiz, *En pos del tributo*, esp. chap. 4; Jacobsen, "Campesinos y tenencia de la tierra."

45. Hünefeldt, "Poder y contribuciones."

46. Jacobsen, *Mirages*, p. 128.

47. Glave, *Vida símbolos*, pp. 203ff.

48. Basadre, *Historia de la República*, 3:155.

49. Glave, *Vida símbolos*, pp. 203ff; Jacobsen, *Mirages*, p. 276.

50. Walker, "Peasants, Caudillos and the State," p. 282, effectively refutes the continued functioning of the colonial compact in early republican communities of Cuzco.

51. Nelson Manrique, "Las comunidades campesinas de la Sierra Central, sigol XIX," in *Comunidades campesinas: Cambios y permanencias*, ed. Alberto Flores Galindo (Chiclayo and Lima, 1987), pp. 116–24. Nelson Manrique, *Mercado interno y región: La sierra central, 1820–1930* (Lima, 1987), pp. 145–56; Manuel Burga, "El Perú central."

52. Carlos Contreras, "Estado republicano y tributo indígena en la sierra central en la post-independencia," *Histórica* 13:1 (July 1989), 9–44.

53. Ibid., 34; there is one small area of Indian communities in southern Peru where a similar development may have occurred during the early post-independence era: the districts immediately surrounding the city of Arequipa (today part of the expanding urban space of that city). There, more and more

Indians also "passed the color line" since the last years of the colonial era, and land in the communities was becoming scarce; although there seem to have been some fraudulent sales and adjudications by local authorities in the wake of the 1820s reform legislation, one suspects that the major reason for this was precisely that more and more families did not identify with the communiites anymore. The circumstances here, of course, were quite similar to those of the Mantaro Valley: intense commercial agriculture and close integration into a nearby urban market. See Sarah C. Chambers, "The Many Shades of the White City: Urban Culture and Society in Arequipa, Peru, 1780–1854" (Ph.D. diss.: University of Wisconsin, Madison, 1992), pp. 144–69.

54. For possible resistance to these transformations, see Olinda Celestino and Albert Meyers, *Las cofradías en el Perú: Región central* (Frankfurt, 1981), chap. 6.

55. Alejandro Diez Hurtado, *Las comunidades indígenas del Bajo Piura: Catacaos y Sechura, siglo XIX* (Piura, 1992), pp. 18–24.

56. Ibid., pp. 28–39.

57. Ibid., pp. 37–38.

58. Ibid., p. 37; Jacobo Cruz Villegas, *Catac Ccaos: Origen y evolución histórica de Catacaos* (Piura, 1982), pp. 289–93.

59. Guano sales abroad had begun a few years earlier, circa 1841, but only began to have a major impact on government budgets in 1847.

60. The powerful impact of 1848 on Latin American polities has been confirmed explicitly for the Chilean and Colombian cases; see José Luis Romero, *La Sociedad de la Igualdad: Los artesanos de Santiago de Chile y sus primeras experiencias políticas, 1820–1851* (Buenos Aires, 1978); Christian Gazmuri, *El '48' Chileno: Igualitarios, reformistas, radicales, masones y bomberos* (Santiago, 1992); David Sowell, *The Early Colombian Labor Movement: Artisans and Politics in Bogotá, 1832–1919* (Philadelphia, 1992). For Peru it is suggested by Gootenberg, *Between Silver and Guano*, p. 89; and by Juan Luis Orrego Penagos, "Domingo Elías y el *Club Progresista*: Los civiles y el poder hacia 1850," *Histórica* 14:2 (December 1990), 317–53; on strengthened liberal influences in Peru after 1850, see also Paul Gootenberg, *Imagining Development: Economic Ideas in Peru's "Fictitious Prosperity of Guano, 1840–1880* (Berkeley, 1993).

61. Carlos Augusto Ramos Núñez, *Toribio Pacheco; jurista peruano del siglo XIX* (Lima, 1993), pp. 102–3.

62. Francisco García Calderon, *Le Perou contemporain: Études sociales* (Paris, 1907), p. 98, as cited in Fernando de Trazegnies, *La idea del derecho en el Perú republicano del siglo XIX* (Lima, 1979), pp. 188–89.

63. Jacobsen, *Mirages*, pp. 234–37; Trazegnies, *La idea del derecho*, pp. 189–93.

64. Ramos Núñez, *Toribio Pacheco*, p. 106.

65. Basadre, *Historia de la República*, 3:155.

66. Garmendia to Ministro de Gobierno, Cuzco, June 2, 1858, in Oviedo, *Colección*, 4:310–11.

67. Ibid., 4:311.

68. Ibid., 15:365–66.

69. That is, land on which no taxes were paid produced no commercial values, and thus really did not constitute productive property. That was the definitional dilemma communal regimes of tenure were facing when liberal thought came to dominate.

70. Garmendia to Ministro de Gobierno, Cuzco, June 2, 1858, in Oviedo, *Colección*, 15:368.

71. Ibid., 15:370–71.

72. It is a widely held view among modern historians that the abolition of *contribución de indígenas* in 1854 immediately gave rise to a wave of landgrabbing in the sierra, as provincial elites now had lost a major tool of surplus extraction from the Indian communities. While this was clearly implied by those authors of the 1850s and 1860s who stressed the need to force Andean peasants to become industrious laborers, the thought and its realization on the ground were not the same thing, and, as we shall see below, the evidence for massive land transfers form communities to haciendas during the quarter century after the abolition of *contribución de indígenas* is relatively scant. For the original modern formulation of this idea, see Pablo Macera, "Las plantaciones azucareras andinas (1821–1875)," in Pablo Macera, *Trabajos de historia*, 4 vols. (Lima, 1977), 4:194–95; for a recent reiteration, see David P. Cahill, "Independencia, sociedad y fiscalidad: el Sur Andino (1780–1880)," *Revista Complutense de Historia de América* 19 (1993), 249–68, esp. p. 267.

73. Gootenberg, *Imagining Development*, pp. 143–63, also notes the stress on "work" in the political rhetoric of the 1860s and 1870s, but links it largely to a politically inclusive strain of *civilismo* exalting the virtues of artisans.

74. *Algunas cuestiones sociales con motivo de los disturbios de Huancané. Al Soberano Congreso* (Lima, 1867), p. 14 passim. Recent authors who have insisted on liberalism's undermining of the communal Andean heritage of landholding, pure and simple, have totally missed the point that authoritarian liberals between the 1850s and 1880s in fact insisted on the notion that community peasants were merely holders of usufruct rights to state lands, the same notion presumably espoused by community peasants themselves. For a recent example of this view, see Thurner, "'Republicanos' and 'La Comunidad de Peruanos.'"

75. Cf. Claudio Osambela, *Investigación de los medios mas oportunos y eficaces de estimular a los habitantes del Perú según la situación social al trabajo mas ordenando y provechoso* (Lima, 1867).

76. In his influential and imaginitive work on Indian communities in Bolivia's Norte de Potosí province, Tristan Platt, in *Estado boliviano*, has

underscored the continued vitality of the "colonial compact" between the state (crown) and the Indian community until the early 1870s. But he completely neglects to consider the sinister side of that notion from the perspective of white elite society in the age of liberalism, namely, that it could serve as vehicle to deny the property rights of Indian peasants to the land in the communities.

77. Basadre, *Historia de la República*, 5:26–28, 43–44, 68–71; for the history of the *contribución personal* between 1879 and 1895, see 6:128, 28, 105–6, 391–92; Jacobsen, *Mirages*, p. 277; the history of *contribución de indígenas* and *contribución personal* in the department of Ayacucho, from independence to 1895, is discussed in Heraclio Bonilla, "Estado y tributo campesino: la experiencia de Ayacucho," in *Los Andes en la encrucijada: Indios, comunidades y estado en el siglo XIX*, ed. H. Bonilla (Quito, 1991), pp. 335–66.

78. On the Bustamante Rebellion, see Emilio Vasquez, *La rebelión de Juan Bustamante* (Lima, 1976); on the Atusparia Rebellion, see William Stein, *La rebelión de Atusparia* (Lima, 1988).

79. [Santiago Tavara], *Emancipación del Indio decretada en 5 de Julio de 1854 por el Libertador Ramón Castilla* (Lima, 1856), pp. 1, 22, 25, passim.

80. Juan Bustamante, *Indios del Perú* (Lima, 1867), p. 124.

81. Miguel S. Zavala, *Protectorado de Indios, o sea proyecto de ley ofrecido a las consideraciones de los H. H. Representantes de la Nación, en la presente Legislatura de 1868, con el fin de mejorar la deprimida condición social del Indio, haciendo realizable sus derechos* (Lima, 1868), pp. 14–21.

82. Ibid., pp. 41–49.

83. Ibid., pp. 33–34.

84. Cf. David McCreery, "'An Odious Feudalism': Mandamiento and Commercial Agriculture in Guatemala, 1858–1920," *Latin American Perspectives* 13 (1986), 99-118.

85. This point is underscored, too single-mindedly in my view, by Hector Omar Noéjovich, "Las relaciones del estado peruano con la población indígena en el siglo XIX a traves de su legislación," *Histórica* 15:1 (1991), 43-62, esp. 58–59.

86. Cámara de Diputados, *Anales del Congreso del Perú*, vol. 13: *1868–69* (Lima, 1955), p. 206.

87. Thomas Davies, *Indian Integration in Peru: A Half Century of Experience* (Lincoln, 1974), p. 32; for the surprisingly laudatory neo-revisionist interpretation of Manuel Pardo's administration, see Carmen Mc Evoy, *Un proyecto nacional en el siglo XIX: Manuel Pardo y su visión del Perú* (Lima, 1994), and Gootenberg, *Imagining Development*, pp. 71–88.

88. It is curious to note that some modern pro-Indian writers arrive at nearly the same conclusion for southern Peru's Indian communities of the late nineteenth century; cf. Nelson Manrique, *Yawar Mayu, sociedades terratenientes serranas, 1879–1910* (Lima, 1988), p. 152.

89. Jacobsen, *Mirages*, pp. 234–35.

90. The following paragraph is based on Glave, *Vida símbolos*, pp. 210–23.

91. W. S. Bell, *An Essay on the Peruvian Cotton Industry*, Working Paper no. 6 (University of Liverpool, 1985), table 12, p. 86; Gregor Wolf, "Die erste Technisierung des Baumwollanbaus in den Flußtälern des Chira und Piura und ihre Rückwirkungen auf die Region (1885–1930)" (Master's thesis: Lateinamerikainstitut, Freie Universität Berlin, 1992), p. 29; Manuel Burgos Cabrejos, "Apuntes sobre la estructura agrarian tradicional: del valle de Piura a fines del siglo XIX" (Piura, 1989), typescript.

92. Diez Hurtado, *Las comunidades indígenas*, pp. 39–44. Miguel Jaramillo (personal communication, January 1995), who is completing a dissertation on Piura's nineteenth century economic history at the University of California, San Diego, confirms my suspicion that until the 1880s most Piura cotton was, in fact, produced by community farmers in Catacaos and Sechura.

93. Cruz Villegas, *Catac Ccaos*, pp. 248–49.

94. Report by Agencia Municipal of Catacaos to Municipalidad de Piura, October 26, 1866, in Cruz Villegas, *Catac Ccaos*, pp. 253–57.

95. Ibid., pp. 261–64.

96. Ibid.

97. Ibid., pp. 266–73.

98. Ibid., pp. 276–86.

99. Diez Hurtado, *Las comunidades indígenas*, pp. 41–46.

100. Mariátegui, *Seven Interpretive Essays*, pp. 53–55.

101. In fact, Mariátegui's vision suffers from several internal contradictions, or at least tensions, that to my knowledge have rarely been pointed out by the commentators on his work. While stressing, on the one hand, the "gradual destruction" of the Andean peasant communities at the hand of *latifundia*, Mariátegui at the same time insisted on their strong survival and their continued capacity to serve as the institutional base for a future Peruvian socialism. More seriously, if he believed even the application of a less ambitious *liberal* modernization of traditional Andean communities to be illusory because it represented artificial, extraneous notions for their traditional customs and institutions, how could the conversion of such traditional communities into *socialist* cooperatives, informed by European universalist progressive values, avoid being even more artificial, not to say utopian? One must suppose that his notion of socialist revolution as myth was meant to bridge this enormous gap.

102. Cf. Gavin Smith, *Livelihood and Resistance: Peasants and the Politics of Land in Peru* (Berkeley, 1989), chap. 2, on the central sierra; and August Plane, *Le Perou*, 2d ed. (Paris, 1903), pp. 64–65, on a case from Quispicanchis province in the department of Cuzco.

103. Mariátegui's claim of the irrelevance of liberalism as an element of nineteenth-century Andean peasants' discourse or ideology has recently been

repeated by Florencia Mallon, *Peasant and Nation: The Making of Postcolonial Mexico and Peru* (Berkeley and Los Angeles, 1995), p. 17.

104. For an interesting attempt to explain varying capacities of communities to withstand elite intrusions in the southern Bolivian department of Chuquisaca through *internal* (ecological and demographic) variables, see Erick Langer, "Persistencia y cambio en comunidades indígenas del sur boliviano en el siglo XIX," in Bonilla, *Los Andes en la encrucijada*, pp. 133–67.

105. Cf. Michael Taussig, *Shamanism, Colonialism, and the Wild Man: A Study in Terror and Healing* (Chicago, 1987); Charles Walker, "El uso oficial de la selva en el Perú republicano," *Amazonia Perú* 14 (1987), 61–89. Even the earliest projects by Peruvian government authorities to colonize the Amazon region and make it useful for national economic development during the 1850s sought to use the natives' labor for establishing market-oriented ranching and farming in the region, without granting them proprietary rights to the lands they were to work. See the plan by Francisco Alvarado Ortíz for agricultural development of the Amazon region, dated July 15, 1855, in Oviedo, *Colección*, 4:251–57, 307–8.

106. Cf. Jacobsen, *Mirages*, pp. 273–84, 339–49; Enrique Mayer, "Tenencia y control comunal de la tierra: caso de Laraos (Yauyos)," *Cuadernos* [del Concejo Nacional de la Universidad Peruana], nos. 24–25 (1977), 59–72.

107. Manrique, *Yawar Mayu*, esp. p. 152, suggests that Cuzco's traditional community authorities had become by the late nineteenth century nothing more than transmission belts in a vast system of resource extraction from the communities in favor of local and provincial *gamonales*, in contrast to the more autonomous, associational communities of the Mantaro Valley in the central sierra. Curiously, such a critique by modern, pro-community historians echoes the critique of authoritarian elite writers of the epoch, who condemned surviving "*caciques y recaudadores*" in Cuzco's communities in precisely the same language. See also Deborah Poole, "Landscapes of Power in a Cattle Rustling Culture of Southern Peru," *Dialectical Anthropology* 12:4 (1987), 367–98. But cf. Jacobsen, *Mirages*, pp. 275–77, for the more ambiguous case of the Peruvian *altiplano*.

108. Carlos Contreras, "Mercado de tierras y sociedad campesina: el valle del Mantaro en el siglo XIX," *Historia y Cultura* 20 (1990), 243–65; Florencia Mallon, *The Defense of Community in Peru's Central Highlands* (Princeton, 1983), pp. 209–13; Gavin Smith, *Livelihood and Resistance: Peasants and the Politics of Land in Peru* (Berkeley and Los Angeles, 1989), chap. 3.

109. Legislative declaration of October 30, 1893, in *LIDP*, pp. 38–39. In her book, *Peasant and Nation*, p. 217, Florencia Mallon places great emphasis on a recently discovered plan by a regional representative of the Cáceres administration in Junin department from 1889 to abolish Indian communities for good and distribute their lands to individual peasants, which assumed that these were still the lands of the state to distribute. The plan must have

been written in response to an as yet undiscovered policy initiative of the central governemt in Lima, as the Biblioteca Nacional contains reports from other departments addressing the same issue. Contrary to Mallon's claims, the 1889 plan does not foreshadow government thought on the community in the decades to come, but rather represents a throwback to liberal agrarian thought—down to its wording—as it developed in Peru following the Bolívarian agrarian reform laws of the 1820s; the plan's non-adoption thus represents evidence for the weakening of liberal-era thought on the community. See "Proyecto de ley sobre repartición de las tierras de comunidad," Tarma, July 11, 1889; "Informe del Prefecto del Drepartamento de Huánuco sobre la consulta hecha por el Director de Gobierno, sobre si conviene—la no abolición de las comunidades indígenas," Huanuco, January 25, 1889; "Expediente sobre el oficio dirigido por el Prefecto de Cajamarca al Director de Gobierno, adjuntandole datos sobre terrenos de comunidad," Cajamarca, November 11, 1889; Biblioteca Nacional, Sala de Investigación, Ms D12842, D11197 and D11376.

110. Davies, *Indian Integration*, chap. 3; Manuel Vicente Villaran, "Condición legal de las comunidades indígenas," *Revista universitaria* [of San Marcos University] (1907), 1–9.

111. Cf. Jacobsen, "Free Trade, Regional Elites and the Internal Market in Southern Peru, 1895–1932," in *Guiding the Invisible Hand: Economic Liberalism and the State in Latin American History*, ed. Joseph Love and Nils Jacobsen (New York: Praeger, 1987), pp. 145–76.

112. This perspective has been pioneered especially by Florencia Mallon; cf. her monographs, *Defense of Community* and *Peasant and Nation*; see also G. P. C. Thompson, "Liberalism"; Thurner, "'Republicanos' and 'La Comunidad de Peruanos'"; Walker, "Peasants, Caudillos, and the State;" Jeffrey L. Gould, "'Vana ilusión!' The Highlands Indians and the Myth of Nicaragua Mestiza," *Hispanic American Historical Review* 73:3 (August 1993), 393–430. But note especially the studies by John Tutino, *From Insurrection to Revolution in Mexico: Social Bases of Agrarian Violence, 1750–1940* (Princeton, 1986), and by Herbert Klein, *Haciendas and Ayllus: Rural Society in the Bolivian Andes in the Eighteenth and Nineteenth Centuries* (Stanford, 1993), for bucking this trend.

113. Werner Conze, "Die Wirkungen der liberalen Agrarreformen auf die Volksordnung in Mitteleuropa im 19. Jahrhundert," *Vierteljahresschrift für Sozial-und Wirtschaftsgeschichte*, vol. 38 (1949), 2–43.

6
Liberalism and the Land Question in Bolivia, 1825–1920
Erick D. Langer and Robert H. Jackson

In Bolivia the disentailment of real estate (both urban and rural) did not reach the same dimensions that it acquired in other Latin American countries. Disentailment of Catholic church properties occurred very early in the history of the new republic, and this prevented large-scale conflict found in many other Latin American countries during the nineteenth century. The survival of corporate Indian communities was a much greater problem for liberal reformers, which in the end was resolved by favoring the expansion of the hacienda at the expense of the communities, beginning in the second half of the nineteenth century.

The struggles over land policy can be divided into two periods. In the first period, concentrated during the first few years after the establishment of the new republic, the struggle with the Catholic church and the partial disentailment of religious properties predominated. In the second period, encompassing the last forty years of the nineteenth century and the first few decades of the twentieth, the expansion of the haciendas at the expense of the Indian communities gained importance. While the actions in both periods are related to the anticorporatist components explicit in liberalism, the two periods must be distinguished because they pertain to two different periods in the development of liberal ideology. For this reason, both the legislation and the effects of these reforms were rather different.

An important characteristic of the first phase of liberal reforms that must be taken into account was that they were undertaken when the country was under the occupation of foreign troops whose leaders also held the reins of power. This fact explains the effectiveness of the some of these reforms and the failure of others in the long term. The Venezuelan Antonio José de Sucre—first president of the Bolivian republic (1826–1828)—did not have to worry about an effective antiliberal opposition in a country decimated by a civil war that had raged for more than fifteen years and where virtually all Bolivian revolutionary leaders had been killed before patriot forces finally triumphed.

The Catholic church also was in a weakened state after this prolonged conflict and was barely able to sustain itself. The vast majority of Upper Peruvian clerics, because they were Spaniards (especially in the regular orders), had been on the side of the royalists and had been either jailed or exiled during the conflict.[1] The occupation of an alien army—composed mainly of Colombians and Venezuelans—without many ties to local elites, and the weakness of the church as a consequence of the civil wars, made possible the implementation of important anticlerical reforms during the short tenure of the Sucre administration.

This was not the case for the Indian communities. Although Simón Bolívar had proclaimed new laws that, in theory, abolished the legal status of the indigenous population as tributaries and divided community lands among its members in decrees issued in Cuzco in 1824 and 1825, this legislation never took effect. The importance of Indian tribute in the fiscal health of the state, and the weakness of the state's ability to repress a potential caste war, convinced the government to postpone any reform of the colonial-era status quo in this matter. Indeed, during the administration of Andrés de Santa Cruz (1829–1830) the state confirmed the legal existence of Indian communities and the tributary system. Only the Melgarejo administration (1864–1871), many decades later, dared attack the land system inherited from the colonial period. During the period under discussion, the discourse among the political elites concerning the Indian communities and their role in society changed from a rather naïve Bolivarian liberalism, which anticipated few problems in abolishing this institution, to a vigorous debate over the fate of the rural majority in the context of the changing national economy.

Liberalism and the Catholic Church

The disentailment of the capital and property of the Catholic church was one of the central elements of liberal reformist politics in various Latin American countries. Church possessions, particularly the rural properties, constituted one of the important resources that, according to liberal ideologues, represented a dead weight on the economy. According to the most common interpretations, church properties could not be sold because they had the legal status of entailed estates. Liberals used the term *manos muertas* (literally, "dead hands") to describe the poor systems of tenancy and exploitation of the religious properties. Moreover, the liberals argued that selling church lands and bringing underutilized land resources into the market would contribute to the growth of modern agricultural systems and thus aid in the development of the national economy.[2]

The first attempt in Spanish America to liquidate church wealth occurred in 1804, when the Spanish government, near bankruptcy because of its participation in the costly wars of the French Revolution, decreed the payment in cash of the nominal value of all *censos* and *capellanías*. The money from this exercise was to provide the backing for the *vales reales* (an instrument of royal credit). According to the decree, the church was to receive three percent interest on the capital deposited with the government. Although the consolidation of the *vales reales* was the consequence of pressure from the extraordinary war expenses on the fiscal structure of the Spanish state, a number of ministers, such as Jovellanos, imbued with Enlightenment ideas in the second half of the eighteenth century had already discussed the need to reform and modernize the agrarian and economic structure of Spain, focusing especially on entailed estates and the goods in *manos muertas*.

The 1804 decree affected the landowners of Latin America in important ways. Nevertheless, there are few studies on this important topic and the majority focus almost exclusively on Mexico.[3] The 1804 decree established the legal basis for later reforms and, in many ways, the debate in Spain in the previous century provided an ideological underpinning for the liberal-reform programs in the nineteenth century. Nineteenth-century liberals took the *consolidación de vales reales* and the liquidation of church capital to its logical conclusion, calling in the capital dispersed in *censos* and *capellanías* and forcing the sale of urban and rural church properties. The schedule of the disentailment varied from country to country; up to now the liberal reforms in Mexico have received by far the greatest attention.[4] Studies on liberal politics in other Latin American countries have described processes that appear to be very similar to the Mexican case.[5]

There are few works on church wealth in Bolivia and even fewer specifically on the politics of disentailment. Moreover, there is little information available on the importance of the church as landowner.[6] As we show below, the development of anticorporatist ideology in Bolivia was very different than in Mexico. The Bolivian government tried to liquidate church wealth at an earlier date, during the Sucre administration, but was only partially successful. The majority of female regular orders did not lose their lands until the twentieth century, and even in some cases not until the Agrarian Reform of 1953. Not all masculine orders were closed either; in addition, the Sucre anticlerical program did not affect parish lands at all.

Another difference with Mexico is that the debate over church wealth did not cause political instability during the first formative years of the Bolivian state (1825–1880); only at the end of the nineteenth century did the subjects of church and lands again become part of the debate. This time the most important manifestation of anticlericalism in Bolivian history concerned the mission lands in the sparsely populated eastern portion of the country. However, inflation pressures in the Bolivian economy in the last years of the nineteenth and early twentieth centuries led the female orders to sell their land and invest the capital in financial instruments that provided a better hedge against rising prices.

The Lands of the Regular Orders in Bolivia

In the late colonial period the church, in particular the regular orders, had a much greater influence on the rural economy than the number of rural estates they possessed might indicate. However, a lack of studies on the role of the church in the Upper Peruvian economy has made possible the proliferation of a series of incorrect hypotheses. We know very little about the motives of the administrators of the convents and monasteries to purchase or invest their capital in real estate or other instruments that brought in stable earnings. It is generally not known that the members of the regular orders were for the most part descendants of the wealthiest families of Upper Peru and that the existence of the regular orders did not threaten the interests of the elites.

Mexican liberals, fiercely anticlerical, in general were not members of the richest families but part of the new bourgeoisie that was not connected to the ecclesiastical hierarchy or the regular orders. In contrast, the evidence for Bolivia suggests that there was no group within the local elites that proposed the disentailment of church wealth as the primary goal of its political program. Herbert S. Klein has claimed that the late colonial Upper Peruvian elites did not worry much about the church: "The Church, although an important source of credit and active through a few powerful convents, was nevertheless a small sector of the hacendado class, indicating the ability of the lay society to maintain a flourishing and independent leadership in agriculture despite its financial dependence on the Church."[7] Different religious institutions owned rural estates and gave out loans; more important as sources of income for the religious communities were the *censos* on rural and urban properties. A number of *censos* can be considered as relatively short-term loans, but the majority functioned as mortgages on properties, with the interests going directly to the convents and monasteries.

The importance of *censos* on the Upper Peruvian economy in the late colonial period is an issue that requires further investigation. Evidence from

Cochabamba indicates the significance of *censos* in the local economy. In 1825, seven convents and monasteries in Cochabamba controlled *censos* worth 637,000 pesos, which produced an annual income of 22,000 pesos; this income was the equivalent of between five and ten percent of the total value of wheat, corn, and other grains, as well as all the flours exported each year from the region at the end of the eighteenth century. This income was extremely important in the individual budget of these religious institutions as well. For example, the Santa Clara convent received forty-one percent of its income from the interests on the *censos*.[8]

The administration of Antonio José de Sucre focused on the issue of the regular orders' wealth. Backed by Venezuelan and Colombian troops, Sucre implemented elements of Simón Bolívar's reform program in Bolivia, reforms that probably did not enjoy the whole-hearted support of local elites. The law of March 29, 1826, ordered the closure of convents and monasteries with few residents and decreed the confiscation of the properties of the suppressed institutions.[9]

Documentation on Cochabamba indicates that Sucre's decree affected primarily the masculine orders. The government closed three monasteries and one hospital and sold their properties. The nine haciendas that previously belonged to the Augustinian monasteries in the city of Cochabamba were included in the sale of confiscated properties, including Hacienda Collpa, which controlled more than eleven hundred hectares of prime land in the Valle Alto of Cochabamba.[10] In La Paz, the regular orders also lost their rural estates. In 1780, thirteen convents and monasteries in the cities of La Paz and Oruro owned fifty-seven rural properties in the department of La Paz. One century later, in 1880, there were six institutions left that controlled only thirty-five haciendas.[11] Unfortunately, however, we have no direct evidence that proves that the diminution of haciendas was due to the Sucre reform program of the 1820s.

During the nineteenth century, the national government did not take other measures to attack the regular orders, nor did it touch the parish lands, usually small or medium-sized properties that sustained the secular parish priests. In the case of the female orders, the convents, in fact, served an important social function for the elites, and for this reason they survived the century. Elite families could deposit their unmarried daughters in the convents and thereby assure that their sexual purity, and thus the families' social prestige, would remain intact.

Indeed, in some cases the feminine regular orders increased the number of rural properties during the nineteenth century, either through donations or through outright purchases. In Cochabamba City, two nuns left Santa Clara in 1867 to establish a new convent. Members of the local elite donated lands for the new institution and, by the end of the century, the new convent owned at least eight rural properties.[12] The regular orders of Cochabamba remained the owners of at least twenty properties at the beginning of this century.[13]

In the first decades of the twentieth century the regular orders had to confront a fiscal crisis that threatened their very existence. Information from the regular orders in Cochabamba indicates that the income from rental of their rural properties did not rise as much as inflation. The administrators of various convents sold these properties and invested their capital in bank mortgages that paid a higher interest than inflation. for example, rental income from Hacienda Cliza (property of Santa Clara convent) increased thirteen percent between 1877 and 1901. During the same years, corn and wheat prices (important indices of regional price movements) went up seventy percent and forty-one percent respectively. Moreover, inflation increased even more after 1900, worsening even more the regular orders' financial situation.[14] In 1911 and 1912 the administrators of the Santa Teresa and Capuchin convents offered various haciendas for sale, citing as their reason "economic necessity."[15] The most extensive sale of lands occurred between 1901 and 1919. In these years the administrators of the Santa Clara convent sold portions of Hacienda Cliza valued at two million Bolivianos to pay the cost of the construction of a new complex of buildings for the nuns, which included a church. The leftover money was invested in mortgage notes.[16]

It is probable that future studies will confirm that the loss of earnings from the *censos*, in combination with the inflation of the late nineteenth and early twentieth centuries, caused an erosion of the regular orders' financial base, and liberal politics, despite its anticlerical cast, was not very important after the Sucre administration. The politics of the Liberal Party (1899–1921) affected rural and urban properties that financed the eastern mission program, but it did not affect the convents and monasteries in the principal cities.

The Case of the Franciscan Missions

It is possible to understand better the relationship between liberal ideology and the church in the way that the Bolivian state treated the case for the missions, although even here the relationship is not completely obvious. To comprehend the changes in state policy toward the missions, it is first necessary to return briefly to the political history of Bolivia. When the Bolivian political system finally stabilized in the late nineteenth century, as in the rest of Latin America, two parties, called Liberal and Conservative, emerged.

Even though they took the traditional names of the two great nineteenth-century political currents of Latin America, they did not fully subscribe to the same ideologies as the parties in other countries. This was partly due to the constant and fierce infighting among elite factions during the nineteenth century.

As Tristan Platt has suggested, both parties in a fundamental sense were liberal in outlook and policies. Among these similarities were the desire to promote free trade, the recognition that the political models that emerged from the French Revolution were superior, and the declaration that the Indian communities should be abolished since they were undesirable colonial residues.[17] Herbert S. Klein has asserted that the only difference between the two parties was the issue of whether to make peace with Chile in 1880: the Conservatives were for reestablishing commercial and political ties with their enemy during the War of the Pacific (1879–1884).[18]

While Klein's interpretation is essentially correct, it is possible to show that the Conservatives assumed the role of defending the Catholic church, whereas the Liberal Party attracted those who were anticlerical. At least in the newspapers of the period the question of the church was a point of vigorous debate, although effectively the hegemony of the Conservatives until the end of the century made the anticlerical bent of the Liberals irrelevant on the national political level. An example of Conservative ideas about the church were the writings of Mariano Baptista, president of Bolivia (1892–1896) and principal ideologist of the Conservative Party. He had defended the Catholic church since the 1860s, when he wrote newspaper articles from Europe in which he showed his profound discomfort toward church persecution by the liberals of that continent. Later in his political life he became the most consistent defender of the Catholic church as an institution. Baptista saw the church as the bulwark of true European civilization and viewed any intent to suppress its privileges as a threat that would inevitably lead the country into anarchy.[19]

The pro-Catholic sentiments of the government also had practical consequences, especially in the reestablishment of the regular clergy. The Jesuit order, when they were readmitted into Bolivia in 1882, did not purchase large properties in the countryside as before, but instead returned in their role as the educators of the Bolivian elites with the establishment of schools in the principal cities of the country. Other orders returned as well and, when possible, reoccupied the buildings in the cities from whence they had been dismissed in the first years of the republic. This was the case with the regular clergy of Santa Ana (1879), Daughters of Charity (1883), Sacred Heart (1883), Buen Pastor (1891), and the Salesians (1896).[20]

Despite these successes, the most important religious order in the nineteenth century was the Franciscan order. The Franciscans were one of the few orders that had not disappeared during the independence struggles. Even during the colonial period they had been the most important missionary order after the exodus of the Jesuits in 1767. Already in 1833, the Franciscan friar Andrés Herrera had gained permission of President Andrés de Santa Cruz to obtain more friars and fortify the convents that still existed in Tarata, Tarija, and La Paz. Herrera traveled twice to Europe and brought back a total of sixty-four Italian and Spanish friars for Bolivia.[21] Consequently, the convents began to open missions among the heathen of the eastern frontier regions and thus obtained control over large expanses of lands there.

The best example of this process were the Tarija Franciscan missions among the Chiriguanos, about which we have a significant amount of information. After Bolivian independence, the only mission still under the Franciscan Colegio de Propaganda Fide in Tarija since the great missionary thrust in the late eighteenth century was located in Salinas, on the eastern frontier in Tarija. Only in 1845 did the friars establish another mission nearby in Itau. Between this date and 1872 the Franciscans of Tarija founded a total of eight missions all along the southeastern frontier. Later, the Potosí convent founded another six missions in the same region between 1876 and 1912. Just in the department of Chuquisaca, the five missions extant at the end of the nineteenth century occupied almost 100,000 hectares of the most fertile lands of the southeastern frontier region.[22]

Given the large expanse of land the missions occupied on the frontier, why didn't nineteenth-century administrations scrutinize these holdings? There are a number of reasons: first, the anticlerical episode of the Sucre administration had resolved most church–state issues in favor of the Bolivian state; second, the missions were located, almost by definition, in marginal regions that were of little interest to most members of Bolivian society. Even if the power of the church had preoccupied the inhabitants of the densely settled highlands, the frontier missions did not represent any danger even to the hegemony of the notoriously weak Bolivian state of the nineteenth century.

The most important reason that permitted the expansion of mission lands—at times at the expense of secular colonists—was that the government viewed the missions not so much as religious institutions, but as organizations that helped develop the frontier regions. After all, the state had few resources of its own to control, much less to repress, the diverse frontier ethnic groups, among which we must count the numerous Chiriguanos, up to a quarter-million strong in the nineteenth century. This situation and the pro-Catholic policies that the ruling Conservative Party showed after 1880 were the most important reasons why the friars received all the aid they requested from the government. Luis Paz, prefect of Tarija department, expressed very well the attitudes of the ruling elites of the period. For this reason, it is worth citing him extensively:

> It is not to be doubted that the Franciscan missions constitute the only serious and helpful colonization program implanted in Bolivia. In every mission an extensive population is supplied with temples and schools, with spacious plazas, with productive meadows and orchards, as well as parks. The mission Indians are supplied with beneficial and permanent occupations, by teaching them trades and first letters, uprooting them from their barbarous state to convert them into useful agents for [the development of] civilization and industry.
>
> The barbarians disseminated in the desert, without unity, without any occupation, a constant and terrifying threat to neighboring settlements, converted into active workers, into elements of progress; that is the great work that the selfless missionaries are realizing.
>
> The government should give them all the support that they need to realize their goals, which will report the greatest and most positive services to the fatherland. It is necessary to reestablish the glorious past of the missions, which transform entire races, enabling them to progress and so that they may protect our frontiers, thus carrying the sign of possession to our deserts.[23]

With this type of discourse the government also admitted implicitly that it did not have other means to make effective its claims over frontier lands. However, in the last years of Conservative hegemony the government's frontier strategy and, with it, the role of the missions changed significantly.

The administration following pro-Catholic Baptista, that of President Severo Fernández Alonso, thought it had found a more effective method in colonizing the frontier by giving large tracts of land to private military enterprises. The Fernández administration continued to recognize the worth of the missionary enterprise, but now characterized it as having "sure results, [but which] by its nature had to be slow" and considered that the missions were "insufficient to guarantee the life and property of the colonists from the attacks of the savages."[24]

There were other very concrete problems that exacerbated the tense relations between the government and the friars at the turn of the century. In 1897, the new prefect of Chuquisaca was annoyed with the missionaries, whom he accused of permitting the contracting of mission Indians as peons in Argentina. In contrast, he exalted the inhabitants of the frontier settlements and militias in the forts for having "assured the tranquility of the population."[25] With these words, the prefect discounted the historic importance of the Franciscan missions in protecting settlers from Indian attacks and ignored the role that local officials also played in the contracting of peons.

One important reason why government officials changed their opinion about the efficacy of the mission system was the fact that the frontier had passed beyond the missions, and the settlers did not fear the attacks of the Chiriguanos or the tribes of the Gran Chaco. In the perspective of the colonists, the missions had served their purpose and so should be secularized. Another reason for the change in attitudes had to do with the large number of indigenous laborers the missionaries controlled, whom the local creoles coveted in the labor-scarce frontier economy.

Once the Liberal Party took control of the national government in the aftermath of their victory in the Federalist War (1898–1899), the undisguised anticlericalism of the new administration worsened relations with the Franciscans. With rising anticlericalism at the end of the nineteenth century, the expansion of church-held frontier territory came to a stop. Even though there were attempts to found new missions during the Liberal regime, the opposition of the settlers took precedence and the new missions were quickly turned back to secular control. This was the case with the two Parapiti missions, founded by one of the most illustrious missionaries in all of the history of the Bolivian missions, Fr. Bernardino de Nino. Established in 1903 and 1905, they were suppressed in 1912.[26] Other, older missions also suffered the same fate during this period.

The most important secularization case was that of the missions of San Antonio de Padua and San Francisco Solano, on opposite shores of the Pilcomayo River, which the government combined to form the town of Villamontes in 1906. Although the Indians of these missions should have received plots within San Antonio and San Francisco, the government turned virtually the whole territory over to Staudt and Company, a German merchant firm that promised to develop the economy of the region. The company almost immediately began to acquire large chunks of land around the settlement and became probably the most powerful and perhaps largest landowner in the whole Bolivian Chaco. The Franciscans complained bitterly, but were unable to regain the missions' lands. Again the model of frontier development based on private enterprise had triumphed, this time at the direct expense of the mission enterprise.[27]

The Problem of the Indian Communities

The elites' debates over Indian communities has been studied extensively, and in many aspects is similar to debates on the same issue taking place elsewhere in Latin America.[28] What we would like to emphasize here is that the state's fiscal needs and the fear of a caste war in a militarily weak state made any meaningful reform impossible until the second half of the nineteenth century. This does not mean that there was no development of ideological positions over the course of the nineteenth century independent of the actual situation in the countryside or the state's capacity to implement any reform measures.

Nevertheless, the 1860s saw an intensification in the debates over the role of the Indian communities in Bolivian social and economic development. Not surprisingly, this was the precise time when liberal ideological currents, which were also to predominate in much of the rest of Latin America, began extending their influence over the elites in Bolivia. The issue of Indian communities was part of a larger debate in the latter decades of the nineteenth century concerning the nature of economic development of the country. This included the ways in which the countryside could be transformed to utilize the land as productively as possible. Liberal ideology postulated that it was necessary to create a free land market to reach this goal. All the authors agreed on this point; what they debated was the best method to achieve these aims.

One influential faction argued that the Indians were incapable of becoming capitalist farmers. Instead, the communities should be reorganized as haciendas in the hands of the elites. One of the most important representatives of this position was José Vicente Dorado, who asserted that the Indians could only prosper under the guidance of creole *hacendados*. The creole landowners, after all, were not only the only ones imbued with a capitalist mentality, but they could also protect the ex-community members from abusive local officials and priests.[29]

Others argued from a different perspective. They also wanted to abolish the Indian communities, but thought that the only way to change the Indians from subsistence-oriented peasants to farmers was to abolish the tribute system and give each community member property rights over the plots that he controlled. Those who made this argument proposed the division of the community among its inhabitants, because only in this fashion would they have the incentive to invest their own capital and labor in the land. To favor the hacienda, or the large property, would be an error because it had already proved to be a relatively unproductive system that would not promote the development of a true land market.[30]

Important regional differences can be discerned in this debate. Those who favored José Vicente Dorado's position were generally from the northern part of the country, around La Paz, where the Aymara communities dominated virtually the whole *altiplano*. The *paceños* felt that their region's economic development was restricted because most of the land around the city of La Paz was in the hands of the Indian communities. They saw as their salvation a hacienda-dominated region such as the Yungas, in the valleys to the east of La Paz, where landowners received excellent returns commercializing *coca* leaves and other subtropical products.

In turn, elites from Cochabamba, Potosí, and Sucre were generally in favor of giving the land directly to the Indians, although each had somewhat different reasons for favoring this policy. In Cochabamba, the pamphleteers looked toward the peasantry's successful participation in the market, in a region where traces of the communities' social and political structures had virtually disappeared. Elites from Potosí and Sucre (many of the latter were also silver-mine owners in Potosí as well) surely took into account the important commercial activity in which the Indian communities engaged in the region, particularly the prolific wheat production that sustained the urban and mining centers. Moreover, they had an acute sense of the power of these communities, given the sporadic Indian revolts that punctuated the nineteenth century.

Despite the arguments of the southerners and their intellectual (and realistic) foundations, the officials of the regime of Mariano Melgarejo (1864–1871), who desperately needed funds to finance the army necessary to put down the chronic attempts at revolution during his administration, ignored these objections. Instead, they favored the hacienda. Thus, to a certain degree, the Melgarejo regime put into effect many of Dorado's recommendations when he put up the community lands for sale. Although the government based its actions on the intellectual justifications of the debate that preceded this sale, it is difficult to believe that the results—the acquisition of funds for the state—was not much more important than any liberal-inspired arguments. Leaving aside the practical motives for these actions, the Melgarejo reforms nevertheless remain important because of the precedents they set and for the creation of a powerful pressure group within the elites that favored the transformation of the communities into haciendas, despite their initial lack of legislative success.

In fact, the 1866 and 1868 sales of *tierras de origen*, as the community lands were called, were not permanent. The revolutionaries who finally overthrew Melgarejo in 1871 had to resort to the mobilization of the *altiplano* Indian communities. The Indians retook the haciendas formed by the sale of community lands (at least in the north of the country) and the new government had neither the will nor the military means to remove the armed Indians from their recently reconquered communities.[31]

Only the 1874 laws of *ex-vinculación*, implemented from 1880 onward, led to the legal abolition of the communities and the slow incorporation of

Indian lands into the "free" land market. The process of *ex-vinculación* was different from the program applied by the Melgarejo administration because the southern interests won the battle over how to implement these reforms. The 1874 laws ordered that the government give the lands directly to the Indians so that the community members presumably could transform themselves into small yeoman farmers according to the Liberal model.

The *ex-vinculación* of Indian lands was a long and drawn-out process and so did not, as had happened in the case of ecclesiastical lands, dump large amounts of lands on the market in one fell swoop. The 1880 implementing legislation for the distribution of community lands called for a relatively complex bureaucratic process. In the first place, commissions had to measure each plot of land to make possible the handing out of titles. This process, called *revisita*, took many years, given the scant resources of the state, and, in many places, was never completed. Moreover, Indian resistance to the measurement of lands was common and in many cases helped postpone—sometimes indefinitely—the *ex-vinculación* process.[32] Another result of this legislation was that, in theory, purchasers of Indian land had to do so plot by plot and could not, as during the Melgarejo administration, acquire whole communities. In practice, however, the process of acquisition showed important regional differences.

In the south and in the center of the country (Cochabamba, Chuquisaca, and Potosí), whole communities were rarely transformed into new haciendas. In Cochabamba this was the case because community lands were scarce to begin with and the communities had already suffered internal divisions in the land-tenure system and in their social organization. In turn, in Chuquisaca and Potosí strong peasant resistance made it difficult for non-Indians to acquire land, at least in great quantities. The great majority of land sales involved only portions of holdings and often to pay off relatively small debts. Where haciendas were carved exclusively out of community land, such as in the case of Hacienda El Carmen in Chuquisaca, the owners had endemic problems with neighboring Indian communities that tried to regain their old properties.[33] In addition, there was not a very strong economic incentive to purchase Indian lands. In the mid-nineteenth century the elites found it much more lucrative to invest their money in silver-mining-company stocks. When the silver mining declined in the south in the last years of the nineteenth century, the region entered into a prolonged period of economic decline that also affected earnings from land.[34]

The situation was rather different in the northern part of the country. The tin boom in the last years of the nineteenth century and the wave of speculation that followed on its heels made it attractive for members of the *paceño* elite to buy Indian lands as a way of gaining collateral to obtain credit and mining company stock. Also, the building of the railroad network on the *altiplano* led to an economic expansion in the northern countryside and to increased land values. Thus, incentives were great to purchase whole communities at low prices, which led to many fraudulent sales and, in some cases, even the use of force. The most striking example of this form of acquisition was President Ismael Montes's purchase of a large part of the Taraco peninsula on Lake Titicaca in the first decade of the twentieth century. When the Indians resisted, Montes sent troops to occupy the territory and make effective his acquisition by force of arms.[35] Even though Erwin Grieshaber has recently questioned the La Paz stereotype of the creation of haciendas from entire communities, this pattern was much more common in the north than in southern or central Bolivia.[36]

Apparently, the racist ideology of social Darwinism, which considered the Indians to be inferior beings destined to be dominated by people of European extraction, had more adherents in turn-of-the-century La Paz than elsewhere in the country. Of course, it also proved to be a very convenient ideology to justify the usurpation of indigenous lands within the Bolivian context.[37] By the early twentieth century it is possible to note a contamination of liberal ideology. At times, members of the elites did not even try to keep up the pretense that the liberal reforms were eventually to benefit everybody and create new opportunities for the peasant majority.

This was the case with the so-called surplus lands in Cochabamba department. The government defined as surplus those lands occupied by community members who controlled more land than the state considered necessary for their subsistence; lands occupied by non-Indians also fell into this category. In the majority of cases, local governments sold or rented those lands, but in Cochabamba the administration, or better said, poor administration of surplus lands caused a political scandal that lasted five years (1909–1914) during the Liberal Party administration.[38]

We have centered our analysis on the administration of surplus lands in the department of Cochabamba (see Table 6.1). Initially, the government sold or rented out surplus lands held by non-Indians and, in some very isolated cases, distributed these lands to ex-community members. In Cochabamba, the municipal council of the capital of the same name received the responsibility of administering the lands of the state. They sold some lands in the Valle Bajo region. Otherwise, there was not much interest in the last decades of the nineteenth century for buying lands in the *altiplano* districts of Cochabamba, and these were rented out. For example, in 1878 José Moscoso, a Cochabamba landowner, annually paid 2,208 Bolivianos rent for state ranch lands in Canton Vacas.[39]

Table 6.1: State-Owned Lands in Cochabamba
in the Early Twentieth Century

Cantón	Ecological Zone	Number of Properties	Hectares
Passo	Valley	10	24.66.12
Tiquipaya*	Valley	6	26.19.06
VilaVila*	Altiplano	1	10,330.56.00
TinTin	Altiplano	1	980.92.50
Vacas	Altiplano	20	5,183.04.80
Tapacari	Altiplano	9	2,446.75.61
Quirquiavi	Altiplano	12	834.33.81

*Lands confiscated for failure to pay land taxes.
Source: Catastro de la propiedad rustica, Archivo de la Prefectura de Cochabamba, various jurisdictions; *El Ferrocarril* and *El Heraldo*.

The law of January 15, 1900, stipulated that the municipal council sell state lands in Cochabamba to pay for schools in the urban centers. The council was to invest funds from the sale of these lands in mortgage notes. However, the council did not attempt to sell the surplus lands; instead, it continued to offer them as rental properties. Only some plots were sold in the Valle Bajo. In 1909 the prefect of Cochabamba and a Liberal Party member, José Santos Quiroga (1908–1910), took advantage of a 1908 law that contradicted the 1900 law and sold the state-held ranches in Canton Quirquiavi (Arque province) under suspicious circumstances. Santos Quiroga only published the land-sale announcements in a temporary newspaper established in 1910 to promote Liberal Party candidates for the elections of the same year, and not in the regular Cochabamba newspapers, as was customary. The purchasers of the ranches were speculators who acquired the lands in anticipation of the arrival of the Oruro-Cochabamba railroad that was to pass through Arque. Before paying the government, the speculators sold the lands at a higher price to third parties.

The opposition Republican Party used the sale of the Quirquiavi ranches to attack the ethics of the government in power. Indeed, the case of the Quirquiavi ranches shows well the way in which local elites used Liberal politics for their own advantage. This case, and that of Taraco, shows clearly the bankruptcy of Bolivian liberalism by the beginning of the twentieth century.

Conclusion

The case of Bolivian liberalism shows well the differences in the treatment of different corporate institutions. On the one hand, the Sucre administration expropriated church lands soon after independence. On the other hand, after about the middle of the nineteenth century it is possible to discern an alliance between the Bolivian state and the religious orders that made possible the establishment of missionary systems on the eastern frontier. Moreover, the female orders were never affected in the same way as those of the men. They emerged relatively unscathed by Sucre's anticlerical program and were able to keep most of their resources throughout the nineteenth century.

In turn, the state's policies toward the Indian communities (the only other important corporate entities outside of the Catholic church) were almost exactly opposite those that applied to the religious communities. At the beginning of the republican period, although the government also tried to abolish the communities and create a class of smallholding farmers, it failed to do so for a number of reasons. Only in the second half of the nineteenth century, with the reforms imposed by the Melgarejo administration, did liberal prescriptions triumph. Even though the Melgarejo reforms did not last, after 1880 the so-called *ex-vinculación* of Indian lands accelerated and led to the expansion of the hacienda as well as the *mestizo* towns' economies in the countryside.

Why these differences? Was it because Bolivian liberals (regardless of party affiliation) were insincere and inconsistent in their beliefs? In fact, we know that Latin American elites did not copy totally liberal ideology brought over from Europe. They always adapted these ideas to the realities of their own countries, although in hindsight it is clear that their perceptions were often distorted because of their own class position and by regional interests to which they were tied.

This, however, is insufficient to explain the apparent contradictions in liberal ideology. Why did they attack one corporate entity and not another? To rely on semantic arguments and assert that the party of the southern silver oligarchs, the Conservative Party, was truly conservative in their outlook cannot be sustained. Despite their name, with the exception of church-related issues, the Conservatives overall followed liberal policies. In addition to the *ex-vinculación* of Indian communities, they established free trade, expanded the transportation network, put the army under civilian control, and implemented other liberal reforms. To resolve this apparent contradiction, it is necessary to take into account three factors: the Catholic church's lack of influence immediately after independence, the relatively great power of the Indian communities, and the important role that the Catholic church played at the end of the nineteenth century in the development policies of the Bolivian government.

The church–state issue had already been decided in favor of the Bolivian government early in the republican period, a remarkable exception to patterns elsewhere in Latin America. Occupied by a foreign army and with a president born elsewhere who could not be pressured by traditional techniques through ties among the elites, the Catholic church did not represent an important political force. The feminine orders were not a political danger, serving instead Bolivian elites in placing unmarried daughters so as not to dilute unduly the inheritance. After the political chaos that followed the fall of the Santa Cruz administration (1829–1839), the church did not play an important role; by this time it already was an institution not worth fighting over. Even the pro-clerical policies of the Conservative Party did not substantially change this situation. The Catholic church was never able to dominate Bolivian society, even with the help of Mariano Baptista's powerful rhetoric or that of his cohorts. At best, the government aided the church in an essentially liberal project: developing the national economy on the frontier fringes.

The Conservatives recognized the role the Franciscans had played since the 1840s in this endeavor, an endeavor that had been approved by previous administrations as well. It is not known whether this was an intentional policy, but even the Conservatives kept the church's influence limited mainly to the sparsely settled frontier areas. As with other administrations, the Conservatives also recognized that the state had insufficient resources to take on the task of developing the frontier itself. However, once strong economic growth took place in the region that made colonization by private entities more likely, the Conservative government favored these over the missionary enterprise. The change in government, from Conservative to Liberal parties, simply accelerated a process begun under the former. As in other aspects, again we see that the Conservative Party was essentially liberal in its ideological orientation.

The case of the Indian communities shows something slightly different. The communities were much more powerful during the nineteenth century than the Catholic church. The history of the attempts to abolish the Indian community as a legal entity goes back to the Sucre administration, but it is clear that the government did not have at its disposal sufficient repressive powers to implement the Bolivarian laws. This suggests, among other things, that the Catholic church suffered much more during the wars for independence than the communities; however, this is a hypothesis that needs further testing. Be that as it may, the reintroduction of the tributary regimen under Andrés de Santa Cruz and legislation introduced by José Ballivian and other administrations until Melgarejo were pragmatic actions intended to maintain fiscal income and thus, implicitly, recognized the severe problems that reforming rural society might have entailed.

Mariano Melgarejo and his advisors believed that they finally did have the resources that made the destruction of the communities possible and thus would reform, according to liberal principles fashionable among intellectuals, the Bolivian land-tenure system. They were wrong. The Indians' movement was crucial in the overthrow of the *caudillo*'s government, and afterward the new rulers returned to the old system. Only a gradual reform, such as that actually implemented after 1880, was possible. Indeed, the process of alienation of Indian lands could only accelerate after the Federalist War, when the national army defeated Pablo Zarate Willka, the military leader of the *altiplano* communities. Again, the Liberal Party inherited a situation in which an essentially liberal policy had already been put into place; it was just that the Liberals were even more vigorous in pursuing this policy than their predecessors.

In this sense, the often great differences in the two cases we have observed virtually disappear. In both cases, the ironically named Conservatives already had begun policies based on liberal principles. They also introduced a measure of political stability and so gained the resources necessary to diminish significantly the power of the church, even in the far frontiers of the republic, as well as to abolish the Indian communities in the center of the country. Thus, the policies of the Liberal Party after 1899 were simply extensions of measures introduced previously. The apparent corruption in the sale of community lands in Cochabamba showed the extremely pragmatic vision of the new government in the case of the Indian communities.

Notes

1. For a description immediately after independence, see Joseph B. Pentland, *Informe sobre Bolivia*, trans. Jack Aitken Soux (Potosí, 1975); and William L. Lofstrom, *La presidencia de Sucre en Bolivia*, trans. Mariano Bapista G. (Caracas, 1987). The fundamental work on the independence period in Bolivia continues to be Charles W. Arnade, *La dramática insurgencia de Bolivia*, trans. Luis Penaloza C. (La Paz, 1972). Also, see René Arze Aguirre, *Participación popular en la independencia de Bolivia* (La Paz, 1979). For the situation of the church, see, for example, Alejandro M. Corrado, *El colegio franciscano de Tarija y sus misiones*, 2d ed., vol. 2 (Tarija, 1990).

2. For a general introduction to the role of the Catholic church in Latin America, see Arnold J. Bauer, "The Church in the Economy of Spanish America: *Censos* and *Depósitos* in the Eighteenth and Nineteenth Centuries," *Hispanic American Historical Review* 63:4 (1983), 707–33. A more detailed study is Michael Costeloe, *Church Wealth in Mexico: A Study of the "Juzgado de Capellanías" in the Archbishopric of Mexico 1800–1856* (Cambridge, 1967).

3. For the antecedents of the *consolidación de vales reales* and Spanish reformist politics, see Richard Herr, *Rural Change and Royal Finances in Spain at the End of the Old Regime* (Berkeley, 1989), especially chaps. 1 and 2. For the implementation of the *consolidación de vales reales* in Spanish America, see Brian Hamnett, "The Appropriation of Mexican Church Wealth by the Spanish Bourbon Government—'The *Consolidación de Vales Reales*,' 1805–1809," *Journal of Latin American Studies* 1 (1968), 85–13; Asunción Lavrin, "The Execution of the Law of 'Consolidación' in New Spain: Economic Aims and Results," *Hispanic American Historical Review* 53:1 (1973), 27–49; Romeo Flores Caballero, *La contrarevolución en la independencia. Los españoles en la vida política, social y económica de México (1804–1838)* (Mexico City, 1969); Masae Sugawara H., *La deuda pública de España y la economía novohispana, 1804–09* (Mexico City, 1976); Margaret Chowning, "The Consolidación de Vales Reales in the Bishopric of Michoacán," *Hispanic American Historical Review* 69:3 (1989), 451–778. The impact of the policies of the *consolidación de vales reales* has received little attention outside of Mexico. For an exception, see Lowell Gudmundson, "The Expropriation of Pious and Corporate Properties in Costa Rica, 1805–1860: Patterns of Consolidation of a National Elite," *The Americas* 39:3 (1983), 281–303.

4. Liberal policies regarding church wealth have been studied in most detail for Mexico, and at times there is a tendency to equate the disentailment process in other Latin American countries with that of Mexico. For an overview of liberal politics in Mexico, see Richard Sinkin, *The Mexican Reform: 1855–1876: A Study in Liberal Nation-Building* (Austin, 1979), especially chap. 7; and Robert Knowlton, *Church Property and the Mexican Reform (1856–1910)* (DeKalb, 1976).

5. For liberal policies in Colombia, including the disentailment of church wealth, see Richard Hyland, "A Fragile Prosperity: Credit and Agrarian Structure in the Cauca Valley, Colombia, 1851–87," *Hispanic American Historical Review* 62:3 (1982), 369–406.

6. Studies on the church and its properties in Bolivia focus either on the activities of the missionaries in the eastern region, or on national-level institutional history. See, for example, Josep M. Barnadas, *La iglesia católica en Bolivia* (La Paz, 1976); David Block, *Mission Culture on the Upper Amazon: Native Tradition, Jesuit Enterprise, and Secular Policy in Moxos, 1660–1880* (Lincoln, 1994); Eudoxio Palacio and José Brunet, *Los Mercedarios en Bolivia* (La Paz, 1975); Walter Hermosa V., *Tribus selvicolas y misiones jesuitas y franciscanas en Bolivia* (La Paz, 1986). There are a number of articles that describe the Jesuit properties after the Jesuits' expulsion by Charles III. See, for example, Rene Arze Aguirre, "Las haciendas jesuitas de La Paz (siglo XVIII)," *Historia y Cultura* 1 (1973), 105–24; and Edgar Valda M., "Datos sobre la Compañía de Jesús en Potosí," *Historia Boliviana* 6 (1986), 43–60.

7. Herbert S. Klein, "The Structure of the Hacendado Class in Late Eigh-

teenth-Century Alto Peru: The Intendencia de La Paz," *Hispanic American Historical Review* 60:2 (1980), 212.

8. Lofstrom, *La presidencia*, pp. 145–46; also, Brooke Larson, *Colonialism and Agrarian Transformation in Bolivia: Cochabamba, 1550–1900* (Princeton, 1988), p. 223.

9. Lofstrom, *La presidencia*, pp. 159–71. According to the work of Thomas Millington, the purchasers of the ex-church properties could acquire the haciendas and cancel the *censos* with internal government debt notes, which lost much of their value on the open market. See Thomas Millington, *Debt Politics after Independence: The Funding Conflict in Bolivia* (Gainesville, 1992), p. 96. For example, the elites in Cochabamba took advantage of the decree of 1826, paying for the confiscated haciendas of the regular orders in certificates with a nominal value of 214,080 pesos, and paid for the *censos* with certificates with nominal values of 37,392 pesos.

10. Robert H. Jackson, "The Alienation of the Lands of the Regular Clergy in Cochabamba, Bolivia, 1826–1882," unpublished manuscript.

11. Klein, "Structure," 202; and by the same author, "The Distribution of Landed Wealth in Late Nineteenth Century Bolivia: The Hacendados of the Department of La Paz in 1881–1882," in *Agrarian Society in History: Essays in Honor of Magnus Mörner*, ed. Mats Lundhal and Thommy Svensson (London, 1990), pp. 71–88.

12. Damian Rejas, *Tercer centenario de la fundación del Monasterio de Santa Clara de Asis en Cochabamba, años 1648–1948* (Cochabamba, 1948), pp. 16–17.

13. Jackson, "Alienation," table 11.

14. Ibid. For an index of agricultural prices in Cochabamba, see Robert H. Jackson, "The Decline of the Hacienda in Cochabamba, Bolivia: The Case of the Sacaba Valley, 1870–1929," *Hispanic American Historical Review* 69:2 (1989), 281.

15. See, for example, the announcement published in *El Ferrocarril*, July 25, 1911.

16. Robert H. Jackson, "Liberal Land and Economic Policy and the Transformation of the Rural Sector of the Bolivian Economy: The Case of Cochabamba, 1860–1929" (Ph.D. diss., University of California, Berkeley, 1988), 214–19.

17. See, for example, Tristan Platt, *Estado boliviano y ayllu andino* (Lima, 1982); also, by the same author, "Liberalism and Ethnocide in the Southern Andes," *History Workshop* 17 (1984), 3–18. The creation of political parties at the end of the nineteenth century is described in Herbert S. Klein, *Parties and Political Change in Bolivia, 1880–1952* (Cambridge, 1971), pp. 17–30. For a general overview of liberalism in Bolivia, see Erick D. Langer, "El liberalismo y al abolición de la comunidad indígena en el siglo XIX," *Historia y Cultura* 14 (1988), 59–95.

18. Klein, *Parties*, pp. 22–23.

19. Mariano Baptista, *Obras completas* (La Paz, 1932–1935), especially 7:142–57, 227–36.

20. Barnadas, *La iglesia*, pp. 99–100.

21. Corrado, *El colegio franciscano*, pp. 301–13.

22. Fermin Prudencio, *Memoria de Guerra y Colonización 1917* (La Paz, 1917), p. 132. Also, see Erick D. Langer, "Mission Land Tenure on the Southeastern Bolivian Frontier, 1845–1949," *The Americas* 50:3 (1994), 399–418.

23. Luis Paz, *Informe que en cumplimiento de la ley eleva el Supremo Gobierno, el Prefecto y Comandante General de Tariaj, sobre la administración del Departamento* (Tarija, 1890), pp. 31–32.

24. Fernando Quiroga S., *Informe de la Prefectura y Comandancia General del Departamento de Chuquisaca* (Sucre, 1897), pp. 25–26.

25. Joaquin Torrelio, *Informe del Prefecto del Departamento de Chuquisaca* (Sucre, 1896), p. 44.

26. Bernardino de Nino, *Las tres misiones secularizadas de la Provincia de Cordillera* (Tarata, 1916).

27. Gerardo Maldini, *Franciscanos en Tarija* (La Paz, 1988), pp. 131–39; Anonymous, *Las industrias del Gran Chaco y la Empresa Colonizadora Staudt y Compañía* (Tarija, 1912).

28. For a general overview of the problem of Indian tribute and the communities, see Langer, "El liberalismo;" Jorge Alejandro Ovando Sanz, *El tributo indígena en las finanzas bolivianas del siglo XIX* (La Paz, 1985); and Erwin P. Grieshaber, "Survival of Indian Communities in Nineteenth-Century Bolivia," (Ph.D. diss., University of North Carolina, 1977).

29. José Vicente Dorado, *Proyecto de repartición de tierras y venta de ellas entre los indígenas* (Sucre, 1864).

30. Pedro Vargas, *Indicaciones economicas para la reforma del sistema tributario de Bolivia* (Potosí, 1864).

31. See Langer, "El liberalismo," 78–79. In the case of Chuquisaca, in the southern portion of the country, many Indians were unable to recoup their lands lost during the Melgarejo administration. See Erick D. Langer, "Persistencia y cambio en las comunidades indígenas surbolivianas (siglo XIX)," in *Los Andes en la encrucijada: Indios, comunidades y estado en el siglo XIX*, comp. Heraclio Bonilla (Quito, 1991), pp. 133–67.

32. Langer, *Economic Change and Rural Resistance in Southern Bolivia, 1880–1930* (Stanford, 1989), pp. 65–66; Platt, *Estado boliviano*, pp. 73–111; Platt, "Liberalism," passim.

33. Langer, *Economic Change*, pp. 43, 79–80, 83–84.

34. See Jackson, "Liberal Land"; and Gustavo Rodríguez O., "Entre reformas y contrareformas: Las comunidades indígenas en el Valle Bajo cochabambino," in Bonilla, *Los Andes*, pp. 277–334, for the Cochabamba case. For Chuquisaca, see Langer, *Economic Change*; for Potosí, see Platt, *Estado boliviano*.

35. Silvia Rivera C., "La expansión del latifundio en el altiplano boliviano: Elementos para la caracterización de una oligarquia regional," *Avances* 2 (178), 95–118. For Taraco, see Silvia Rivera C., *Oprimidos pero no vencidos: Luchas del campesinado aymara y qhechwa, 1900–1980* (La Paz, 1986), p. 32.

36. Erwin P. Grieshaber, "La expansión de la hacienda en el Departamento de La Paz, Bolivia, 1850–1920: Una versión cuantitativa," *Andes: Antropologia e Historia* 2–3 (1990), 33–83.

37. Langer, "El liberalismo," pp. 85–86.

38. Some historians have examined the impact of the implementation of the law of *ex-vinculación* on other regions of Bolivia, but have not identified the important category of lands defined by the state as "surplus lands." The sales of communities in the 1860s included this category of lands.

39. Protocolos notariales (Cochabamba City) 1878, Archivo Historico Municipal de Cochabamba.

7
Community and Hacienda in the Bolivian Highlands
Changing Patterns of Land Tenure in Arque and Vacas
Robert H. Jackson

In the late nineteenth and early twentieth centuries patterns of land tenure in Bolivia experienced rapid change. Efforts to liquidate the corporate indigenous community met with varying degrees of success in different parts of the country, and the hacienda either expanded or was fragmented.

This essay briefly explores changing community and hacienda tenure in two highland regions in Cochabamba department, Arque province, and Vacas. Prior to its administrative subdivision in the early twentieth century, Arque province consisted of three different ecological zones: high altitude plains and the mountains of the eastern Andes cordillera, often in excess of fifteen thousand feet in elevation, the narrow Arque River Valley cut through the Andes Cordillera, and the lower elevation Capinota and Caraza valleys. Corporate communities existed in the Capinota Valley, and Quirquiavi in the highland section of the province. Privately owned haciendas dominated much of the rest of the province. Vacas, a high altitude plain that borders the Valle Alto, was dominated by corporate indigenous community lands and to a lesser extent by haciendas.

This essay briefly outlines changing land tenure in the communities and haciendas in both areas. The first sections document government policy toward the communities in the middle and late nineteenth century and the impact of the law of *ex-vinculación* (1874), which attempted to liquidate the communities. A discussion of highland haciendas, changes in hacienda tenure, and changing patterns of landownership in Arque province follows these sections.

Recreating the Community in the Mid-Nineteenth Century

Beginning in the 1570s, during the administration of Viceroy Francisco de Toledo (1569–1581), the colonial and later the republican administrations in Upper Peru/Bolivia assumed an active role in defining the structure and extent of the corporate indigenous community. The Toledan reforms of the early 1570s included the policy of *reducción,* the resettlement of spatially dispersed Indian populations into more compact settlements with clearly defined land rights. During the early colonial period, the government defined two classes of tributaries who paid different tribute levels depending on their legal status. *Originarios,* community members with full rights to community lands, paid higher tribute levels than did *forasteros,* Indians who had left their native communities and settled in haciendas, the emerging Spanish towns, or other communities.[1] Throughout the colonial period, tribute constituted an important source of government revenue, although the number of *originarios* steadily declined during the seventeenth and eighteenth centuries due to disease and out-migration from the communities as the weight of tribute payments and service in the mining mita in Potosí and elsewhere became too burdensome.

In the early 1790s and in the 1840s and 1850s, the state took a more active role in defining the internal structure of the corporate community by converting *forasteros* to the legal status of *originarios* with an obligation to pay higher tribute levels. For example, between 1793 and 1795, under the direction of Intendant Francisco de Viedma, officials in Cochabamba settled *forasteros* on community lands and legally transformed them into *originarios*.[2] While trying to increase the amount of tribute collected, government officials also re-created the community by assigning community lands to *forasteros*.

During the fifty years following Bolivian independence, politicians debated the future of the corporate indigenous community in Bolivia, and passed a series of laws designed to define the status of the communities. However, since the Bolivian government still heavily depended on tribute as a source of revenue, little was done to implement the anticommunity legislation.[3] In the 1860s and again in the 1870s, the Bolivian government passed legislation that terminated the special legal status of the communities and started the process of alienating community lands. However, there was one last instance of the re-creation of the corporate communities through the settlement of *forasteros* on community lands, in the late 1850s and early 1860s, following a severe mortality crisis in 1856 that reduced the number of *originarios* in several communities.

The 1856 epidemic significantly reduced the Indian population and the number of tributaries throughout Cochabamba department. The Indian population of six provinces in Cochabamba department reportedly dropped from 50,770 in 1852 to 35,454 in 1858, two years following the epidemic.[5] The number of tributaries in different parts of Cochabamba dropped. The number of tributaries in Cercado province (Cochabamba City, Itocta, CalaCala,

Sacaba, Colomi, and Tablas) dropped from 507 in 1850, 448 in 1855, to 181 thirteen years later in 1868.[6] Similarly, the number of tributaries in selected jurisdictions in the Valle Alto and adjoining highland areas (Paredon, Punata, San Benito, Arani, and Tiraque) declined from 495 in 1850 to 263 in 1867.[7] Following the epidemic, on July 25, 1857, the government enacted a law that mandated the redistribution of lands left vacant by the epidemic to "honorable" Indians, which led to the redistribution of some community lands.[8]

The tribute records for Cantón Capinota document the creation of new *originarios* following the passage of the 1857 law. Prior to the epidemic in 1856 there were 81 *originarios* with land in Capinota, 199 *originarios* without land, and 166 *forasteros* (see Table 7.1). In the wake of the epidemic, landless *originarios* and *forasteros* were resettled as landed *originarios*. The tribute censuses of 1858, 1863, and 1871 record 115 *originarios*, who controlled a community territory that embraced a total of 3,696.91.64 hectares of land.[9] Nevertheless, disputes over community land did occur in the decade following the epidemic and creation of new landed *originarios*. For example, in 1867, during the regime of Mariano Melgarejo (1864–1871) and during an effort to sell community lands, the government announced the sale of six parcels of land in IrpaIrpa, with a total area of 18.96.33 hectares reportedly usurped by *originarios* who, according to the government, had no right to use the disputed lands.[10]

Cantón Quirquiavi, located in the highland section of Arque, provides a more complex example of state-directed change in the internal structure of a community. The tribute censuses show that in 1858 there were 359 landless *forasteros* and no landed *originarios* (see Table 7.2). In 1862, the government conducted a *deslinde* (examination of land titles and boundaries) prompted by a revolt on the privately owned property that had previously dominated the area.[11] According to the tribute censuses prepared in 1863

Table 7.1: Tributaries by Category in Cantón Capinota in Selected Years

Year	*Originarios* with Land	*Originarios* without Land	*Forasteros* without Land
1850	79	197	178
1856	81	199	166
1858	115	97	Not Available
1863	115	0	99
1871	115	18	74

Source: Padrones de Tributarios, Archivo Nacional de Bolivia, Arque Province, Selected Years.

Table 7.2: Tributaries by Categories in
Cantón Quirquiavi in Selected Years

Year	Originarios with Land	Forasteros without Land
1858	0	359
1863	317	83
1871	324	122

Source: Padrones de Tributarios, Archivo Nacional de Bolivia, Arque Province, Selected Years.

and 1871, respectively, there were 317 and 324 landed *originarios* in Cantón Quirquiavi, and only 83 and 122 landless *forasteros* (see Table 7.2). In other words, the 1862 *deslinde* resulted in the distribution of land to more than 300 newly created *originarios*.

The distribution of land in Quirquiavi in 1862 transformed the structure of land tenure. The Jesuits owned Hacienda Quirquiavi until their expulsion in the late 1760s, and after the expulsion the government administered the estate.[12] A private family bought Hacienda Quirquiavi, most likely in the 1820s. In 1860, the hacienda was divided into four sections in order to realize the division of an estate for inheritance. After 1862, no private properties existed in Quirquiavi. Writing in the *Diccionario Geográfico de la República de Bolivia*, Dr. Federico Blanco noted of Quirquiavi that "Es bastante extenso y antes formaba una sola comunidad" [It is very extensive and before formed only one community].[13] Altogether, the government distributed some 6,687.98.52 hectares of land to the new *originarios*, a calculation based upon data from the cadastral survey.[14] In addition to the lands assigned in Cantón Quirquiavi, the Indians of Quirquiavi apparently pooled their resources and bought Hacienda Challoma Grande, located in Cantón Tacopaya, along the Arque River and at a lower elevation than Quirquiavi, from one Dr. Samuel Gonzales Portal. The cadastral survey prepared around 1916 recorded an area for the property of 258.84.76 hectares.[15] The acquisition of Challoma Grande reflected the strategy of controlling lands at different ecological niches.

The Impact of the Law of Ex-Vinculación, *1874–1929*

The Bolivian politicians who drafted the law of *ex-vinculación* in 1874 envisioned a radical transformation of land tenure in the country. Many members of the elite wanted to see large haciendas absorb former community

COMMUNITY AND HACIENDA   197

lands, which would put large quantities of land in the hands of white landowners who, from the point of view of government officials and politicians influenced by social Darwinism, were more qualified to exploit them. However, in the case of large parts of Cochabamba department the legal abolition of the community in the long run did not lead to the creation of new haciendas or the expansion of existing estates. Rather, in the fifty years following the passage of the law of *ex-vinculación* agricultural land in sections of Cochabamba department experienced rapid fragmentation, and thousands of former community members, landless peasants, and artisans retained or acquired small plots of land.

Much of the community land in Cantón Capinota passed into the hands of a sizable group of smallholders. According to the cadastral survey prepared about 1916, there were 814 separate properties in Cantón Capinota with a size of less than 10 hectares; 89.7 percent of all properties in the jurisdiction, occupied 26 percent of the land registered in the cadastral survey. Large haciendas with an extension of more than 100 hectares occupied only 21.1 percent of the land in the jurisdiction. Land in Cantón Capinota was fairly evenly distributed between small (less than 10 hectares), medium (10–99.99 hectares), and large (more than 100 hectares) properties (see Table 7.3).

Cantón Quirquiavi offers a more complex pattern of change in the structure of land tenure in the years following the passage of the law of *ex-vinculación*. The original legislation passed in 1874 attempted to abolish all forms of communal land tenure and force community members to take individual title to their lands. However, in the early 1880s the government

Table 7.3: Structure of Land Tenure in Cantón Capinota, ca. 1916

Size of Parcel in Hectares	Number of Properties	%	Area in Hectares	%
0–0.99	527	58.0	204.41.08	4.6
1–4.99	224	24.8	499.28.51	1.2
5–9.99	63	6.9	456.94.04	10.2
10–19.99	42	4.6	600.19.42	13.4
20–49.99	23	2.5	661.34.99	14.8
50–99.99	17	1.9	1,102.87.03	24.7
100–499.99	3	0.3	325.08.88	7.3
500–999.99	1	0.1	615.86.64	13.8
Size Not Given	8	0.9		
Total	908		4,466.00.59	

Source: Catastro de la Propiedad Rústica, Archivo de la Prefectura de Cochabamba, Capinota Province, Cantón Capinota.

made a number of modifications of the law. For example, a law passed on August 16, 1880, at the height of the War of the Pacific, when most of Bolivia's army was on the coast in Tarapaca, allowed community members to receive title in an undivided communalist *pro-indiviso* tenure.

To carry out the task of measuring the individual parcels to be granted to community members and to distribute individual titles, the government created *mesas revisitadores* (land commissions). The land commissions began the task of measuring lands in 1876, but with mixed results. Community members in Potosí, Oruro, and La Paz departments actively resisted the visits of the land commissions. As a result, the work of distributing land titles lasted longer than had originally been anticipated, and in some areas the land commissions never completed their work.

The land commissions worked slowly in Quirquiavi, adjudicating title to community lands in 1880, 1883, and again in 1897. Most of the *estancias* located in Quirquiavi remained in the hands of community members in the *pro-indiviso* tenure (2,835.47.41 hectares). The commissions granted individual title to thirty-six estancias to community members (3,018.17.30 hectares) and returned twelve properties (834.33.81 hectares) to the public domain. However, the cadastral survey prepared ca. 1916 shows that the 483 originarios of Quirquiavi ayllu controlled 48 estancias in the jurisdiction.[16] Most likely during the *revisitas* conducted in 1880 and 1883, the land commissions granted title to thirty-six *estancias* to individual community members and title to the remaining twelve *estancias* in *pro-indiviso* tenure. The 1897 land commission may have reversed the work of the previous commissions and granted title to all forty-eight *estancias* in *pro-indiviso* tenure.

Because of Quirquiavi's relative isolation from regional markets and the lower quality of its land, fewer sales of community land followed the passage of the law of *ex-vinculación*. Between 1895 and 1928, only thirty-eight land sales were recorded in Cantón Quirquiavi. Eleven sales registered in 1909 and 1910 were related to the auction and resale of the twelve state-owned properties in the jurisdiction.[17] In the late 1940s, on the eve of Bolivia's agrarian reform, fifty-two community-owned *estancias* in Quirquiavi embraced some 5,746.00.02 hectares of land, or 98 percent of the land reportedly controlled, according to the cadastral survey prepared about 1916.[18]

Hacienda Challoma Grande, located in Cantón Tacopaya, passed into the hands of private individuals through a series of sales recorded between 1888 and 1916. One Pablo Cespedes, a merchant who resided in Quirquiavi town and possibly a member of Quirquiavi *ayllu* who entered creole society, purchased shares to Challoma Grande from individual members of Quirquiavi *ayllu* in small transactions. In 1888, 1890, and 1894, for example, Cespedes bought twenty-nine parcels or shares in Challoma Grande.[19] According to the cadastral survey prepared about 1916, Cespedes owned 238.01.60 hectares in Challoma Grande. Miguel Leque, also a member of Quirquiavi *ayllu*, owned 11.90.60 hectares of land, and Miguel Ortiz owned a parcel of 8.92.56 hectares.[20]

The second case study of the impact of Bolivian community legislation in highland Cochabamba is Vacas. Prior to 1878, community lands in Vacas occupied some 7,484 hectares of land, or 58.5 percent of the registered agricultural lands in the jurisdiction.[21] Haciendas (*estancias*) specializing in the production of potatoes and other tubers controlled the rest of the land in the jurisdiction.

In 1879, the land commissions distributed individual title to community members in Vacas of standard-sized parcels of 8.64 hectares. In the early 1880s, the government distributed additional lands to former community members. A law passed on October 1, 1880, stipulated that title to "excess" lands could be adjudicated to former community members. For example, in 1879 Petrona Mamani received title to a standard parcel measuring 8.64 hectares in the *estancia* Muyocchipa, and an additional 106.56 hectares of land four years later in 1883.[22] In addition, the land commissions returned twenty properties classified as excess, unused, or usurped lands to the public domain. The twenty *estancias* occupied an area of 5,183 hectares, a total of 40.5 percent of the land registered in the *cantón* and 69.3 percent of the former community lands.[23] The Cochabamba City municipal council administered the state-owned *estancias* on behalf of the national government, and generally rented the estates to members of the local landowning elite. The first renter of the Vacas *estancias* was José Moscoso, who paid an annual rent of 2,760 pesos.[24]

Small and medium-sized properties were common in Cantón Vacas. Three large *estancias* had an extension of more than 1,000 hectares. According to the cadastral survey prepared about 1916, 410 properties with an extension of less than 50 hectares (90.8 percent of all properties) occupied 23.9 percent of the registered agricultural land in Vacas. Nineteen large *estancias*, including three with an extension of more than 1,000 hectares, occupied 71.9 percent of the land (see Table 7.4). Two of the large estates were state *estancias* taken from former community land, and the third was an *estancia* with an area of 2,400 hectares owned by one Clemencia de Soriano.[25]

The greatest loss of community land resulted from the return of the twenty *estancias* to the public domain. There was little increase in the number of properties in the *cantón*, which can be shown by documenting the number of private properties in the jurisdiction. The 226 private properties that already existed in Vacas in 1882, taken with the 199 subsistence parcels of community land, give a minimum of 425 properties following the passage of the law of *ex-vinculación*. To this total must be added the twenty state

Table 7.4: Structure of Land Tenure in Cantón Vacas, ca. 1912

Size of Parcel in Hectares	Number of Properties	%	Area in Hectares	%
0–.99	55	12.2	29.41.08	0.2
1–4.99	131	29.0	391.88.40	3.1
5–9.99	120	26.6	926.24.29	7.2
0–49.99	104	23.0	1,708.17.05	13.4
50–99.99	9	2.0	535.58.52	4.2
100–499.99	16	3.5	3,980.24.34	31.1
1,000–4,999.99	3	0.7	5,221.33.00	40.8
Size Not Given	14	3.1		
Total	452		12,793.14.49	

Source: Catastro de la Propiedad Rustica, Archivo de la Prefectura de Cochabamba, Arani Province, Cantón Vacas.

estancias, which gives a total of 445 properties.[26] In about 1916, there were 452 properties registered in Vacas. The modest increase in the number of properties most likely can be attributed to a small number of land sales and to the division of lands for inheritance.

A detailed examination of the internal structure of land tenure in two former community *estancias* provides further insight into the change in land-tenure patterns in Vacas. Muyocchipa was divided between small and medium-sized properties, three of which were state-owned *estancias*. Twenty-five properties with an area of less than 10 hectares occupied 36.8 percent of the land, and fifteen *estancias* with an area of from 10 to 50 hectares controlled the rest of the land (see Table 7.5). Yanatama was similarly divided between small and medium parcels and a large state-owned *estancia* with an extension of 267.34.60 hectares. Twenty-four properties with an area of less than 10 hectares occupied a quarter of the land in Yanatama; two properties with an extension of 10 to 50 hectares occupied 6.1 percent of the land; and the large state-owned *estancia* 68.1 percent (see Table 7.6).

The *estancias* in Cantón Vacas remained in the hands of the national government until the 1953 agrarian reform, although the service tenants living on the *estancias* gained effective control over the lands after 1936. In 1929, the service tenants in the Vacas *estancias* complained to the Cochabamba City municipal council that the individual renting the lands was attempting to redefine the relationship between the service tenants and renter by extracting additional labor while at the same time reducing the amount of land assigned to them for their subsistence needs. The municipal council sent a picket of troops to repress the growing peasant unrest on the Vacas *estancias*.

However, seven years later, in 1936, the service tenants organized a *sindicato* (peasant league), and, with the support of a reform-minded national government, rented the Vacas *estancias*.[27]

Haciendas in Arque Province

The highland hacienda controlled large extents of land, but the land was of varying qualities. Estates located in the lower-elevation valleys in Arque province controlled more fertile and well-watered lands. A detailed inventory of Hacienda Sicaya in the highland section of the province, prepared in 1860, described the extent and quality of the hacienda lands. Hacienda Sicaya embraced 714.21.01 hectares of land. High quality irrigated lands totaled 103.91.11 hectares located primarily in the Arque River Valley, or 14.6 percent of the area of the estate. Unirrigated lands, much of it described as rocky, covered 68.88.45 hectares, or 9.6 percent of the area of the hacienda. The *serrania*, lands in the mountains on both sides of the Arque River, covered 541.41.45 hectares, or 75.8 percent of the hacienda. The *serrania* was used for the dry farming of potatoes and grains, such as *quinua*, which were adapted to higher elevations; the grazing of livestock; and the collection of building materials.[28] Labor on haciendas in Arque province came from two sources. Most haciendas had a permanent labor force of service tenants known as *colonos*, who provided labor for the hacienda *demesne* in exchange for a subsistence plot. In 1882, there were 4,978 *colonos* in Arque province, 4,830 in about 1902, and 4,412 around 1916.[29] Hacienda owners could also draw upon seasonal laborers.

In the late nineteenth century Arque haciendas experienced a degree of subdivision, although the partition of the hacienda was not as extensive as in the neighboring central valley districts. One reason was the declining profitability of haciendas, and their partition for inheritance. Table 7.7 summarizes a sample of haciendas divided in the late nineteenth century for inheritance. The partition and later administration of Hacienda Sicaya is typical of the subdivision of estates in the province due to inheritance (see Table 7.8). In 1860, four members of the Antezana family divided the hacienda for inheritance. Over the next forty years the hacienda experienced further subdivision. The four Antezana heirs—two women, a man, and a boy—rented and sold sections of their lands. In 1860, following the initial subdivision of the hacienda, Maria and Gregoria Antezana rented their shares of the hacienda. Evidence from throughout the Cochabamba region shows that women more commonly rented their lands. In 1861, Mariano Antezana

Table 7.5: Structure of Land Tenure, Estancia Muyocchipa, ca. 1912

Size of Parcel in Hectares	Number of Properties	%	Area in Hectares	%
1–4.99	9	22.5	29.33.71	6.7
5–9.99	16	40.0	132.39.59	30.1
10–49.99	15	37.5	277.78.80	63.2
Total	40		439.52.10	

Source: Catastro de la Propiedad Rustica, Archivo de la Prefectura de Cochabamba, Arani Province, Cantón Vacas.

sold lands in Sicaya to Vicente Granes for Bs. 3,520. Transactions in the 1870s and 1880s included one land sale and several rental contracts. The regional economic crisis of the 1890s can be seen in the sale of additional lands.

The 1890s was a period of crisis for hacienda owners throughout the Cochabamba region, but especially for hacienda owners in Arque province. The completion of the Antofagasta-Oruro railroad significantly reduced transportation costs between the Pacific Ocean and the Bolivian *altiplano*. Large quantities of cheaper and higher quality Chilean wheat flour entered the country for the first time, and undersold Bolivian wheat flour. The contraction of markets, coupled with periodic ecological crises and growing tax obligations, ruined many Cochabamba hacienda owners, who frequently responded by selling their entire estates or smaller parcels of land.[30] The economic crisis of the 1890s was particularly difficult for hacienda owners in Arque province. Many haciendas in the region, including Sicaya, included mills that ground wheat and corn into flour for sale in the Bolivian *altiplano*, which provided much of the income from the haciendas. Moreover, Arque was a center of the grain trade between Cochabamba and the *altiplano*. With

Table 7.6: Structure of Land Tenure, Estancia Yanatama, ca. 1912

Size of Parcel in Hectares	Number of Properties	%	Area in Hectares	%
0–99	1	3.7	0.37.19	0.09
1–4.99	16	59.3	40.72.45	10.4
5–9.9	7	23.9	60.24.78	15.4
10–49.99	2	7.4	23.80.16	6.1
100–499.99	1*	3.7	267.34.60	68.1

*state-owned *estancia*.
Source: Catastro de la Propiedad Rustica, Archivo de la Prefectura de Cochabamba, Arani Province, Cantón Vacas.

Table 7.7: Selected Haciendas in Arque Province Divided for Inheritance, 1860–1895

Year	Cantón	Property	Area in Hectares	Shares
1860	Quirquiavi	Quirquiavi	?	4
1860	Sicaya	Sicaya	714.21.01	4
1863	Capinota	Pampa Capinota	23.71.47	2
1864	Arque	Curumi	127.68.06	?
1864	Caraza	Guanacota	30.76.50	4
1869	Caraza	Baqueria	?	4
1875	Caraza	Sausini	575.74.50	2
1875	Caraza	Caporaya	220.23.84	5
1875	Sicaya	Guicha	162.03.75	?
1895	Caraza	Chiuni	330.15.40	8

Source: Cochabamba City Notarial Protocols, Archivo Histórico Municipal de Cochabamba, various years.

the importation of Chilean flour the Arque grain trade collapsed, and mill owners lost most of their business. The economy of the region, especially the highland sections of the province, did not improve in the early twentieth century.

Between 1850 and 1929 the number of private properties in Arque province grew, from forty-five estates in 1856 to 2,263 properties of all size in about 1916. The number of properties nearly doubled again between 1930 and 1945. There were 4,465 properties in the jurisdiction in about 1945 (see Table 7.9). The growth in the number of private properties resulted from the

Table 7.8: Transactions Involving Hacienda Sicaya, 1860–1899

Year	Sale/Rental	Price in Bolivianos
1860	Rental	738.40/year
1860	Rental	1,060.80/year
1861	Sale	3,250.00
1864	Rental	?
1877	Sale	2,400.00
1883	Rental	400.00/year
1883	Rental	1,440.00/year
1890	Rental	640.00/year
1891	Sale	2,600.00
1892	Rental	800.00/year
1894	Sale	3,000.00
1899	Sale	6,400.00

Source: Cochabamba City Notarial Protocols, Archivo Histórico Municipal de Cochabamba, various years.

Table 7.9: Number of Properties in Arque Province

Year	Number of Properties
1856	45
1882	770
ca. 1902	2,086
ca. 1916	2,263
ca. 1945	4,465

Source: Padrones de Tributarios, Archivo Nacional de Bolivia, Sucre, Arque Province, 1856; Honorio Pinto, *Bolivia tierra y población 1844–1939* (Lima, 1978), pp. 21–22, 32–34; and Rafael Reyeros, *El pongueaje. La servidumbre personal de los indios bolivianos* (La Paz, 1949), p. 216.

subdivision of community lands, especially in Capinota, and the partition of haciendas into small-, medium-, and large-sized parcels.

The greatest degree of subdivision occurred in Cantón Capinota, as noted above, and in Cantón Caraza. In about 1916, there were 748 separate properties in Caraza, 690 (92.2 percent of all properties) with an area of less than ten hectares occupied 25.8 percent of the land in the jurisdiction censused in the cadastral survey. Fourteen properties with an area of more than fifty hectares (1.9 percent of all properties) controlled 54.1 percent of the land in the *cantón*.[31] Land was fairly evenly distributed in Caraza.

The hacienda continued to dominate the rest of the Arque region. Properties with an area of more than fifty hectares controlled 76.5 percent and 86.1 percent, respectively, of the land in Cantón Sicaya and Cantón Vilcabamba.[32] Similarly, middle- and large-sized haciendas in the highland sections of the region (the smaller Arque province following the subdivision of the jurisdiction, including Cantón Quirquiavi) controlled 78.8 percent of the land registered in the cadastral survey.[33] However, the large colonial-era haciendas had been considerably subdivided. Whereas there were only forty-five haciendas in Arque province in the mid-1850s, in about 1916 there were 200 properties with an area of more than fifty hectares.

Conclusion

Agricultural land in some districts in Arque province experienced considerable fragmentation after 1850, particularly in the years following the passage of the law of *ex-vinculación* and the economic crisis of the 1890s. Community lands in Quirquiavi remained in the hands of former community members, whereas the lands of Capinota community were subdivided into a mosaic of small parcels owned by former community members and others. In Vacas former community lands experienced subdivision, but the greatest loss of land occurred from the state appropriation of community lands. The evidence for both Arque and Vacas neither indicates that existing haciendas expanded at the expense of community lands nor demonstrates that, as was the case in the Bolivian *altiplano*, especially in the area around Lake Titicaca and La Paz, a significant number of new haciendas were created.

Haciendas experienced subdivision through inheritance and also because of the economic difficulties of the 1890s and the early twentieth century. However, the degree of subdivision varied in the different ecological zones in the region. The greatest degree of fragmentation occurred in the Capinota and Caraza Valley, districts with large expanses of fertile, well-watered agricultural land that was in greater demand. In the highland sections of Arque province, on the other hand, the number of *piqueros* was considerably smaller, and middle- and large-sized haciendas continued to control most of the land. Quirquiavi, the one highland community in the jurisdiction, retained control over most of its land, and no new haciendas were created from the lands still in the hands of the community after the passage of the law of *ex-vinculación*.

Notes

1. For a discussion of the formation of the Toledan *reducción* policy and the tribute system in Upper Peru/Bolivia, see Nicolas Sánchez-Albornoz, *Indios y tributos en el Alto Peru* (Lima, 1978).

2. Ibid., pp. 180–85.

3. For a discussion of anticommunity legislation in Bolivia see Erick Langer, "Liberalism and the Abolition of Indian Communities in Nineteenth-Century Bolivia," paper presented at the ICLA-MALAS meeting, Chicago, November 6–7, 1987. On the continued dependence of the Bolivian government on tribute as a source of revenue, see Sánchez-Albornoz, *Indios,* pp. 187–218.

4. For a discussion of the short-term consequences of the 1856 epidemic in Chayanta, see Tristan Platt, *Estado tributario y ayllu andino tierra y tributo en el norte de Potosí* (Lima, 1982), chap. 2.

5. Erwin Grieshaber, "Survival of Indian Communities in Nineteenth Century Bolivia" (Ph.D. diss., University of North Carolina, Chapel Hill, 1977), p. 294.

6. Padrones de Tributarios, Archivo Nacional de Bolivia (hereafter cited as PT,ANB), Cercado Province, selected years.

7. PT,ANB, Cliza Province, selected years.

8. Escrituras Públicas, Archivo Historico Municipal de Cochabamba (hereafter cited as AHMC), expediente no. 108.

9. Federico Blanco, *Diccionario geográfico de la República de Bolivia: Departamento de Cochabamba* (La Paz, 1902), p. 22.

10. Escrituras Públicas, AHMC, expediente no. 113.

11. Escrituras Públicas, AHMC, expediente no. 109.

12. Brooke Larson, *Colonialism and Agrarian Transformation in Bolivia Cochabamba, 1550–1900* (Princeton, 1988), p. 225, n. 47.

13. Blanco, *Diccionario geográfico*, pp. 115–16.

14. Catastro de la Propiedad Rústica, Archivo de la Prefectura de Cochabamba (hereafter cited as CPR), Arque Province, Cantón Quirquiavi.

15. Registro de Derechos Reales (hereafter cited as DR), Arque Province.

16. CPR, Arque Province, Cantón Quirquiavi.

17. DR, Arque Province.

18. Rafael Reyeros, *El pongueaje la servidumbre personal de los indios bolivianos* (La Paz, 1949), p. 219.

19. DR, Arque Province.

20. CPR, Arque Province, Cantón Quirquiavi.

21. This figure is calculated as the total number of *asignaciones* reported following the passage of the law of *ex-vinculación*, plus lands returned to the public domain. See CPR, Arani Province, Cantón Vacas; Blanco, *Diccionario geográfico*.

22. DR, Punata Province, 1902.

23. CPR, Arani Province, Cantón Vacas.

24. Cochabamba City Notarial Protocols, AHMC, 1878.

25. CPR, Arani Province, Cantón Vacas.

26. Blanco, *Diccionario geográfico;* Honorio Pinto, *Bolivia tierra y población, 1844–1939* (Lima, 1978), pp. 32–34.

27. Robert H. Jackson, *Regional Markets and Agrarian Transformation in Bolivia: Cochabamba, 1539–1960* (Albuquerque, 1994), p. 200.

28. Cochabamba City Notarial Protocols, 1860, Archivo Historico Municipal de Cochabamba.

29. Robert H. Jackson, "Evolución y persistencia del colonaje en las haciendas de Cochabamba," *Siglo XlX* 3:6 (1988), 145–62.

30. See Jackson, *Regional Markets;* Robert H. Jackson, "The Decline of the Hacienda in Cochabamba, Bolivia: The Case of the Sacaba Valley, 1870–1929," *The Hispanic American Historical Review* 69 (1989), 259–81.

31. CPR, Capinota Province, Cantón Caraza.

32. CPR, Capinota Province, Cantón Sicaya, Cantón Vilcabamba.

Conclusion

The essays in this volume have presented case studies of the formulation and particularly the implementation of liberal anticorporate land policies in Mesoamerica (Mexico and Guatemala) and the Andean region (Peru and Bolivia). Useful comparisons can be made of the two regions by focusing on three parallel processes: the implementation and impact of anti-church policy; the implementation and impact of anticorporate indigenous community policies; and state building as reflected by the ability of governments to translate liberal ideas into concrete policies.

Antichurch Policies

In Mexico and Guatemala the conservative–liberal ideological debate became polarized and violent, and the Catholic-church hierarchy frequently took a direct if not an indirect interest in national politics in support of the interests of church privileges such as the fuero (special judicial jurisdiction) or the integrity of church wealth and status. Mexican and Guatemalan liberals attempted to enforce anticlerical policies, and conservatives frequently allied with the church blocked these policies wherever possible. A useful comparison can made between anticlerical policies in Mexico and Bolivia.[1]

The Mexican liberal attack on church wealth was framed as part of a larger program to promote economic development. Liberal ideologues such as Mora argued that the different constituent bodies of the Catholic church held considerable wealth in a form that did not circulate and could not be tapped to finance economic development. In the mid-1850s the liberals attempted to disamortize church wealth. This entailed the sale of church-owned real urban and rural property, but the church retained control over their capital. Instead of being invested in real property, church capital would be fluid and could be invested in productive enterprises. There was also a pragmatic side to this program: the government levied a tax on property sales.

Resistance to disamortization and the outbreak of civil war that lasted from 1858 to early 1861 radicalized the Juárez government. Shortly after the end of the civil war Juárez nationalized church wealth, including unsold church-owned real property. This was both a punitive and pragmatic measure. The proceeds from the sale of confiscated real property went to the government, which was desperate for funds after a long civil war. The sale of confiscated real property was also an attempt to restore the value of government debt certificates. The buyers of confiscated properties could partially pay the already discounted price for rural or urban property in depreciated government debt certificates. This measure helped to retire debt certificates and, to a certain extent, shored up the value of the certificates since it potentially created some demand for them among individuals interested in buying confiscated properties at only a fraction of their true value.

The Bolivian anticlerical program was similar to the Mexican in some respects but very different in others. In 1826 Antonio José de Sucre decreed the closure or consolidation of the convents and monasteries with only small numbers of residents and the confiscation of the real property and, in some cases, even the buildings of the suppressed institutions. The government sold the confiscated properties and also encouraged foreign-born officers serving in the army stationed in Bolivia to invest their bonuses in land. Moreover, as was also the case in Mexico following the confiscation of church real property, the purchase of confiscated church lands could be made with a combination of cash and depreciated government debt certificates. Sucre's assault on church lands was limited only to the regular orders, and not local parishes. Well into the twentieth century parishes owned rural real property.

The impact of Sucre's anticlerical program on convents, monasteries, and the Catholic church in general was quite different. The immediate consequence was the closure of mostly male monasteries and the confiscation of the lands of the male institutions. The populations of the male institutions were low following the independence struggle in Bolivia that began in 1809, especially following the expulsion of Spanish-born clerics who had supported the royalist cause. Most of the female institutions, on the other hand, survived Sucre's decree relatively intact and retained their urban and rural real property. Most nuns were not Spanish-born and were not subject to expulsion as were the male clerics. Moreover, in a small and close-knit elite in Bolivia nunneries served the important function of providing a place for surplus daughters who could not be married off to improve the status of the family. As such, the female orders continued to attract new nuns.

The female orders not only survived the Sucre policy of the 1820s but grew or at least maintained population levels. Moreover, the social importance of the female orders continued, and during the course of the nineteenth century a number of the female orders received new donations of urban and rural real property. The late nineteenth century also witnessed a renewed interest in Bolivia in male and female regular orders, and new institutions were established in the major cities with donations of land. It was only in the early twentieth century that the anticlericalism of the Bolivian Liberal Party coupled with economic dislocation resulted in the male and female orders losing most of their rural lands. Nevertheless, many convents and monasteries adjusted to the new conditions, and most survive even today.

The Mexican church survived the liberal assault of the mid-nineteenth century, but did so under new circumstances. The 1857 and 1917 Mexican constitutions contain strong anticlerical provisions that have been enforced selectively on the basis of the philosophy of each presidential and gubernatorial administration. However, the different groups within the church did not regain the lands alienated as a consequence of the disamortization and later confiscation of church-owned real property. Moreover, as implemented, the Mexican program did not exempt selected institutions as did the Bolivian. Indeed, the Mexican government went so far as to confiscate the dowries of the nuns and, in some instances, used the dowries to support public education. One explanation for the difference in the treatment of the nunneries may be the social status of the reformers. Most Mexican liberals were not members of the colonial-era elite that had endowed and placed their daughters in convents, and many viewed the convents and monasteries as being unproductive drains on Mexican society.[2]

The development of Guatemalan anticlerical policy parallels the Mexican case somewhat. In the 1830s, as in Mexico, liberal reformers attempted to recast the role of the Catholic church in Guatemalan society, only to be overthrown in 1840 by conservatives who reversed the liberal measures. The 1830s reforms included the institution of public education and suppression of the religious orders. Liberals regained control of Guatemala in 1871 and once again assaulted the position of the Catholic church. The government expelled the Jesuits and suppressed the other religious orders. The government further confiscated the property of the orders.

Corporate Indigenous Community Land Policy

Reform-minded liberal politicians in Mexico, Peru, and Bolivia viewed corporate indigenous communities and community ownership of large areas of prime agricultural land as an impediment to modernization and economic development. Liberal reformers in all three countries attempted to legislate communal corporate indigenous community land tenures out of existence in the name of integrating the indigenous population into society, of creating a free and unencumbered land market, or of putting community lands into the hands of more industrious and capable nonindigenous landowners. However, the intent of anticommunity policy often was blunted by the political realities of the countryside and the conflicting interests of local and regional elites and politicians.

Mexican liberals in the mid-1850s included corporate indigenous community lands in the legislation that attempted to disamortize all corporate forms of land tenure that the reformers claimed existed in a form of *mortmain*. Earlier laws had attempted to force the division of community lands but for a number of reasons had not been enforced. As Knowlton shows in his essay on land sales in the Guadalajara area, some communities divided and sold off *ejido* lands, but in the same state indigenous peasants revolted against government authority, particularly in the 1850s, as the disamortization law first went into affect. Ducey, on the other hand, shows a complex pattern of land-tenure change in Huasteca communities. State government and the courts interpreted the intent of the disamortization law, and local politicians and elites had conflicting interests in the implementation of the law. As was the case in other parts of Mexico such as Oaxaca,[3] the division and later alienation of Huasteca community lands occurred in the late nineteenth century during the Porfiriato (1876–1910), when the national government was finally stable and strong enough to enforce its will in the countryside and to use force to suppress peasant resistance.

The Bolivian experience was similar in many respects to the Mexican. Early anticommunity legislation designed to force the division of corporate indigenous community lands remained on the books but was not enforced. An effort in the mid-1860s to sell community lands had to be abandoned in the aftermath of a large-scale uprising that included thousands of community members and overthrew the government. A decade later, the Congress passed a law of *ex-vinculación* that legislated the division of community lands.

Various governments attempted to enforce the new law between 1874 and 1920, with mixed results. The community members in the Valle Bajo of Cochabamba readily accepted the division of community lands and joined the ranks of the growing number of *piqueros* (smallholders), whereas many communities in highland and *altiplano* (high altitude plains) districts resisted. The disastrous War of the Pacific (1879–1884) modified the implementation of the law of *ex-vinculación*. For example, in 1880, the government allowed undivided *pro-indiviso* tenures that, for all intents and purposes, negated the effort to privatize community lands. Community lands in Quirquiavi remained in *pro-indiviso* tenure. In Chayanta, in Potosí department, communities retained most of their lands. In La Paz and Oruro, on the other hand, the division of community lands led to the creation of new haciendas from former community lands and the expansion of existing estates. At the end of a civil war in 1899 thousands of community members from the *altiplano* refused to demobilize and resisted the government they had just helped to put into power.

The history of Peruvian community policy is far more complex than the Bolivian case. Geography and the location of important urban centers and the seats of power were two factors. A large percentage of Peru's population was located on the coast, where the indigenous population had disappeared relatively quickly in the decades following the Spanish conquest and few corporate indigenous communities survived into the nineteenth century. Moreover, Lima, the national capital and largest city in Peru, is located on the coast. Nineteenth- and early twentieth-century Peruvian politics was fragmented and complicated by the confrontations of regional interests and, especially, the coast and sierra and by the construction and collapse of coalitions between *gamonales* (rural highland political bosses) and coastal politicians. The economic and political impact of the guano boom of the mid-nineteenth century, along with the political consequences of the Peruvian defeat during the War of the Pacific and the arming of highland indigenous peasants during the guerrilla campaign at the end of the war, further complicated the formulation and particularly the implementation of government policy regarding the highland corporate indigenous communities.

Unlike Mexico, Bolivia, and Guatemala, there was no systematic Peruvian anticommunity campaign. Highland hacienda owners had the greatest interest in breaking up the corporate indigenous communities and acquiring new land and labor. However, the *gamonales* had to share power with coastal elites and politicians who did not have the same interest in the destruction of the corporate indigenous communities. Moreover, the *gamonales* were not always in a position to influence the formulation of national policy to their favor. As Jacobsen points out in his study of Peruvian community policy, the Peruvian government passed more laws regarding communities in the 1920s and 1930s than had been legislated in the previous century.

In Bolivia, on the other hand, the major cities (La Paz, Oruro, Potosí, and Cochabamba) were all located within short distances of large concentrations of indigenous populations living in corporate indigenous communities. Regional economic interests also existed in Bolivia, but the coastal–highland nexus was absent as a defining parameter in Bolivian politics. Bolivian political leaders may have differed on issues such as free trade, monetary policy, and the social and economic role of the Catholic church, but all had to address the so-called Indian problem since it had considerable import for hacienda owners, merchants, and miners.

State Building

The ultimate objective of liberal reformers was the creation of strong and modern states with vibrant economies. Some politicians such as Bolivian President Ismael Montes, who reportedly acquired large tracts of former community land on the shores of Lake Titicaca at a fraction of its value, also saw the division of community lands or the confiscation of church property as an opportunity to acquire land at a relatively cheap price. The ability of liberal reformers to implement reformist programs, particularly anticommunity legislation, and to suppress opposition to the new policies provides an indication of the relative strength of national states. Mexico and Bolivia provide the best comparisons.

Stevens[4] provides important insights into the divisions among Mexico's political elite that dated to the independence wars and significantly polarized politics in a country that had already been militarized at the end of the colonial period by the creation of a standing army. These divisions resulted as much from social status, class background, and the sides chosen during the independence wars as from abstract ideological differences. In the first decades following independence the army continued to grow in size and importance. Instability marked by frequent changes in government, civil wars, and failed military coups sapped Mexico's strength and left Mexico vulnerable to partition at the hands of the United States following the Mexican-American War (1846–1848). In defending its position, the Catholic church contributed to instability. In the aftermath of the war, liberals gained influence and, in 1855, seized power and put into place reform legislation that attacked corporate landownership. However, it would be another twenty years before political stability was finally established, and this followed a three-year civil war and the long French occupation of much of the country. Continued instability and war delayed the effective enforcement of the desamortization program.

The establishment, after 1876, of stability during the Porfiriato also led to the construction of railroads that tied the country into a single unified market with strong links to foreign markets, particularly the United States.

The construction of railroads also created new demands for agricultural lands spurred by new market opportunities and growing pressure to divide community lands that also caused increased incidents of resistance to land consolidation.[5] However, the Mexican government was now in a position to effectively suppress much of the unrest resulting from the accelerated campaign to liquidate the corporate indigenous communities.

Similarly, political instability and economic stagnation left the Bolivian government weak for some fifty years following independence, and the government could not enforce legislation that aimed to liquidate the corporate indigenous communities. Moreover, with a large indigenous population the government relied on tribute as an important source of revenue. The gradual revival of the silver industry after about 1850 contributed to the growth of state power, and in the 1880s and 1890s Bolivia began the development of a railroad system that fully integrated the major regions of the country. The passage of the law of *ex-vinculación* in 1874, only four years after thousands of community members participated in the overthrow of the Melgarejo administration, reflected the perception of growing strength. However, the War of the Pacific clearly suggested the limits of state building. From a position in the late 1870s of trying to enforce the division of corporate indigenous community lands, the Bolivian government was forced to make concessions to communities, including the approval of *pro-indiviso* tenures.[6]

The War of the Pacific had an impact on Bolivia similar to the impact of the Mexican-American War on Mexico. Military defeat led to political reorganization and the establishment of greater political stability as well as military reorganization and professionalization. As the pace of the alienation of former community lands quickened after the war, especially in La Paz and Oruro, the Bolivian government faced serious indigenous resistance. However, the government was able to effectively suppress resistance, as exemplified by the crushing of the 1899 indigenous uprising and the 1921 uprising at Jesús de Machaca, both of which occurred in the *altiplano*.[7]

With the exception of the Cochabamba region of Bolivia, the division of community lands in Bolivia resulted in land consolidation by the creation of new haciendas or the expansion of existing estates. The Cochabamba *piqueros* in the early twentieth century, however, were not the yeoman farmers idealized by Thomas Jefferson and other early American republicans who influenced early Spanish American liberals. In fact, Cochabamba hacienda owners bemoaned the weakening of the old rural society dominated by haciendas and the competition they faced in local markets from *piqueros*. Ironically, the growth in the number of *piqueros* was a consequence of the liberalization of trade coupled with the modernizationist goal of building railroads.

Cochabamba haciendas that traditionally produced corn and wheat could not compete with cheaper grains imported over the new railroad system.[8] As in Peru, hacienda owners did not dominate the government. Although favored by the passage of the law of *ex-vinculación* in 1874, development policies such as the construction of railroads adopted to promote the growing mining industry had greater priority, and in the Cochabamba case these policies contributed to the demise of the hacienda owners.

This final observation regarding the impact of economic modernization policies on traditional Cochabamba hacienda owners points to one final important facet of nineteenth-century Spanish American liberalism: its fundamental pragmatism. Liberalism was more than anything else a blue print for modernization and economic and social development. Liberal ideologues such as José Mora dwelled, for example, on the impact of the dead weight of church wealth on the Mexican economy, the common perception that corporate indigenous community members did not exploit agricultural land in a rational fashion to maximize productivity, and the need to integrate the indigenous populations more fully into national political life. Both liberals and conservatives could and did embrace the objective of economic development and modernization, although they sometimes disagreed on which pragmatic economic policies best suited the needs of the nation. Disputes also arose over economic issues such as trade policies. But in these cases the debate over free trade versus protected markets was also fundamentally pragmatic.

Notes

1. The discussion for Mexico is based on Jan Bazant, *Alienation of Church Wealth in Mexico: Social and Economic Aspects of the Liberal Revolution 1856–1875*, trans. and ed. Michael Costeloe (Cambridge, 1971); Charles Berry, *The Reform in Oaxaca, 1856–76: A Microhistory of the Liberal Revolution* (Lincoln, 1981).

2. See Donald Stevens, *Origins of Instability in Early Republican Mexico* (Durham, 1991).

3. Berry, *Reform in Oaxaca*.

4. Stevens, *Origins of Instability*.

5. See John Coatsworth, *Growth against Development: The Economic Impact of Railroads in Porfirian Mexico* (DeKalb, 1981), chap. 6.

6. Robert H. Jackson, *Regional Markets and Agrarian Transformation in Bolivia: Cochabamba, 1539–1960* (Albuquerque, 1994), especially chaps. 2–3; Erick Langer, *Economic Change and Rural Resistance in Southern Bolivia, 1880–1930* (Stanford, 1989).

7. Ramíro Condarco Morales, *Zarate El "Temible" Willka: Historia de la rebellión indígena de 1899* (La Paz, 1983); Roberto Choque Canqui, *La Massacre de Jesus de Machaca* (La Paz, 1986); Silvia Rivera, *"Oprimidos pero no vencidos": Luchas del campesinado aymara y qhechwa de Bolivia, 1900–1980* (Geneva, 1986).

8. Jackson, *Regional Markets and Agrarian Transformation*.

Index

Academy of Studies, 100–101
Agrarian crisis of 1856, 41
Agrarian reform: Bolívar, 130–31; Bolivia (1953), 7, 173, 200; Mexican commission, 69; Peru, 128, 159
Agrarian reform laws of 1824–1828 (Peru), 135; ignored, 143; Indian status as proprietors, 141; Juan Bustamante on, 144; mestizos, 138; taxes and racial descent, 137
Agricultural modernization, 3, 156–57
Agriculture, commercialization, 5, 37
Alcabalas, 18
Alcohol, 98
Alexander VI (pope), 95
Alvarez, Juan, 38
Amezaga, Mariano, 139
Anarchism, 153
Andean region, 123–206
Anticlericalism: Bolivia, 7, 174, 176, 177, 178, 180, 207, 208–9; Guatemala, 107–8, 110–11, 112–13, 116, 207, 209; Mexico, 4, 110, 174, 207–8, 209; political coalitions and, 8. *See also* Catholic church
Arce, José Manuel, 98
Armed bands, 38, 40, 80. *See also* Bandits

Arroyo, Angel, 115–16, 104n., 122
Atusparia Rebellion (1885), 143
Ayllus, Peru, 126, 128, 136, 147, 7n., 161
Aymara, 181–82
Ayuntamientos: Guadalajara, 14–17, 22; as landowners, 19–20, 22

Baldíos, 126
Ballivian, José, 187
Banco Agrícola Hipotecario, 111, 112
Banco Nacional (Guatemala), 112
Bandits: 40; of Alica, 52, 62n., 64; Lozada rebellion, 51, 52. *See also* Armed bands
Baptista, Mariano, 177, 187
Barrios, Justo Rufino, 102–3, 107–8, 111, 114–15, 124
Barrundia, José Francisco, 99, 101
Benitez, Ángel, 39
Bethlemita order, Guatemala, 113, 78n., 120
Bolívar, Simón, 128–30, 172, 175
Bolivia, 171–88, 193–205; Arque province, 7–8, 185, 193, 201–4; Chuquisaca, 178, 179, 183; Cochabamba, 7, 8, 175–76, 182, 183, 184–85, 188, 194–95, 197, 199–201, 201–4, 210, 213; Lake

217

Titicaca, 184, 205, 212; Oruro, 198, 211, 213; Parapiti, 180; La Paz, 182, 198, 205, 211, 213; Potosí, 178, 182, 183, 198, 211; Sucre, 182; Tarija, 178; Vacas, 193; Villamontes, 180; Yungas, 182
Bourbon reforms, 127, 130; church, 96–97
Bustamante, Juan, 144–45
Bustamante Rebellion (1866–1868), 142, 144–45

Cabeceras, 66, 70, 81
Cabecillas, 80
Cacicazgos, 9–10
Caciques, 130, 135, 141; *caciques recaudadores*, 148
Cadastral surveys, 10, 198
Caja de Censos, 134
Camarena, Jesús, 40
Cantón, 14
Capellanías, 173
Capuchin order, 108, 109, 78n., 120
Cargo system, 136
Carmelite order, Guatemala, 114
Carrera, Rafael, 101, 105
Casaus y Toreres, Ramón (archbishop), 97, 98, 99
Castas, 137, 142
Caste war in the Huasteca, 69, 79–80
Castilla, Ramón, 141, 143
Castillo, Apolinar, 75
Castro Pozo, Hildebrando, 123
Catacaos, 137–39, 149–52
Catholic church: antichurch policies compared, 207–9; attacked, 107; Bolivia, 171, 172–80, 177, 186–87, 207, 209; charity criticized, 112–13; concordat, 102, 106; *diezmos*, 95, 101, 102, 106–7; disentailment, 171; Guatemala, 95–117, 207, 209; independence and, 97, 187; Mexico, 38, 40, 71, 110, 207–8, 209, 212; *patronato real*, 95–96, 98, 99, 102, 110; religious holidays, 98; separation of church and state, 107, 110; tithes, 99
Cattle, 67; Veracruz, 77, 79
Censos, 173, 174–75
Central America, 95–117
Centralism, 37
Cerna, Vicente, 102
Cevellos, Octavio, 46–47
Chicherías, 150
Chile, 177
Chiriguanos, 178, 180
Christianization, 96
Church landholdings. *See* Religious corporate holdings
Citizenship and property ownership, 132
Civil Code (Peru), 139–40
Civil War (U.S.), 149
Clientelism, 147, 148
Coca leaves, 182
Coffee industry, 6, 102, 103–4, 146
Collective memory, 160
Colonial era: Bolivia, 193–94; local government, 69–70; Peru, 125–27; terminology and offices, 73
Colonos, 144, 201
Communal lands: Bolivarian era, 127; Bolivia, 124–25; communal rotation, 136; Habsburg era, 126; Indian possession of, 131–32; legislation, 74–75; liberal view, 73–74; pasture, 148; Peru, 152; Peruvian independence, 128–32; pro-Indian writers, 123; uses of, 69–73
Communistic peasantry, 153, 154, 158–59
Comonfort, Ignacio, 38, 39
Comuneros, 72, 76
Condueñazgos, 76–77, 80, 81, 83, 84, 14n., 87

Confraternities, 111, 113
Conscripción vial, 157
Conscription, 57
Conservative rebellions, 105
Conservatives: Bolivia, 176–77, 178, 186, 187, 188; Mexico, 51, 52
Conspiracy, 54, 99
Constitutions: Central America (1824), 100; Central America (1825), 97–98; Guatemala (1851), 102, 114–15; Guatemala (1879), 116; Mexico (1857), 13, 40, 44, 85, 107, 209; Mexico (1917), 209; Peru, 141, 159; Spain (1812), 97
Contraband, 51
Contribución de indígenas: abolished, 141, 142, 143, 72*n*., 166; as head tax, 132; Indian local authority, 137, 148; Indian peasants and, 136; as tribute, 130
Contribución personal, 141, 142–43, 144, 148
Corporations, defined, 2*n*., 25
Cotton, 149, 150–51, 157
Council of Government (Peru), 131
Crown lands, 126

Daughters of Charity, 177
Dávila, Gregorio, 39
Dawes Severalty Act (1887), 9
Debt certificates (Mexico), 208
Degollado, Santos, 13, 38, 39
Degollado decree, 14–15, 19–20, 22
Dehesas, 15
Delgado, José Matías, 97
Despoblado, 138
Díaz, Porfirio, 83
Dictatorship, "transitory," 103, 115
Disamortization, Mexico, 8, 23, 207–8, 209. *See also* Ley Lerdo
Disentailment: Bolivia, 171, 173; Bolivia and Mexico compared, 173–74; law of *ex-vinculación*

(Bolivia, 1874), 7, 182–83; *vinculaciones* prohibited (Guatemala), 115
Dominican order, Guatemala, 99, 100, 102, 109, 112
Dorado, José Vicente, 181, 182
Drought, 41

Echenique, José Rufino, 141
Economic development: Bolivia, 178, 181, 187; church property and, 111–12; communal tenure and, 9; Guatemala, 103–4, 108, 111–12, 113, 114, 116; liberalism and, 3, 214; Peru, 143
Education and religious instruction, 104, 109, 112, 177, 178
Ejidos, 5; concept, 15, 17; exemptions, 18*n*., 27–28; Guadalajara, 14, 15; Peru, 126; sales, 22*n*., 28; urban, 14, 15; Veracruz, 69, 70
Elites: Bolivia, 175, 179, 208; conflicts with government officials, 5; effect of independence on rural, 79; implementation of laws, 9; liberalism influences, 3; Mexico, 209, 212; Peru, 124, 135, 149–52, 159; Positivism, 6; prosography, 4; water issues, 149–52
Emigration, 56–57
Encarnación (mother superior), 113
Enlightenment ideas, 100
Enríquez, Juan de la Luz, 73
Epidemics, 158, 194–95; cholera, 41, 20*n*., 60, 101; typhoid, 41
Escuela Politécnica, 112
Espinosa y Dávalos, Pedro (Bishop), 39, 40
Espinosa y Palacios, Francisco, 106, 108, 111
Ethnic indigenous status, 138–39
Ethnic relations, Mexico, 5–6
Europe, revolutions of 1848, 7

Europeans, Tepic, 51
Exports, 139, 152; coffee, 6; cotton, 149; guano, 7; tin, 183–84

Fajardo, Rosalindo, 81
Federalism, 37–38
Federalist War (1898–1899), 180, 188
Fernández Alonso, Severo (president), 179
Feudal order: Europe, 128; Peru, 154
Food shortages, 41
Forasteros, 130, 135
Forced labor, 103, 146; *conscripción vial*, 157
Forced loans, 57
Foreign clergy, 172, 208
Foreign interests, Peru, 133
Foreign intervention, in Mexico, 22, 38, 41, 57
Foreign merchants, 51, 149, 180
Foreign occupation, 171, 172
Foreign publications, 109–10
Forests, controlling, 81
Franciscan order: Bolivia, 177–80, 187; Guatemala, 99, 108, 112
Free trade, 177, 186, 214
Fueros, 96, 97
Fundo legal: Guadalajara, 15, 17; Jalisco, 47, 55, 61*n*., 64; Veracruz, 70, 76

Gaínza, Gabino (General), 95
Gálvez, José, 139
Gálvez, Mariano, 98, 100, 101
Gálvez, Pedro, 139
Gamonales, 135; land grabs, 140, 157; Peru, 148, 107*n*., 169, 211
García Calderón, Francisco, 140
García Granados, Miguel, 102, 103, 105, 107–8, 109, 114
García Peláez, Francisco de Paula (archbishop), 106
Garmendia, Francisco, 140–41

Gavillas, 38, 40, 48, 52, 56; Antonio Godines, 54; emigration, 57; Tolotlán, 54
Glen Grey Act (1894), 9
Godines, Antonio, 54
Guano exports, 7, 139, 141–42, 156, 59*n*., 165, 211
Guardia Nacional (Mexico), 80
Guatemala, 95–117; Los Altos, 104; Antigua, 105; Oriente, 105, 106, 111; Quezaltenango, 103, 104
El Guatemalteco, 114

Habsburg land policies, 125–26
Haciendas: Andean, 128; Bolivia, 8, 175, 176, 182, 201–4; in crisis, 134; Jalisco, 46–47, 54–55; Peru, 135, 153, 211, 214; *pueblos extinguidos*, 47; Veracruz, 67, 69, 77–78, 79
Herrera, Andrés, 178
Hilbck family, 151
Honduras, 98
Hunger, 41, 20*n*., 60–61

Immigration issue, 99
Imperial Law of Revision, 22
Independence wars: effect on pueblos, 9; elite divisions, 212; foreign soldiers, 7; Peru, 127; political future and, 3
Indian community landholdings, Bolivia, 180–85, 186, 187–88, 193–205, 209–12
Indian community landholdings, local politics, 135
Indian community landholdings, Mexico: agrarian associations, 76; armed peasants, 5; compared to Peru and Bolivia, 209–10; *condueñazgos*, 76–77, 82; conflicts with mestizos, 77–78; Huasteca, 5, 65–86; Jalisco, 23, 24;

joint possession, 23; land rights, 5n., 25; large landowners and, 24; Ley Lerdo, 44–46; means of defending, 79–82; Puebla highlands, 5; *pueblos extinguidos*, 47
Indian community landholdings, Peru, 123–60, 130, 131–32, 139–40, 146–52; compared to Mexico and Bolivia, 209, 211; Mariátegui on, 153–54, 155; pressures, 156–57, 158
Indian rebellions: Bolivia, 6, 188, 211, 213; Mexico, 52, 55, 80–81; Peru, 143
Indians: campaign of Tepic, 52; Coras, 51; Huicholes, 51; Jalisco, 23, 24; protective legislation, 131; *pueblos extinguidos*, 47; rights, 144–45
Indians, view of: Bolivia, 172, 179; Central America, 99; Mexico, 73; Peru, 123, 133, 139–40, 142, 144–46
Indians, wealthy, 71, 72
Indian uprisings, Mexico, 46
Indigenismo, Peru, 7, 123, 153, 154, 160
Indigenous corporate holdings. *See* Indian community landholdings
Individualism, 153
Inflation, 176
Inheritance, 136, 201
Irrigation, 149, 150–51
Iturbide, Agustín de, 97

Jalisco, 5, 13–35, 37–58; Los Altos, 44; Santa Anita, 54; Bolaños, 54; Chalco, 46; Chapala, 44, 47, 53; Chimaltitán, 54; Colotlán, 51, 54; Guadalajara, 5, 13–35; Hejuquilla, 54; Jamay, 46, 47; Mamatla, 54; San Martín, 54–55; Mezcala, 53; Mezquitic, 54; Otatán, 46; Tala, 46; Tamaní, 46; Tepic, 51, 53; Tizapán el Alto, 47; Tolotlán, 54; Tomatlán, 47; Tonalá, 54; Totatiche, 54; Tuxcacuesco, 47; village of Santa María, 23; Zapopan, 21
Jefes políticos, 82, 84
Jesuits, expulsion of: Bolivia, 177, 178, 196; Guatemala, 103, 104–5, 106, 107–8, 209; Latin American liberals and, 96
Jovellanos, 173
Juárez, Benito, administration, 4, 22
Judicial system, Guatemala, 101
Juez divisor de tierras, 150
Julius II (pope), 96

Kurakas, 10, 127, 129

Labor drafts, 81
Labor services, 84, 135
Labor tenants, 154, 18n., 162
Labor tenants, 200–201
Lainfiesta, Francisco de, 108
La Mojonera ranch, 20–21
Land auctions, 10, 198
Land commissions, 198
Land conflicts: civil war and, 41; Peru, 148
Land disputes: arbitration system, 74; Bolivia, 195; court records, 10; invasions, 68–69; Jalisco, 46, 47, 51, 55; liberal legislation and, 74; San Luis Pochititan, 55; motives, 48–49; San Pedro Tequepespan, 55; population increase, 56; *pueblos extinguidos*, 47; Rivas revolt, 54–55; Veracruz, 68–69
Land divisions, 74–75, 78–82, 80; Veracruz, 82–83
Land markets: fluctuations, 19; Guadalajara, 17, 19, 20; Jalisco, 5, 21–22; Juan Orozco, 20–21;

multiple property transactions, 20–21; sales agreements, 19
Land-measurement systems, 10
Landownership: Bolivia, 6; Mexico, 6
Land question, 65–66
Land rentals: Bolivia, 185, 199, 201, t. 7.8, 203; ejidos, 19; Guadalajara, 17; Mexico, 8, 70–71, 84
Land sales: Bolivia, 198; Mexico, 24; Peru, 138
Land tenure: Bolivia, 8, 193, 196–201, 211, 213; Guadalajara, 5; Indian influence, 81; Mexico, 5; *pro-indiviso*, 8, 76, 198, 211, 213; sources, 10
Land values, Guadalajara, 19
Larrea y Loredo, José de, 130
Latifundia, 153–54
Laurent, Francois, 109, 110
Law of *ex-vinculación* (Bolivia, 1874), 7, 8, 182–83; enforcement, 210; impact, 196–201, 204; railroads, 214; state building, 213; triumph, 186
Leguía, Augusto (president), 157, 159
Lerdo de Tejada, Miguel, 13
Lerdo Law. *See* Ley Lerdo
Ley de Pavón (Guatemala, 1852), 109
"Ley de perro," 101
Ley Juárez, 39, 12*n*., 60
Ley Lerdo: contrast with Peru, 140; Jalisco, 5, 13–23, 18*n*., 27, 37–58, 32*n*., 62; nature of, 74; Veracruz, 71, 75–76
Liberalism: basic tenets, 96; Bolivia, 7, 171, 181–88; Catholic church and, 172–80; classical, 73–74, 124; economic, 4; economic and trade policy, 123; Indian problem, 2*n*., 86; Indians adopt, 151–52; liberal project (Mexico), 73–78, 85–86; liberal project (Peru), 146; Mariátegui critique, 152–54, 155; as moral statecraft, 124; Peru, 7, 123–24, 139, 151–52, 156; "popular liberalism," 66, 80; pragmatism, 214; protection of Indians, 145–47; studies discussed, 4
Liberal party: Bolivia, 176–77, 180, 209; Mexico, 4; *moderados* and *radicales*, 39; Peru, 7
Liberals: alliance with peasants, 81; church question, 97, 110; Guatemala, 97–117; Lozada rebellion, 51, 52; relationship to indigenous communities, 65; Veracruz, 65–86
Libraries, 99
Llave, Ignacio de la, 74
Local government: land question and, 65, 66, 82–84; peasant agency and, 85; Peru, 125, 135; political manipulations, 82–84
López, Diego, 54
Lozada, Manuel, 50–53
Lozada Rebellion, 50–53, 55

El Malacate, 104, 107
Mandamiento decrees, 146
Manos muertas, 172, 173
Mariátegui, José Carlos, 123, 152–54, 101*n*., 168
Maximiliano (Archduke), 22, 51–52
Measures, table of, 33
Melgarejo, Mariano, 172, 182–83, 186, 187–88, 195
Mesoamerica, 4, 13–122
Mestizos: Bolivia, 186; Juan Bustamante on, 144; land conflicts, 77–78, 83; land divisions, 75; Peru, 131–32, 138, 144; Veracruz, 67, 77–78, 83
Mexican-American War (1846–1848), 212
Mexican Revolution, 84, 85
Mexico: Chiapas, 86; contrast with Peru, 140; Guanajuato, 57; Guer-

rero, 80; Huasteca, 5, 210; Jalisco, 5, 13–35, 37–58, 74, 210; Michoacán, 14, 74; Oaxaca, 210; Puebla, 80; state of Mexico, 74; Veracruz, 65–86
Meza, Pio Benigno, 147
Mezcala revolt, 53
Migration, 137
Military rule, 53
Mining, 183, 194
Missions, religious, 174, 177–80
Mistis, 148
Mita, 127, 194
Modernization, 37, 214
Montes, Ismael (president), 184, 212
Montúfar, Lorenzo, 115
Mora, José María Luis, 110, 112, 207, 214
Moral "statecraft" tradition, 124
Morazán, Francisco, 98–99, 101
Mortmain, 3
Muleteers, 137
Municipal structures, Mexico, 70–73, 81–82

Nationalism, 153, 159
Nationalization decree (Mexico, 1859), 22
National Patronage of the Indigenous Race, 157
Nayarit, Tepic, 51, 53
Nino, Bernardino de (Fr.), 180
Notarial records, 9, 24
Notaries, 14, 18–19

Onofre, Lugardo, 46
Originarios, 130, 135
Orozco property transactions, 20–21, 24, *t.* 1.2, 34–35
Ortiz Urrutia, Mariano (bishop), 106

Palacios, Enrique, 111
Papantla rebellion, 80–81

Parcialidades, 147
Pardo y Aliaga, Felipe, 141
Parrodi, Anastasio (General), 39, 40, 41–42, 57
Peasant conflicts, Peru, 149–52
Peasant rebellions: Santa Anita, 54; Antonio Godines leads, 54; Bolivia, 195; Carlos Rivas leads, 54–55; causation, 48; causes, 56, 1*n*., 58–59; Chapala, 53; *contribución personal*, 148–49; fears of, 79; Huasteca, 79, 82–83; Lozada rebellion, 50–53; Mezcala, 53; national policy in Mexico, 53; numbers in arms, 48, 50; offensive action, 47; Peru, 148–49, 18*n*., 162; population increase, 56; Tala, Jalisco, 55; Tolotlán, 54; Tonalá, 54
Peasant resistance, Bolivia, 183
Peasant unrest, Bolivia, 200–201
Peasant uprisings: armed mobilization and, 40–56; Jalisco, 5, 37–58; Mexico, 39; number of, 41, 42–44, 57
Pérez, Rafael, 105, 106
Peru, 123–60; Amazon rain forest, 154–55, 105*n*., 169; Canas, 148; Catacaos, 149–52; Cuzco, 134–36, 140–41, 148; Huancané, 148; Junin, 136–37, 159; Mantaro Valley, 136–37, 156; La Mar, 148; north coast, 155; Piura, 137–39, 149–52; Puno, 134–36, 148
Piñol y Aycinena, Bernardo (archbishop), 104, 106
Piqueros, 7, 8, 205, 210, 213
Poblaciones, 13
Population decline, 47
Population growth, 56, 158, 194
Porfiriato: *despojo* of village lands, 82, 210; land question, 66; railroads, 212–13; rural land concentration, 13

Positivism: Bolivia, 125; Guatemala, 103, 104, 109; influences elites, 6; Peru, 153, 157
Prado, Mariano Ignacio, 151
Prisons, 100
Private property: Bolivarians and, 130–31; Bolívar on, 129; Bolivia, 195, 203–4; concept (Mexico), 74; Juan Bustamante on, 144, 145; liberal legislation, 78; liberal view, 124; local government and, 84–85; Peru, 132, 136, 140–41, 148, 155, 156
Privatization, 75, 77
Progress, idea of, 73–74, 96
Propios: concept, 15; Guadalajara, 15, 17; Veracruz, 70–71
Prosography, 4
Protector of Indians, 145–46, 157
Public education: church properties and, 8–9; Guatemala, 100–101, 104, 209
Pueblos extinguidos, 47, 56
Pueblos sujetos. See *Sujeto* communities
Putumayo rubber fields, 154

Railroads, 184, 185, 202, 212–14
Rancheros, 71
Recollect order, Guatemala, 99, 109, 112, 78*n*., 120
Reconquista, 96
La Reforma: anticlericalism, 4; Jalisco, 39
Reducción, 194
Religious corporate holdings: Bolivia, 6–7, 8–9, 172–80; Central American confederation, 99, 101–2; Guatemala, 6, 100, 109–10, 112, 113; liberalism and, 96; Mexico, 4, 22; Mora on, 110; national policies compared, 207–9; Peru, 6–7

Religious issues, 55
Religious orders, 99, 108–9, 134, 186
Religious orders, female: Bolivia, 7, 9, 173, 174, 175–76, 177, 208–9; Guatemala, 110–11, 113–14, *t.* 4.1, 115; Mexico, 209
Religious orders, male: Bolivia, 7, 9, 173, 175, 177, 208, 209; Guatemala, 108–9
Religious toleration issue, 99, 102
Reparto, 46, 58, 32*n*., 62
Repúblicas de indios, 69–70
Restored Republic (Mexico, 1867), 57, 77
Revisitadores, 141, 183, 198
Revoltosos, 47; Carlos Rivas, 54–55; Manuel Lozada, 50–53; numbers, 48, 50
Revolution of Ayutla, 38
Revolutions of 1848 (Europe), 139
Río, Manuel del, 134
Rivas, Carlos, 54–55
Rivera Paz, Mariano, 101
Rodríguez Blanco, José María, 14
Rodríguez de Uluapan, María Josefa, 67
Rojas y Briones, Pedro de, 132–34
Román, Martín, 14
Romero family, 151
Romero Rubio, Manuel, 83–84
Rosa, Ramón, 105
Rural unrest, 10
Rural violence, Guadalajara, 5

Salesian order, 177
El Salvador, 97
Samoyoa, José M., 109
San Martín, José de, 125, 127, 128
Santa Anna, Antonio López de, 38
Santa Cruz, Andrés de, 172, 178, 187
Santos Quiroga, José, 185
Scientific racism, 157, 184

INDEX 225

Sechura, 137–39, 149, 151
Secularization: as church goal, 96; of education, 100, 104, 109
Servicios personales, 136
Sharecroppers, 151
Sindicatos, 7, 201
Sisters of Charity, Guatemala, 104n., 121–22
Smallholders: Bolivia, 197; ideal of, 3; Peru, 129. See also *Piqueros*
Social Darwinism, 125, 184, 197
Socialists, 153
Social mobility, 137
Social protest: reactive, 38; violent, 37
Sociedad Amiga de los Indios, 144, 145, 146
Sociedad de Agricultura, 150–52
Sociedades de beneficencia pública, 134
Society of Jesus. See Jesuits, expulsion of
Solares, 15
Soto, Manuel, 73–74
Soto, Marco Aurelio, 105, 107, 108
Sources and records, 9–11, 48
Spain, 97, 127
Sucre, Antonio José de: church wealth, 173, 175, 186, 208; opposition, 171–72
Suertes, 15
Sujeto communities: 66, t. 3.1, 68, 70, 72–73, 77; municipal resources, 81–82
Surveys, land, 71

Tacalá irrigation canal, 150–51
Taracena, Francisco W., 111, 114
Tavara, Santiago, 143–44
Taxes: Bolivia, 124; exports and, 139; head tax, 84, 124, 132, 141, 143; Indian lands and, 136; on industrial production, 142; Mexico, 57, 84; Peru, 130, 132, 141, 142–43; property, 18, 142, 143; tax collectors, 130
Tejeda, José Simeón, 139, 141
Telléz, Andrés, 104, 107
Terratenientes, 47
Texas, 71
Tiburcio, Simón, 81
Tierras de comunidad, 129
Tierras del común, 148
Tierras de oficio, 130
Tierras de origen, 182
Tierras de repartimiento, 17, 70, 71–72, 75
Tierras realengas, 126, 134
Toledo, Francisco de (viceroy), 193–94
Transportation, 103
Tribute: abolished, 126, 127, 128; Bolivia, 172, 187, 194, 213; Bourbon era, 127; colonial institution, 126; *contribución de indígenas*, 130; *forasteros*, 194, 195; head tax replaces, 124; *originarios*, 194; Peru, 127, 130; *recaudadores de tributo*, 135; reintroduced, 130
Túpac Amaru rebellion (1780–1781), 127

Ubico, Manuel, 105
Uluapan, marquesa of, 67
Unanue, Hipólito, 130
University of San Carlos, 100

Valcarcel, Luis, 123
Vales reales, consolidación de, 173
Vassalage, 126, 127, 136
Veracruz: Amatlán, 69, 79; Chicontepec, 75–76; El Espinal, 68–69, 83–84; San Gerónimo, 75; Huasteca, 65–86; Huautla, 71; Santa María, Ixcatepec, 68; Mextitlán, 71; Panatela, 82–83; Papantla, 76; state land law, 76; Temapache, 67,

73, 77, 78, 80, 83; Temazola, 72; Texcatepec, 67, 84; Tuxpan, 67–68
Victoria, Guadalupe (President), 67
Viedma, Francisco de, 194
Vincention order, 112

Wages (Peru), 142
War of extermination, 52
War of the Pacific (1879–1884), 177, 198, 210–11, 213
War of the Reform, 22; Jalisco, 40; land sales, 24, 140
Water issues, 149–52
Women, 20, 201, 208–9

Yanaconas, 151
Yarlequés family, 151

Zarate Willka, Pablo, 188
Zavala, Miguel, 145–46, 147, 157

Contributors

Dawn Fogel Deaton is a doctoral candidate at the University of Chicago. She is completing her dissertation entitled, "The Riotous Peasantry: Rural Social Protest in Jalisco, Mexico, 1825–1885." She is also the author of "La protesta rural durante el siglo XIX en Jalisco," in *Elite clases sociales y rebelion en Guadalajara y Jalisco, siglos XVIII y XIX* (ed. Carmen Castaneda, 1988).

Michael Thomas Ducey received his Ph.D. from the University of Chicago. He teaches Latin American and Mexican history at the University of Colorado at Denver. He is currently finishing a book manuscript on rural social and political movements in Veracruz, Mexico during the late eighteenth and early nineteenth centuries.

Robert J. Knowlton, Professor Emeritus of the University of Wisconsin-Stevens Point, received his Ph.D. from the University of Iowa. His specialization is the nineteenth century Mexican Reform era. He is the author of *Church Property and the Mexican Reform, 1856–1910* (1976).

Robert H. Jackson received his Ph.D. from the University of California, Berkeley. He currently teaches at Texas Southern University. He is the author of *Indian Population Decline: The Missions of Northwestern New Spain* (1994); *Regional Markets and Agrarian Transformation in Bolivia: Cochabamba, 1539–1960* (1994); with Edward Castillo, *Indians, Franciscans, and Spanish Colonization: The Impact of the Mission System on California Indians* (1995); and co-editor with Erick Langer, *The New Latin American Mission History* (1995).

Nils Jacobsen received his Ph.D. from the University of California, Berkeley. He currently teaches Latin American history at the University of Illinois, Urbana-Champaign. He is the author of *Mirages of Transition: The Peruvian Altiplano, 1780–1930* (1993).

Erick D. Langer received his Ph.D. from Stanford University. He teaches Latin American history at Carnegie-Mellon University. He is the author of *Economic Change and Rural Resistance in Southern Bolivia* (1989), and co-editor with Robert Jackson of *The New Latin American Mission History* (1995).

Hubert Miller, Ph.D., Professor Emeritus at the University of Texas-Pan American, has published on Church-state relations in Guatemala during the national period. His major work is *La iglesia y el estado en Guatemala, 1871–1885* (1976).

About the Book and Editor

Liberals, the Church, and Indian Peasants
Corporate Lands and the Challenge of Reform in Nineteenth-Century Spanish America
Edited by Robert H. Jackson

The control and use of land were fundamental issues throughout Spanish America in the nineteenth century. This volume is the first comprehensive treatment of this topic. The seven original essays in this book explore how governments and local officials, following the tenets of economic liberalism, forced changes in land ownership after Independence and what resulted from their reforms.

Leaders in newly independent countries in Mesoamerica and the Andean region attacked as inherently unproductive the large land holdings of the Church, charitable institutions such as orphanages, and Indian communities. Liberals believed that breaking up communal land holdings and selling these to individuals spurred economic development and modernization. Each chapter addresses how, by transfer of ownership, lands were—to varying degrees—incorporated into the nineteenth-century expansion of agriculture. The social and political changes associated with land tenure reforms are carefully considered, too.

Robert H. Jackson is professor of history at Texas Southern University and the author of several books on related topics.